LAWN GEEK

LAWN GEEK

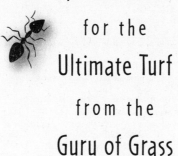

Tips and Tricks
for the
Ultimate Turf
from the
Guru of Grass

TREY ROGERS

 NEW AMERICAN LIBRARY

New American Library
Published by New American Library, a division of
Penguin Group (USA) Inc., 375 Hudson Street,
New York, New York 10014, USA
Penguin Group (Canada), 90 Eglinton Avenue East, Suite 700, Toronto,
Ontario M4P 2Y3, Canada (a division of Pearson Penguin Canada Inc.)
Penguin Books Ltd., 80 Strand, London WC2R 0RL, England
Penguin Ireland, 25 St. Stephen's Green, Dublin 2,
Ireland (a division of Penguin Books Ltd.)
Penguin Group (Australia), 250 Camberwell Road, Camberwell, Victoria 3124,
Australia (a division of Pearson Australia Group Pty. Ltd.)
Penguin Books India Pvt. Ltd., 11 Community Centre, Panchsheel Park,
New Delhi - 110 017, India
Penguin Group (NZ), 67 Apollo Drive, Mairangi Bay,
Auckland 1311, New Zealand (a division of Pearson New Zealand Ltd.)
Penguin Books (South Africa) (Pty.) Ltd., 24 Sturdee Avenue,
Rosebank, Johannesburg 2196, South Africa

Penguin Books Ltd., Registered Offices:
80 Strand, London WC2R 0RL, England

First published by New American Library,
a division of Penguin Group (USA) Inc.

First Printing, March 2007
10 9 8 7 6 5 4 3 2 1

▥ REGISTERED TRADEMARK—MARCA REGISTRADA

LIBRARY OF CONGRESS CATALOGING-IN-PUBLICATION DATA

Rogers, Trey.
Lawn geek: tips and tricks for the ultimate turf from the guru of grass/Trey Rogers.
p.   cm.
ISBN : 978-0-451-22035-6
1. Lawns.   2. Turf management.   I. Title.   II. Title: Tips and tricks
for the ultimate turf from the guru of grass.
SB433.R76   2007
635.9'647—dc22   2006029842

Set in 11pt Baskerville
Designed by Patrice Sheridan

Printed in the United States of America

PUBLISHER'S NOTE
Accordingly nothing in this book is intended as an express or implied warranty of the suitability or fitness
of any product, service or design. The reader wishing to use a product, service or design discussed in this
book should first consult a specialist or professional to ensure suitability and fitness for the reader's particular lifestyle and environmental needs.
   The publisher does not have any control over and does not assume any responsibility for author or
third-party Web sites or their content.

ACKNOWLEDGMENTS

First, I would like to thank Sonia Castleberry. Her tireless efforts as well as her quickly acquired knowledge and expertise were very impressive. Next, there is Alec Kowalewski, my illustrator. Amazingly, he was always able to read my mind.

The next set of thanks goes to my colleagues at Michigan State University, Jim Crum, Kevin Frank, Joe Vargas, and Ron Calhoun. Thanks for listening to my ideas and schemes. These are guys who never get tired of talking about turf.

Next I would like to thank all of my students, graduate and undergraduate, all one thousand (and counting) of you. I have learned something from everyone.

I would also like to thank my friends at Briggs & Stratton, Rick Zeckmeister, Anita Fisher, Monica Baer, and Terri Kaminski. These are the people who helped start the Lawn Geek, a.k.a. Yard Doctor. It has been an unbelievable journey.

I would be remiss if I did not thank Tracy Bernstein and all of her gang at New American Library. After all, the book was as much their idea as anyone's. Thanks for being so encouraging, patient, and nurturing.

Finally, I would like to thank my wife, Michelle, and our children, Rebecca, Miranda, and Evan. You are everything I ever dreamed, more than I could ever ask for, and far more than I deserve. I have loved every minute with all of you.

CONTENTS

What a lawn is and isn't, from the soil on up. How lawns differ
depending on where you live. The history of lawns in America,
and why we're so passionate about our green spaces.

All about cool-season grasses, the ones that can survive subzero
temperatures and still look like rock stars (as long as you treat
them right).

Grasses that can take the heat without breaking a sweat.

Want to ensure a love affair with your lawn? Choosing
the right grass by knowing your zone is a great way to start.

LAWN GEEK

INTRODUCTION

The way I see it, when it comes to lawns, there are three basic types of people.

You've got your lawn snobs, folks who appreciate a magnificent, lush, well-kept lawn, but from arm's length. They're not going to get down and dirty with their turf. Instead, they'll gladly pay others to do it for them. You've got your lawn slobs, the people who couldn't care less about what their lawns look like, and it shows. And you've got your lawn geeks, the ones who care maybe a little too much about the green stuff and have the calluses on their palms and the permanent black stuff etched under their fingernails to prove it.

I am decidedly a member of the third group. And I'm proud of it. Although I sometimes bristle at being classified as a geek, I've become convinced that being a lawn geek is not necessarily a bad thing. In fact, it's far from it. Like computer geeks who understand things like kilobytes and seek rates and whatnot, and can use these terms in coherent sentences, we understand things like evapotranspiration rates and fertilizer ratios. And we can use them in sentences, too. It's nice to know a geek or two when certain problems erupt. When it comes to lawns, lawn geeks are the go-to guys.

Being a lawn geek gives you license to spend time with the object of your affection and not make any excuses for it. You can stuff your snout deep into a choice divot of turf, inhale the warm, organic mustiness of good soil, and not be branded a weirdo. You can be an amateur geek or actually get paid for doing things like spending long hours staring at grass or getting down on your hands and knees for a bug's-eye view of the world. You can be a groundskeeper at a golf course or oversee the turf in athletic fields. Or you can take the career path I did and sign on at a major university that has a turf sciences program and bear responsibility for turning out the next generation of lawn geeks as well as conduct research for current and future lawn geek generations to use.

I've made a good living doing what I love, which is working with the green stuff that grows under our feet. While my real obsession is playing fields, I often get called on to transfer my knowledge of them into smaller areas, such as lawns. I provide information on a large scale as a consultant for Briggs & Stratton, the lawn mower people. As the "Yard Doctor," I do radio shows, make television appearances, and answer questions online at my Web site (www.yarddoctor.com). But I also make house calls. A lot of house calls. When it comes to helping people with their lawns, I just can't get enough.

In the professional world of turf management, people like me spend a lot of time researching things like water application, mowing, and weed-control strategies for commercial turf. It makes sense for us to do so, being that folks depend on the results of our efforts to guide theirs. But our efforts sometimes . . . well, maybe more than sometimes . . . range beyond the call of duty. Some might call it an obsession. I'm not sure I'd go that far, but I do know that just about everyone I've ever met who deals with turfgrass, professionally or not, does so out of an abiding love for the green stuff. As such, there's a deep connection between us and everyone else who is passionate about having a great-looking lawn. Kind of a brotherhood of the green. Or, for that matter, a sisterhood. Geekiness knows no gender.

This thing, this great-looking lawn, it's like a Holy Grail to lawn geeks. But here's the thing: Like the Holy Grail, or, for that matter, any grand pursuit, great-looking lawns don't just happen. Look at any broad, verdant, weed-free stretch of green, and I'll bet you dollars to doughnuts there's at least one guy (or gal) responsible for putting in lots of hours to get it there.

To me, lawn care is a lot like taking care of your teeth. Fertilizing and irrigation are like brushing and flossing. Do it regularly and the chances of having a great lawn, and a great smile, are substantially improved. Do it when you happen to think about it or have a spare moment, and you'll end up with crummy-looking grass and root canals.

A little preventive maintenance goes a long way, too. Just like you should visit your dentist regularly for checkups and cleanings, you should inspect your lawn regularly (or have someone do it) to look for things like weeds, insects, and diseases.

Nothing good comes from neglecting your teeth. Nothing good comes from neglecting your lawn, either.

The lots of hours part might be a deterrent, especially at first and especially if you're still figuring out if you really want to be a lawn geek or not. But I'm not going to blow smoke at you. A great-looking lawn does take work. You have to mow. You have to water. You have to fertilize. These are the big three practices—cultural practices, in turfgrass parlance—and there are others, too. But here's the good thing: Do them right and often enough, and eventually the amount of time you have to spend on them lessens, if that's what you're after. Lawns can be as high-maintenance or low-maintenance as you want them. They can fit your lifestyle. You don't have to alter yours to fit theirs. This, to me, is the ultimate goal when taking care of any lawn. You calling the shots, instead of feeling like a slave to what can be an extremely demanding entity.

So, why this book? There are a bunch of different reasons, but they all boil down to one basic truth: I'm passionate about grass and I love sharing what I know about it with others. That passion developed pretty early on, as a teenager, in fact. I started playing golf. Soon, life without golf was unimaginable. Like most serious golfers, I wanted to learn more about the stuff I was playing on. Lucky me, I got the chance to do that and spend a lot of time with the object of my affection while working as a golf course groundskeeper in my hometown, Fort Smith, Arkansas.

Some sort of grass studies would have made the most sense for me when it came time for college, but like most kids at that stage of life I had to make at least one wrong turn before I figured that out. I started as an engineering major, but—I can't resist the pun here—grass kept on cropping up in the back of my mind. Pretty soon, with my family's blessing, the inevitable won out and I switched to agronomy, the science of soil management, land cultivation, and crop production. And I never looked back.

To some people grass is a nuisance; it's in their yard and they have to take care of it. Then there are people like me to whom grass is the first thing they think about every day when they get up. I've spent the majority of my life figuring out what's right and wrong about turf and various types of grass. As a turf specialist, I've worked on projects ranging from high school soccer fields to the world's largest enclosed golf course. I've advised turf lovers around the world, from heads of state to groundskeepers to home owners. I've helped folks across the United States achieve the lawns of their dreams. I was a grass consultant to the Athens Olympic Games, and I'm helping the folks in Beijing get their playing fields in shape for the next Summer Olympics.

My turf expertise has even gotten me involved in a murder investigation (I was asked to determine how long a stop sign had been lying in the grass at an accident site) and a lawsuit over First Amendment rights stemming from the 2004 Republication National Convention in New York City. A group of people were told they couldn't hold a rally in Central Park. The stated reason? They would ruin the grass. My job was to try to determine how many people could assemble in Central Park and not ruin the grass. The answer? It all boils down to the things I'm going to show you in the chapters ahead, things like how the grass is mowed, how it's watered, and how it's fertilized.

For my efforts, I've earned the nicknames "Sultan of Sod" and "God of Grass." They're pretty lofty titles, in my book, and I'm proud of them. But, when all is said and done, I'm still a lawn geek. Nothing makes me happier than the sight of a healthy, well-groomed patch of residential green.

In my experience, lots of people make the care of their residential green spaces more difficult than it needs to be, and that frustrates me. They give various reasons for this; I often hear explanations like "my father always did it this way, so I do," or "the guy at the home store recommended I do thus and so." Neither are necessarily bad things, but your father's way of taking care of his lawn might be outmoded or simply wrong. So too might be the home store guy's advice.

The better approach, it seems to me, is to learn and understand the fundamentals of lawn care as they are today. The basics don't change all that much; how grass grows hasn't changed and isn't going to change, that's a simple fact of nature. But, thanks to research, we know a lot more about what we can do to make it grow better and what we can do to keep our lawns healthier and happier in general. When you combine the basics with best practices gleaned from the front lines—from experts like me, who spend their lives focused on such things—the Holy Grail, the great-looking lawn, can happen. If you're battling a bad-looking lawn, you'll be able to look beyond what it is now, know how your efforts are going to pay off, and see the future. A green, lush, glorious future.

Throughout this book, I'll give you the real deal, the facts on what growing and maintaining a great lawn is all about, gleaned from many hours of doing what I do and know best. We'll start with what grass is, and what you can and should do to make it be the best it can be. We'll

Just about everyone uses the terms "turf" and "grass" interchangeably when talking about lawns. I do, too, but they aren't exactly one and the same in the turfgrass industry. Technically speaking, and I'm quoting from a glossary of turfgrass terms published by the American Society of Agronomy here, turf is "a covering of mowed vegetation . . . growing intimately with an upper soil stratum of intermingled roots and stems." In other words, it's what you get when you grow lots of grass plants in a defined area—your yard, an athletic field, a playground, what have you. Grass is "any plant of the family Poaceae," which might seem like Greek to you now, but *Poaceae* is actually Latin and you'll learn lots more about this part of the plant kingdom in the pages ahead. And, of course, there's turfgrass, which is "a species or cultivar of grass, usually of spreading habit, which is maintained as a mowed turf." That said, what you call your own green space is entirely up to you; it can be lawn, grass, turf, turfgrass, whatever works for you.

talk about what you can do to keep good grass from going bad and what you can do if, because or in spite of you, it does anyway. This book will help you if you have to establish a lawn from scratch or if you just inherited the lawn from the dark side. Even if you've been at it for a while, I'm confident that you'll find a few tips that will help you do things better or—and this is my favorite—easier.

My overall goal is to give you the best advice I can about modern turfgrass management, directly from the front lines, and make it make sense to you. As such, I'll break down the science and put things as simply as I can. I'll also minimize the use of technical terms, but you will see them when and where they make sense. Being a lawn geek requires knowing some of them, anyway. The key here, though, is not just being able to throw out terms to awe and impress. The key is to know at least a little bit about the science behind them, to have an understanding of what they really mean.

I'll also stay away from referring to plants by their scientific names, for one simple reason: Unless you're at the high end of lawn geekiness and the people you hang out with say things like *Festuca rubra* or *Bouteloua gracilis* and you feel you need to be on par with them, there's little to no need to know them. Instead, I'll use their common names— red fescue, blue grama, and so on.

I'm assuming that you picked up this book because you're either (a) an avowed lawn geek, (b) a closeted lawn geek, or (c) an aspiring

Each grass has a two-part scientific name. The first part of the name identifies the genus—its official classification or category—and is always capitalized. The second part identifies the species and typically refers to a distinctive feature of the plant, such as its growing form, the area in which it was discovered, sometimes even the person who discovered it, and is never capitalized. As an example, Kentucky bluegrass's scientific name is *Poa pratensis*. *Poa* is the genus name; *pratensis* means, roughly, growing or found in meadows. The scientific name for the most common form of zoysiagrass is *Zoysia japonica*, in honor of where it was first found.

lawn geek. Regardless of your specific geek status, there's one thing that unites you with all other lawn geeks: You're a hands-on person. For whatever reason, you take pride in rolling up your sleeves and caring for your lawn. There's something about it, some little piece of DNA programming, that keeps you connected to your agrarian past. You might grumble about it, you might do more than grumble when you have to haul out your mower, your rotary spreader, your hose-and-sprinkler combo, but you yield to that siren call, that small voice in the back of your brain that cues you when it's time to commune with your green stuff.

The connection between you and your turf is one of the healthiest and most rewarding things going, for both you and your lawn. You are working with a living, growing entity, which readily shows the result of your efforts, and you can take pride in the very visible proof of your work and dedication. Lawn care can provide a good aerobic workout, if you're after that. The time you spend with your turf can even be meditative if you want it to be. As your relationship with your lawn develops, your lawn care knowledge will deepen along with it. Even more important, so will your understanding of your lawn's likes and dislikes. You'll be able to spot small problems before they become big ones. You'll know which areas are prone to snow mold, and you'll know what to do to keep it at bay. You'll be able to tell when it really needs water instead of just flipping the switch on your irrigation system out of habit. You'll know if it needs fertilizing, and what kind and how much.

"Lawn" can mean different things to different people, but for the purposes of this book it means turfgrass, which is defined as grasses that are designed for mowing. This isn't to say there aren't different kinds of lawns, nor is it to cast aspersions on the others in any way. But my professional focus has been on turf since the beginning. Not on ground covers, not on meadows, not on xeriscaping. Turf. The green stuff. It's my passion, and I'm assuming it's yours as well.

By the time you're done reading, you should have a newfound regard and respect for your geekiness, if you don't already have it. At the very least, you should know a heck of a lot more about taking care of your own patch of green. Your lawn. Your turf.

PART ONE

Lawn Basics

CHAPTER 1

Beginning at Grass Roots

What a lawn is and isn't, from the soil on up. How lawns differ depending on where you live. The history of lawns in America, and why we're so passionate about our green spaces.

Early in my career, this girl I was dating (now my wife) asked me a serious question. "What's so hard about grass?" she queried. "You mow it, you water it, you fertilize it."

I wanted to argue, but she was right. Lawn care isn't rocket science. It might seem like it at times, and parts of it, like figuring out why one tiny patch of your lawn turns brown year after year no matter what you do, can be a little challenging at times. But when it comes to the basics of taking care of turf—mowing, watering, and fertilizing—there's nothing all that difficult about any of it. What's more, there never was. We've refined turf care over the years, and certain aspects of it have benefited by scientific discoveries and developments, but its effects are the same now as they were centuries ago.

The centuries ago part is a little intriguing. I've often wondered how ancient people figured out that certain plants had a higher purpose. Like, what stroke of brilliance led to the first boiled artichoke? Popcorn I can understand—get any kind of dried kernels too close to heat and they'll explode. But artichokes? Have you ever seen these things in the wild? They look like giant thistles, which, actually, is exactly what they are. How anyone ever thought they could be edible is beyond me.

And grass. Of all the green things that grow underfoot, what led the ancients to focus on this particular plant as the basis for creating outdoor play spaces and living areas? Sure, animals liked it—well, they ate it anyway—but there's a big cognitive jump from forage food to living carpet. Or is there?

FROM PASTURES TO GARDEN CARPETS TO LAWNS

We'll never know exactly how that cognitive leap happened, of course, but one likely scenario goes something like this: People lived more closely with their animals back then, and they spent a lot of time observing them. Over time, they noticed that certain grazed plants grew a little differently than those in ungrazed fields. Specifically, they grew more vigorously—they were fuller, lusher, and they contained fewer undesirable plants (read weeds). Other factors, like water and sunlight, being the same, the answer had to be in how the plants responded to grazing.

Such reasoning was right on the money, by the way. I'll go into more detail on this later, but of the more than ten thousand grass species, only a handful of them, about fifty or so, have the physical characteristics not only to stand up to grazing—or the human equivalent, mowing—but to actually benefit from it.

Still, when it came to creating the green spaces in ancient landscape designs, grass wasn't the plant of choice. The Persians, for example, chose low-growing flowering plants, not grasses, for the "garden carpets" in their legendary gardens, which historians date to sometime around the sixth century BC. It wasn't until quite a bit later, around the thirteenth century or so, that grass became part of the equation. Exactly how it did is another thing we'll never know for sure. What we do know is that "lawn gardens" composed of grasses and short-stemmed

Another piece of knowledge that's lost to the ages is where the word "lawn" came from. Some sources tie it to the Middle English *launde,* used to describe a field of wildflowers. Others believe it is derived from the French city Laon, which was once famous for its "laonnes."

flowers were part of the medieval gardens grown throughout Europe, and especially in monasteries, where monks drew inspiration and found peace in their tranquil green spaces.

European gardens in general were private and walled, in keeping with their cloistered heritage. The medieval world was often violent; enclosing garden spaces not only provided peace and tranquillity, but also gave much-needed protection. Turfed seats—seats or benches covered in grass, built against walls, trees, or fountains—were common features of these gardens.

Europe wasn't the only area where grass was grown to carpet outdoor spaces. In Japan, zoysiagrass played a key role in gardens built for tea ceremonies and was cultivated as sod for this purpose as early as the mid–twelfth century, if not before.

Grasses were also part of the acreage surrounding castles and manor houses, but just part. Their star turn here was still in the future. For the time being, they shared the bill with herbs and wildflowers in "flowery meads." Grazing animals—sheep and goats—kept these expanses to a height that lords and ladies could navigate, and kept the plants from reverting back to wild meadows.

The French drew the line between lawns and meadows as early as the sixteenth century. To them, meadows were agricultural in nature, rural areas where animals were raised and fed. Lawns were the opposite—established and tended as part of residential properties. While grazing might control the length of the grasses that comprised them, animal husbandry wasn't their primary purpose.

ESTABLISHING ROOTS IN THE NEW WORLD

Finding comfort in the familiar is part and parcel of human nature, so it only makes sense that the fondness for lawns jumped the pond from Old World to New with the people who did the jumping. The grasses they encountered in the New World, however, were far from the lush green plants back home. But that quickly changed. The indigenous strains, for the most part, couldn't keep pace with the demands of the animals that grazed them. As native species died out, the settlers replaced them with species imported from their homelands. Some seeds made the trip in a more organic, natural way. I'm thinking you can draw your own conclusions here, but if not, consider this equation: animals + food = manure.

Like the land around manors and castles, the areas around the new settlements resembled grassy meadows more than manicured green spaces. Lawns, the stands of single-species grasses as they had come to be developed in Europe, weren't common. Only the wealthy could afford both the seeding and the upkeep.

Over time, however, lawns became an indelible part of the American landscape, just as they were in Europe. Lawn mowers, which came along in the nineteenth century, removed a key barrier of entry to garden carpets. No longer did you have to own goats or sheep or know how to wield a scythe. Now all you had to do was push a machine fitted with cutting blades.

The housing boom and the growth of affordable housing developments after World War II launched lawns into the stratosphere. Almost every new home came with a square of turf in front and a square of turf in back. Lawns, and especially the front lawn, became a measure of who and what you were. Not only were more Americans home owners, they had more leisure time than ever before. Interest in recreational sports—golf, in particular—also boomed. As it became the common man's game, people wanted to transfer what they liked on the golf course to their home turf.

The demand for grasses that would trump the neighbors' patches of green and make home owners feel like they were living on golf courses led to the first cultivated grass varieties. With the new varieties also came new, improved equipment to take care of them.

Today, you're in the minority if you don't have a lawn. According to the Turf Resource Center, in 2002 (the most recent figures available), nearly 80 percent of all U.S. households had private lawns. There was an estimated 40 million acres of tended lawn in the United States, with the average lawn covering one-fifth of an acre, or 8,712 square feet.

Our passion for the green stuff fuels enormous turfgrass and lawn-care industries. According to the 2003 Lawn & Garden Market Statistics Study, conducted by the National Gardening Association, we spent more

The numbers are equally staggering when it comes to hiring turfgrass help. There are more than forty thousand landscape contractors and forty-five hundred lawn-care companies in the United States.

than $38.4 billion on do-it-yourself gardening and landscaping in 2003. This equates to an average of $457 per household. Expenditures on things like lawn mowers, irrigation supplies, and other assorted power equipment and nursery products total another $35 billion annually.

The numbers tell the story. We're grass-oholics, no doubt about it. For whatever reason, we have formed a close, personal bond with the green stuff under our feet. And we definitely prefer life with lawns to life without them. While lawn alternatives are becoming a greater part of our national landscape, they're still very much in the minority. We're turf folks, for the most part, and we're proud of it.

YOU AND YOUR GRASS

Now that you know a little more about how lawns came about, let's go back to our original axiom: Taking care of them isn't rocket science. It never was, but over the years turf care has become even easier, thanks to research and development focused on making it so.

Modern research efforts began in the early 1900s when the U.S. Department of Agriculture and the U.S. Golf Association set out to find

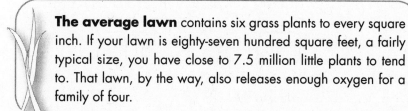

The average lawn contains six grass plants to every square inch. If your lawn is eighty-seven hundred square feet, a fairly typical size, you have close to 7.5 million little plants to tend to. That lawn, by the way, also releases enough oxygen for a family of four.

and develop the best grasses for U.S. climates. Today, thanks to their efforts and those of many others, we have grasses that resist disease, stay green longer, and are more tolerant of things like drought and heat. We also have more choices when it comes to the kinds of grasses we can grow. We can match our lawns to our lifestyles—specifically, the amount of time and money we want to spend on them, as well as the amount of time we want to spend being on them—instead of the other way around.

No matter how much time and effort is spent on developing new and better grasses, however, the basic grass plant remains pretty much the same. Its defining characteristic is that it can be cropped relatively short on a regular basis. Lop off the top of other plants a few times and they'll die. Grasses, on the other hand, thrive. The difference between them? Most plants grow from their tops—the ends of their stems. Grasses, on the other hand, grow from points low to the ground called crowns, where both leaves and roots start from.

Since we'll discuss specific parts of grass plant anatomy throughout this book, knowing a little bit about them is a good idea. The illustration here doesn't identify every plant part, just the ones that a good lawn geek should be able to recognize.

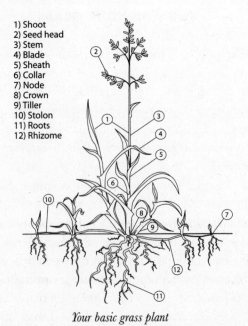

1) Shoot
2) Seed head
3) Stem
4) Blade
5) Sheath
6) Collar
7) Node
8) Crown
9) Tiller
10) Stolon
11) Roots
12) Rhizome

Your basic grass plant

Above the ground:

All aboveground parts are generally referred to as the shoots of a grass plant.

- seed head—the flowering or seeding part of the plant
- stem—the vertical center of the grass plant that supports the seed head of a plant
- blade—the upper portion of the leaf
- sheath—the tubular portion at the base of the leaf that wraps around and encloses the stem
- collar—the part of the leaf where the blade and sheath join together
- nodes—enlarged portions on grass stems where new leaves, shoots, or roots develop

What you're mowing 99 percent of the time are shoots and leaves. If the plant's allowed to go to seed, then you'll be mowing the stem as well.

All of a grass plant's food production comes from what's above the ground. When you cut grass, you remove part of the engine behind this production, which is why mowing heights are so important, and why you'll see me harp on something called the "one-third rule": Never cut off more than one-third of the entire length of a grass blade and/or shoots when you mow.

At ground level:

- crown—the center of the grass plant where the leaves, roots, and stems originate
- tillers—grass shoots that develop from the crown. All grasses form tillers.
- stolons—lateral, jointed stems that originate from the crown, travel above the ground, and develop new shoots and roots along the way. Some grasses have them, but not all.

What happens at ground level is a very big deal. Scalping a lawn—that is, mowing way lower than you should—can damage the crowns, hamper or eliminate new growth, and open the plants up to a world of hurt in the form of turfgrass diseases and insect infestations. Plus, your

Grass plants can live if their roots and/or tops are damaged as long as the crown, which is where all growth emanates from, is still viable. Damaged crowns, on the other hand, typically result in dead grass.

lawn will contain more weeds, as they'll be more than happy to move into the open turf where grass plants should be growing.

Below the ground:

- roots—the underground network that anchors the plant and provides water and nutrients to support its growth
- rhizomes—also jointed stems, but these travel underground. Again, not all grasses have rhizomes.

Grass spreads by tillering or creeping. Tillering grasses add new growth to the main plant only, which means that these plants only grow by expanding outward from one main crown. They're also called bunchgrasses, as they look like bunches or clumps when they grow. Ryegrasses and tall fescue are bunchgrasses. Creeping grasses spread by sending out stolons or rhizomes, which support the baby plants until they can grow on their own.

Being a lawn geek requires more than a passing relationship with the green stuff we call turfgrass. Like any good relationship, the more

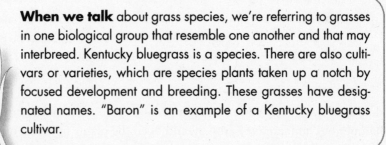

When we talk about grass species, we're referring to grasses in one biological group that resemble one another and that may interbreed. Kentucky bluegrass is a species. There are also cultivars or varieties, which are species plants taken up a notch by focused development and breeding. These grasses have designated names. "Baron" is an example of a Kentucky bluegrass cultivar.

time you spend on the front end, really getting to know it, the better your chances for success in the long run.

It's important to know the kind of grass you're growing, as it will help you avoid stupid decisions or snap judgments regarding your lawn. Say, for example, it looks sparse and clumpy. It could be because it has problems. It could also be because the type of grass in it grows that way.

If you already have a lawn, you might already know what's in it. If you don't, or if you're lawnless and you need to choose a grass to grow, the next couple of chapters are for you.

CHAPTER 2

The Big Chill

All about cool-season grasses, the ones that can survive subzero temperatures and still look like rock stars (as long as you treat them right).

It would be difficult—if not impossible—to be a lawn geek without knowing a lot about the object of your affection. A passing knowledge might be enough if all you're going to do is gaze upon your lawn and entrust its care to someone else, but if you're serious about being a lawn geek, you really have to know about the different types of grasses. People will expect it of you. Plus, it's just kind of cool to be able to look at a stand of grass and call it by name.

What follows in this chapter and the one after it might be—well, okay, probably is—more detail than you'll ever need, and it might seem incredibly anal to you, especially if you already know what's growing in your yard, but bear with me here. There's a method to the madness, and trust me on this, you'll be glad you learned this stuff. Plus, it's information you definitely want to have if you're faced with starting a lawn from scratch for any reason.

I'm going to begin like I would if I were teaching Grass 101 with a group of grasses that date back to when my family came to the New World. My ancestors (on my mother's side) were on the second boat after the *Mayflower*. I like to think that they were personally responsible for bringing those first grasses from Europe to North America, which is a great way of showing my association with all the grasses we use today (it's a great story, anyway). But if they weren't, they definitely were part of the gang responsible for it.

There was grass here; in fact, there were hundreds of native strains. But the animals that the settlers brought along with them made short work of many of these native grasses. Fortunately, the colonists had thought to bring grass seed, and what they brought was hardier stuff that could stand up to the demands of their livestock. For the most part, it came from northern climates, where folks tend to spend a lot of time shaking water off slickers and piling on thick sweaters under them. Someone somewhere along the line saw fit to call them cool-season grasses. The name took, and that's what we call them today.

As their name suggests, these grasses like cool temperatures. This doesn't mean they don't grow when it's hot out, as they definitely do, but they don't grow as fast. They're at their best in the spring, when temperatures are below 75–80°F, and in the late summer and fall, when temps drop back down again. (If you're wondering if you're in cool-season territory, turn to chapter 4 and take a look at the zone map there.)

As a group, again thanks to their misty heritage, cool-season grasses like to drink. Keep them plied with moisture and they'll reward you by staying green throughout the summer. Deny them water and they turn brown. Do it long enough, and especially if it's hot and dry for more than just a couple of days, and they'll quit growing altogether and sit things out until conditions are more to their liking.

If summer temperatures climb pretty high where you live or water's in short supply, your lawn will be brown for at least part of the summer if it's planted with cool-season grasses. If summer means green lawn to you, and you have a choice between cool- and warm-season grasses, you might like the latter better. On the other hand, in warm climates where the ground never freezes, lawns planted with cool-season grasses can stay green, and typically do, through the winter.

If you live substantially above sea level, in the mountains even, cool-season grasses can be good choices if they get enough moisture. They're also happy at sea level as long as temperatures aren't too warm; heat and humidity combined can do them in.

If you've ever played golf in Arizona in January or February and marveled over the lushness of your surroundings even though you're in the middle of a desert, you've seen cool-season grasses on a busman's holiday. In the South and the West, certain grasses in this group are the secret to keeping turf green during the winter. Grass seed—typically fast-growing perennial or annual ryegrass—is spread into the turf before it goes dormant for the winter. When temperatures heat up in the spring, the over-seeded grass dies out as the warm-season grass beneath it turns green again.

Most cool-season grasses, in keeping with their agrarian heritage, are better suited to livestock grazing and aren't used in lawns. But others are decidedly turfgrass worthy, as we're about to see.

SINGING THE BLUES

Of the some two hundred different bluegrass species, Kentucky bluegrass reigns supreme. It's also the grass that, for me and just about every other lawn geek I've ever met, defines the perfect lawn. No other grass has its deep green, knock-your-socks-off color, and yes, it absolutely can look blue in some light, and especially if you're looking at it through sunglasses. Nor can other grasses match its texture, which is as fine and silky as they come, or its thick, dense sod, which simply begs for a bare-foot run-through.

If you want a grass you can brag on, this is it. Or, better put, it can be. Many older Kentucky blues can come down with various diseases, and almost all of them—even newer cultivars—are lousy shade performers. If your landscape sports a lot of well-established trees, Kentucky bluegrass probably isn't the grass for you.

Kentucky bluegrass isn't just a beauty queen; it's a durable grass, too. It spreads via tough, underground rhizomes, which means it can take a fair amount of abuse, such as heavy foot traffic and low mowing, and recover pretty quickly, which is why turf professionals like it for things like schoolyards and athletic fields. It stands up to

Turfgrasses are often described as coarse- or fine-textured. This has to do more with the width of their blades than how they feel in your hand. Wide blades are called coarse or rough grasses; narrow blades are called fine-textured grasses.

fairly cold temperatures better than some other cool-season grasses. It also performs well in drought conditions; if water is scarce or nonexistent, it will quit growing and turn brown. Turn the water back on, and those underground rhizomes will send new green shoots right back up.

Kentucky bluegrass is the most planted turfgrass in the United States, and, well, because we live in a consumer-driven world that's always searching for the next best thing, grass seed producers have dedicated lots of time and money to developing new and better varieties of it over the years. As a result, some one hundred varieties have been introduced in the past twenty-five years alone. The newer Kentucky blues are typically better at dealing with things like temperature variations. They fend off diseases better, are darker and richer in color, grow or green up earlier in the spring, have higher shoot densities (a fancy way of saying thicker turf), grow more aggressively, and recover from abuse faster.

Bluegrass is one of the most widely adapted cool-season grasses. It's found in practically every European country, northern Asia, and in the mountainous areas of Algeria and Morocco. Some bluegrass species, such as Canada bluegrass, are native to North America. Kentucky bluegrass probably came from seed brought by my ancestors and other early colonists, although some research suggests that it came to the United States from Labrador or Alaska and was here when the settlers arrived. Either way, they—and their animals—were the ones who spread it about.

> **Shoot density,** or just density, describes the number of plants in a defined area. This varies quite a bit by grass type; some grasses simply create thicker turf than others. How you take care of your lawn and environmental factors will also affect turf density.

Why I'd tell you to plant it.

Simply put, Kentucky bluegrass is a beautiful grass. It's also a fairly forgiving grass. It tolerates drought conditions well and recovers from abuse quickly.

Why I wouldn't.

If your yard is heavily shaded, Kentucky bluegrass isn't going to grow well. It's bad shade grass. Growing it from seed takes some patience; this grass can take more than three weeks to germinate, making it among the slowest of all turfgrasses to spring up when planted.

> **You'll hear people** talk about *Poa annua*, also known as annual bluegrass. Some people call it a weed, some people don't (especially in the North, where it can coexist nicely with other grasses), but keeping it out of lawns is like keeping a crowd calm when someone yells fire. It ain't gonna happen. It will show up no matter what because it sets lots of seeds. If there's one annual bluegrass plant in a neighborhood, it could be in everyone's yard in five years.
>
> I don't recommend eradicating it if you live in the North. As mentioned, it gets along okay with other grasses and it's more trouble than it's worth to take out. If you're in the South, and it's causing major disruptions in your turf, see chapter 11 for tips on getting rid of it.

COUSINS OF THE BLUES

While Kentucky bluegrass is the undisputed king of the bluegrasses, some of its relatives make my short list for bluegrasses worth knowing about for special situations, particularly shade:

- Supina bluegrass is a recent European import that's gaining attention for its shade and wear tolerance. I have studied this grass extensively and have found it to be a solid performer in shady, cool-season lawns, especially if it gets enough water. It's expensive, though, running thirty-five to fifty dollars a pound because the seed's imported from Germany. You can cushion the hit to your wallet by planting it as a mixture with other grasses (check chapter 6 for more information on doing this). It can be tough to find, but worth seeking out if it fits your needs.
- Rough bluegrass is a good grass for wet, shady areas. Anywhere else, avoid using it for anything other than overseeding warm-season grasses in the winter. There are simply better grasses for growing, period. If Supina isn't available, you might go with it.

The bottom line here: Don't fret too much if you have annual bluegrass. People have gone to great lengths and expense to try to keep it off their property, and you'll hear golf tournament commentators talk about it, too, as the golf industry has spent millions on growing it (it is used on some putting greens) and how to kill it.

About ten years ago, I was visiting an exclusive golf club in Ohio where the management was under the impression that their course had no annual bluegrass and intended to keep it that way. When I arrived the clubhouse staff asked for my shoes. When I asked why, they told me they were going to fumigate my shoes to kill any stray seeds I might have drug in with me. They now have annual bluegrass, by the way, and they are managing it just like the rest of us. So, take heart; even the big boys don't know how to keep it out.

Why I'd tell you to plant them.

I'd tell you to plant Supina if you have a heavily shaded lawn. It's the best cool-season grass for dense, shaded areas. If you need grass in the shade, this is your guy. Plant rough bluegrass if you can't get Supina or if you want a grass that's not as aggressive a grower as Supina is.

Why I wouldn't.

Both need more water than the other bluegrasses, so they're not good choices if you can't water them. They're also not good choices if you're going to object when they invade other parts of the yard, since they grow by stolons. Once you plant them, you're not going to get rid of them. They're both a little lighter in color than other bluegrasses, so they'll show up if they start to invade. Rough bluegrass also doesn't handle traffic well.

COMING THROUGH THE RYE

What I love about ryegrass is that it germinates quick. It can fill in bare areas fast; I can go from bare ground to mowing a thick turf in twenty-one days.

There are annual ryegrasses and perennial ryegrasses. Both are bunchgrasses, and can be planted on their own or used in mixtures. For my money, you'll use perennial ryegrass ninety-nine times out of a hundred; because it's a perennial, it's not going to die off every year.

But this doesn't put annual ryegrass on the "never, ever plant" list. It's not a grass to ignore. In fact, it's far from that. Annual ryegrass is a good choice for overseeding dormant or semidormant warm-season grasses during the winter. It's also an option if, let's say, you just moved into a new house, it's too late in the season to plant seed, and you can't afford sod but you really need to see some green outside your front door to feel like you're home. Annual ryegrass is one of the few true "throw and grow" seeds, meaning you can simply toss it out and let it take hold. No tilling, no digging, no scratching it in like you have to do with other grass seed. (Of course, you'll come back the next spring and put in a proper lawn, right?)

> **A little bit** of insider info: Perennial ryegrass is the grass of choice
> for the two most famous and hallowed pieces of turf ground in the
> world—Augusta National Golf Club (the home of the Masters
> golf tournament) and Wimbledon Tennis Club. Both replant it
> every year, as neither venue stays open year-round and it's
> easier and cheaper than keeping the grass alive. So you're
> seeing brand-new grass (and the players are playing on a
> brand-new surface) every time you see it on television.

Because it germinates so quickly, seed producers used to include annual ryegrass in lots of seed mixes, but you don't see it as often these
days. It's a pushy little grass and will fight for turf dominance with
other, more desirable perennial grasses. And, as mentioned, it dies off
when the growing season's over. Enough said.

Perennial ryegrass is a whole different story, and a better one, too.
It's a tough, low-maintenance grass that forms dense, insect- and
disease-resistant turf. It too can be grown on its own, but its strong
points—fast germination, disease resistance, and all-around ruggedness—
make it a good partner to Kentucky bluegrass and fine fescues, and it's
often included in mixes with these grasses.

Why I'd tell you to plant it.

Perennial ryegrass germinates quickly—you can go from bare
ground to dense lawn in twenty-one days.

Why I wouldn't.

Damaged ryegrass turf won't fill in at all due to this grass's bunch-type growth habit. If your turf is going to serve as the neighborhood playground and you want to plant perennial ryegrass
exclusively, plan on overseeding bare areas throughout the year.
Mowing with a dull blade will shred the heck out of it; newer cultivars
are less susceptible to this problem. Older varieties are a bit coarse in
texture. It's not a good choice in very cold climates, such as those
found in northern Minnesota, Wisconsin, and Michigan, as severe
winters can kill it.

FEISTY FESCUES

Until fairly recently, turf professionals (me included) didn't think too highly of fescues. While they had some good traits—heck, some great traits—such as being real tolerant of poor growing conditions, they had other qualities that, frankly, weren't so hot. Some fescues looked pale or anemic when compared with other grasses. Others had undesirable textures. Many didn't tolerate heat well (a fair number still don't) and were prone to insect infestations and diseases.

If fescues were used at all as turfgrass, they were typically part of shade-tolerant seed mixtures. But fescue's positive qualities led to dedicated breeding programs, and today there are improved cultivars that have made many of this grass's earlier problems history. Many newer strains even look a lot like bluegrass, at least color-wise. Their textures are better, too. Plus, they're more tolerant of heat and drought, and they're more disease resistant.

Fescues come in lots of different sizes and shapes. Some are extremely short with very fine, threadlike leaves. Others have broader leaves and can get up to six feet tall. In the middle of these extremes are some species that are becoming increasingly popular for lawns.

There are about a hundred different fescue species. Those that are used for lawns fall into two categories—coarse and fine—based on their leaf texture. Within these categories, however, is some confusion, and here's why: Some of the newer coarse fescue cultivars—the tall fescues in particular—have finer leaves than their ancestors and are sometimes referred to as "fine-leaved tall fescues." They're more refined when compared with earlier cultivars, but they're still pretty robust when compared with their true, fine-fescue cousins. A better term for these improved grasses is "turf-type tall fescue," and you'll sometimes see them called that, too.

As a Matter of Course

In the United States, tall fescue is the grass most commonly used from the coarse fescue group. It's a deep-rooted grass that likes moist environments best, but it also tolerates drought well and will survive dry periods by going dormant. It likes clay soils (see chapter 5 for more on this) with lots of organic matter, but it does okay in others, too. It's also pretty shade-tolerant, and it can take a fair amount of foot traffic, too.

Tall fescue likes heat better than cold, which, coupled with its ability to survive in drought conditions, makes it a good choice for areas where summers are too hot and humid for cool-season grasses and winters too cold for warm-season grasses. It will stay green when other cool-season grasses go dormant.

Before it came in from the pasture and became the focus of concerted breeding efforts, tall fescue was, to put it kindly, a little ugly. It had coarse leaves and its color wasn't anything to write home about. It had to be mowed fairly high, so lawns that were planted with it never looked particularly well groomed. And it was prone to fungal diseases.

Newer tall fescue cultivars have better color, better texture, and can be mowed shorter. Many are specially bred to take advantage of a naturally occurring fungus called an endophyte (from the Greek *endo*, meaning inside, and *phyton*, meaning plant) that improves their resistance to drought, insects, and some diseases.

Why I'd tell you to plant it.

Tall fescue tolerates hot, dry conditions better than most cool-season grasses, which makes it a good choice in areas where neither cool- nor warm-season grasses do particularly well. It's shade-tolerant and will handle a fair amount of foot traffic. If your kids like to play on your lawn, or your dog likes to run along your fence line, this grass will handle the abuse better than most.

Why I wouldn't.

If you want a lawn with a silky texture, this isn't the grass for you. Even newer strains result in coarse-textured lawns when compared with most other cool-season grasses. It tolerates heat much better than cold; severe cold can cause serious damage and result in sparse, extremely

The major trick to a tall fescue lawn is in its establishment. You have to make sure to cover the ground well with the seed (nine to ten pounds per thousand square feet) and apply it in three directions.

coarse turf. Plus, this grass is a bunch-type grass and will need reseeding when worn down or bare. Unlike perennial ryegrass, it doesn't establish quickly, and establishing it in general can be frustrating.

Fine, Just Fine

I have to admit, I have a lot of respect for fine fescues. They're extremely shade- and cold-tolerant—in fact, they have the highest tolerance in both areas of all the cool-season grasses. This quality typically lands them in mixtures with Kentucky bluegrass for shade areas, but these days you can find them on their own as well. If you're looking for a low-maintenance grass, and summers aren't too hot and dry where you live, fine fescues might just fit the bill. They don't need much fertilizing—in fact, they really don't like it—and they will thrive in dry, unfertile soil. They're slow growers; if left uncut they'll only reach about eight to twelve inches. While they don't like drought conditions, they also don't like too much water. They actually do better with a bit of neglect. Pay too much attention to them and they'll reward you by getting a little puny. These plants really like the shade. If you have a lot of dry, shady spots in your yard, fine fescues will grow in them. If you want to keep fine fescue the dominant species, don't overwater and don't overfertilize.

Of the fine fescues, the following are most often planted as turf-grasses:

- Hard fescue. This grass's strong bunching habit makes it look less refined than other lawn grasses, but it can be a good choice for difficult sites that are unusually cold, windy, and dry. Since it doesn't grow very tall, or very fast, it's also an option for low-maintenance lawns.

An interesting aspect of fine fescue is that because it survives on low amounts of fertilizer and water, a properly maintained fine fescue lawn will attract very little annual bluegrass (which loves both). Turn on the water and fertilizer, though, and you'll have annual bluegrass in a hurry.

Is there one perfect grass among the cool-season grasses? Not really, as there's no one perfect grass, period, but I sure get asked that question a lot. That said, I do have a personal favorite, and it's Kentucky bluegrass. Like most folks, I tend to measure all other grasses against this one. For most home owners, however, I recommend a mixture of Kentucky bluegrass, perennial rye-grass, and fine fescue, as it covers the gamut of conditions. Start with this combination and move out from there and you'll be fine.

- Chewings fescue. Another tough little fescue, this one tolerates poor soil, shade, and drought. It doesn't handle wear well, however, and it doesn't recover from damage quickly. It's often mixed with Kentucky bluegrass for shady, low-maintenance lawns.
- Red, or creeping red. Unlike the other fescues, which are bunchgrasses, this grass also spreads via very short rhizomes, hence its name. It's a deep green, very fine-leaved grass that likes cool, shady areas. It needs quite a bit of shade to do well in the heat. It grows very slowly, which makes it a poor choice for lawns that get a lot of use.

Why I'd tell you to plant them.

Fine fescues are good choices for bad soil, they'll survive periodic droughts, and they love the shade. If you're after a lush, softly textured lawn, you'll like them; fine fescues are just about the finest-textured grasses out there.

Why I wouldn't.

None of the fine fescues are good for yards that get lots of use. Some species can be aggressive and will take over other turfgrass in your yard. Most are bunchgrasses, which means they don't recover quickly from damage. They can produce a lot of plant detritus—also known as thatch, which you'll learn a lot more about in later chapters—and they don't do well in high heat.

 **Bentgrasses** get their name from their odd growth habit. Unlike all other grasses, if they get more than an inch tall, they bend to the side and grow that way instead of upward toward the sun.

GETTING BENT

If you've ever stepped onto a golf course so green that it took your breath away, it was probably planted with a bentgrass, in particular creeping bentgrass, as it's widely used on golf courses, and especially on greens. And that, I have to say, is about the only place you should see any of the bentgrasses, aside from similarly short-cropped places like badminton courts, grass tennis courts, lawn-bowling greens, and whatnot. Anywhere else, forget about it.

Considered by some—well, golfers mostly—as the most beautiful of grasses, you'll recognize bentgrasses by their fine texture, deep green color, and their thick, low-to-the-ground growth. They're shallow rooters and need frequent feeding and watering, as they're lousy at pulling nutrients and moisture from the soil.

Three types of bentgrasses—creeping, colonial, and velvet—are commonly found in the United States, but you won't find them in this book, as I don't consider any of them good choices for home lawns. If you have a bentgrass lawn, you know why. If not, and you're wondering just how bad they can be, go back to the description of their growing habit. Get out a ruler and measure the distance between the tip of your forefinger and the knuckle closest to it. If you're like most people, there's probably about an inch, give or take, separating them. Now think about what it would take to keep an entire yard mowed to that height, if not shorter. More important, think about why you'd even want to. Then add in bentgrass's cultural requirements. This should be enough to quash any thoughts of planting this grass.

Why I'd tell you to plant it.
I wouldn't, as the reasons for staying away from it, in my book, far

outnumber the reasons for growing it. That said, if you want a yard that looks like a putting green and feels like a plush Oriental carpet underfoot, bentgrass is the choice.

Why I wouldn't.

This should be crystal clear by now, but if it isn't . . . bentgrasses are high-high-maintenance plants, although some newer cultivars are less needy. Still, they all need more coddling than most grasses or they'll develop disease and pest problems. All but the newer strains of colonial bentgrass have to be mowed very short, and preferably with a reel mower to keep stress levels low. Bottom line, they're a good choice only if you really want a yard that looks like a golf green and you have the skills, the time, and the money to maintain it. Or you're willing to pay someone else very well to do it.

Now that you've met the grasses that don't come in from the cold, let's take a look at the grasses that like things hot.

CHAPTER 3

Some Like It Hot

Grasses that can take the heat without breaking a sweat.

If there were such a thing as a perfect grass, it might be in this section. The reason I say this is that warm-season grasses, in general, are deeper rooted and grow by rhizomes and stolons. They'll fill in if traffic wears them down; they don't have to be reseeded like cool-season grasses do. This ability to repair themselves goes a long way toward that Holy Grail, the maintenance-free lawn that everyone's looking for.

The knock on warm-season grasses: it has to be warm. If it gets cold, they're not going to grow, and if it gets cold enough, they're not going to survive.

Like cool-season grasses, most of the warm-season grasses are imports. A few came with early colonists; most are later arrivals, some even as late as the twentieth century. Unlike their cool-season kin, warm-season grasses are almost all from the tropics, and many of their variety names reflect their heritage. This group also includes two grasses native to the United States that are increasingly cropping up in lawns where other grasses are difficult to grow.

For the most part, warm-season grasses are the diametric opposite of their cool cousins. In the great circle of life, they're the yang to the cool-season grasses' yin. They like long, hot summers and mild winters. High temperatures paired with high humidity don't faze them, but they'll go dormant and turn brown when temperatures drop below their comfort zone. In severe cold snaps, some warm-season grasses will die off altogether. But don't for a minute think these grasses are wimps. Compared with cool-season varieties, warm-season grasses are generally more robust, especially when temps are high, and they're nowhere near as picky about their growing conditions.

It's not hard to tell cool- and warm-season grasses apart. Warm-season grasses usually have wider leaves. They can be mowed shorter in general, so you'll typically see them mowed pretty short.

Many warm-season grasses spread by aboveground runners, or stolons, and they grow like weeds. "Aggressive" isn't too strong a term here. Many—especially the nonnatives—are noted for their ability to choke out other plants, which can be a good thing where weeds are concerned, but not so good if the other plants they're choking out are other grass species in your neighbor's yard. With warm-season grasses, and especially with some of the common varieties more than the hybrids, this can definitely happen.

This growth habit is also a big thatch producer, which, in addition to being unsightly, can lead to disease and pest problems. The most popular warm-season grasses—bermudagrass and zoysiagrass—spread by both rhizomes and stolons. This makes them very durable as they tolerate heavy use and recover well from it. It also makes them very hard, if not impossible, to totally eradicate—so be careful what you wish for.

BERMUDA SHORTS

If you live in the southern United States, it's a good bet that you have a bermudagrass lawn, especially if you're living in an older home. Bermudagrass is as popular in the South as Kentucky bluegrass is in the North, largely because it's one of the first warm-season grasses introduced here; it made its debut in the mid-1700s from—gotcha—Africa, not Bermuda. But bermudagrass doesn't win the popularity contest just because it's been around the longest. It has other qualities that make it a top pick for southern lawns. It has adapted well to many different growing conditions. It can handle poor soil and it tolerates salt spray. It can survive drought conditions and high heat, thanks to its deep roots. It tolerates foot traffic and can be mowed low. If you want a durable lawn, bermudagrass is a top pick.

Common bermudagrass produces seeds and is a vigorous spreader. Ignore it a bit and it can run wild, taking over flower beds and other areas where it's not welcome, like a fox in a henhouse. Once it does, it can be tough if not impossible to remove, so you're better off not having to deal with the problem in the first place, especially if the flower beds and other areas where it's not welcome are in your neighbor's yard. Regularly weed it out of areas where it's creeping in or spot spray it with a nonselective herbicide like glyphosate, which you'll read more about in the chapters ahead.

There are hybrid bermudagrasses, which some experts feel are better choices for lawns, as they produce sterile seeds and are less likely to grow where they're not welcome. But they'll still invade flower beds if given the chance, and they're big thatch producers. Hybrids are finer textured than common bermudagrasses, which makes their invasiveness and thatchiness a little easier to tolerate. But just a little. Between the two, common bermudagrass is the better choice in most situations, as they need less care than hybrids do.

In general, neither common nor hybrid bermudagrasses handle cold weather well, although some of the common bermudagrasses and some newer hybrids tolerate it better. When temperatures start to dip down below 60°F, they'll start to go dormant. If temperatures drop low enough in the winter, they won't just go dormant, they'll die.

Bermudagrasses are big into sunbathing and don't do well in the shade. You might see shade-tolerant claims on some newer cultivars, but, like sales pitches for Florida swampland, it's best not to believe them.

Both common and hybrid bermudagrasses are meant to be grown as monostands—in other words, not mixed with other genuses or species. Mix them and you'll get patchy growth, as they won't intertwine like cool-season grasses do.

Common bermudagrass originally came to the United States for planting in pastures, not in lawns, as its coarse texture wasn't something most people wanted in their yards. But this grass's positive traits outweighed its negatives, and by the early 1920s it was appearing on golf courses and in lawns.

Why I'd tell you to plant it.

Bermudagrass is a fast grower and will quickly fill in bare spots. It's a tough grass, tolerant of heat, salt, drought, wear, and low mowing. These qualities make it the most popular and best choice for sports fields in areas warm enough to grow it. Also, it's easy to overseed a cool-season grass into it during the winter for year-round color.

Why I wouldn't.

This grass does not like shade or cool temperatures. Hybrids aren't available by seed and must be established vegetatively—that is, by sticking small parts of the plants in the ground. Hybrids also need more tending and must be mowed shorter (less than one and a quarter inch) to look their best. Common bermudagrass can look good at two to three inches tall.

TEEING IT UP WITH ZOYSIA

Zoysiagrass (pronounced ZOY-shuhgrass) came to the United States from Korea in the early 1900s. It's a dark green, stiff grass with fine-to-medium-textured blades that's popular on golf courses, as golf balls tend to sit high on it instead of digging in, as they do on softer grasses.

Zoysiagrass is a deep-rooted, tough plant that resists drought and stands up to wear. But it can be frustrating as heck to grow. Seeds can take forever to sprout, so if not sodded, it's typically established by planting plugs or sprigs, which leaves lots of open space between each vegetative piece. Those spaces will eventually fill in, as zoysiagrass spreads by both rhizomes and stolons, but it does so very, verrrrry slowly.

Zoysiagrasses are native to Japan, China, and other areas of Southeast Asia. They were named to honor Karl von Zois, an eighteenth-century Austrian botanist; but the variety most commonly used in the United States is called Meyer, for Frank N. Meyer, a Department of Agriculture plant explorer who first collected the seed in Korea in 1905.

If you have the patience of Job and don't mind a yard that looks like it's under construction for a couple of years, you might like this grass. But, let me repeat this, you might have to wait two to three years to see if you do (unless you put in zoysiagrass sod, in which case it's wonderful from the start), as it can take this long for your yard to look really good planted with it. Once it does fill in, however, zoysiagrass makes for a handsome lawn with thick, dense turf.

Another drawback with this grass is that it turns brown pretty quick in the fall. When temperatures dip down below 55°F, it gives up the ghost. And it's slow to recover in the spring, which means a zoysiagrass yard is going to look brown longer than some others during the winter. Overseeding typically doesn't work well with zoysiagrass; it's so dense that overseeded cool-season grasses have a hard time establishing themselves. So you'll have to deal with a brown yard. Since zoysiagrass is also one of the lowest-maintenance grasses out there, it's a trade-off many home owners don't seem to mind making.

Soon after it came to the United States, zoysiagrass was touted as the miracle grass that could solve all yard problems, since it can grow almost anywhere and it doesn't get weedy. You'll still see some of this hype today. Because it's more cold-tolerant than most warm-season grasses, the fact that it can grow almost anywhere is technically true. It will even grow as far north as the Canadian border. But will it do well there? Not really. If you think zoysiagrass grows slow in the South, it literally creeps at a snail's pace up north.

The part about it being a virtually weed-free grass (once it gets established, that is) is also technically true. It's still not a good choice in colder climates. Remember, weed-free or not, zoysiagrass turns brown very quickly in the fall and stays brown long into the spring. When all the other lawns around you, lawns planted with cool-season grasses like Kentucky bluegrass, ryegrass, and the like, are green in fall and spring, yours will be brown. I can always count on a few calls in the spring from new owners of older homes who think their lawns are dead because everyone else's are green and theirs aren't.

Zoysiagrass's deep roots are invasive. You wouldn't necessarily find this a problem, but your neighbor might if your zoysiagrass decides to wander into his yard in search of water, which it most likely will. In the fall, if he's growing a cool-season grass, his turf will have

It's easy to see who falls for zoysiagrass hype in cool-season land. Just cruise the neighborhoods in early spring and look for brown patches surrounded by green. That's the dormant zoysiagrass surrounded by cool-season grasses.

big, brown, dead-looking spots where your zoysiagrass has taken up residence. He might think there's something really wrong when the only problem is invasive, dormant zoysiagrass, thanks to you. And he'll have to deal with the same thing in the spring when his cool-season grass greens up on schedule, weeks before zoysiagrass breaks its slumber.

Not exactly neighborly of you to cause this problem, is it? And while zoysiagrass can be eliminated, it's not easy. You can avoid the problem entirely by not believing the hype on this grass, and being judicious about using it. On a relative scale, however, zoysiagrass isn't as aggressive as bermudagrass, which is something to keep in mind if you're thinking about planting either of them.

Why I'd tell you to plant it.

Zoysiagrass can be planted almost anywhere and survive. It tolerates cold and drought. Since it grows so slowly, it doesn't need to be mowed as often as other grasses. A mature zoysiagrass lawn rarely has problem weeds and is relatively disease- and insect-free as well. It will outperform bermudagrass in shade if you are choosing between the two. It also tolerates fluctuating temperatures and salt spray, which makes it a good choice for coastal lawns.

Why I wouldn't.

If you want a lawn that feels good underfoot, zoysiagrass's stiff blades aren't for you. It establishes slowly, turns brown quickly in the fall, and recovers late in the spring. It's not a good choice for heavy-traffic areas because it grows so slowly.

The bottom line on zoysiagrass and bermudagrass, if you're trying to choose between them, is that bermudagrass is going to be a lot easier to establish. Zoysiagrass is also more expensive because it's not readily available. Not many seed growers grow it; it's as hard for them to grow as it is for you.

THE GREAT SAINT

St. Augustinegrass is a very good grass for the southern part of the United States, particularly in shady areas. Its biggest issue is its inability to tolerate cold weather, which limits its use to Gulf Coast states, Georgia, and South Carolina. Some newer cultivars are more cold-tolerant, but even the best ones don't compare to zoysiagrass or even bermudagrass in this regard.

It's not hard to tell St. Augustinegrass from other warm-season grasses because it has wide blades. Once you learn how to identify it, you can't miss it. I can fool you on zoysiagrass and bermudagrass for a long time; I can legitimately say you would need a magnifying glass to tell the difference between them, but you'll never need one with St. Augustine's large, flat stems and broad, coarse leaves.

You'll have to irrigate St. Augustinegrass because most of the time it's growing in sandy soils without much water in them. In a Gulf Coast state, St. Augustinegrass is a very logical choice. It's going to tolerate a wide range of soil conditions, and though it's going to need some water it will stay green year-round.

Fungal diseases, in particular brown patch, are a serious issue with

If you live in South Carolina, you might know St. Augustinegrass as Charlestongrass.

St. Augustinegrass. So too is a virus called St. Augustinegrass Decline, or SAD. It's a big problem in Texas and Louisiana, and there's no known cure for it beyond making sure you plant SAD-resistant cultivars. (For you trivia buffs who want to really impress someone or need to make a few bucks on a wager, SAD is the only known disease-causing virus in the turfgrass world.) Grubs and chinch bugs like St. Augustinegrass, too.

Why I'd tell you to plant it.
It's probably the easiest grass to grow in the coastal areas of Gulf Coast states and it will stay green year-round.

Why I wouldn't.
This grass does not tolerate cold weather. Period.

BOOGYING DOWN WITH BAHIA

I'm not going to gain a lot of brownie points with the bahiagrass people, but here's the story: If you ever wanted a grass that looks like it came out of the pasture, this one's it. It was first used as a forage grass in the South. When the snowbirds moved down to Florida (not the ones who owned the million-dollar homes but the ones who owned the twenty-thousand-dollar trailers in trailer parks carved out of cow pastures), they needed a lawn grass that they could establish and ignore. They didn't want to take care of a lawn—if they wanted that they'd move back north—but they also didn't want to come home and see their trailer park washed away. So they looked across the road and saw what was planted in the cow pastures and drug it over.

The bottom line on bahiagrass is that even on its best day it's not very good-looking. It's not a thoroughbred, it's a plowhorse. This doesn't mean it doesn't do its job, if its job is to provide cover to keep soil from eroding. It's just not going to be a real good-looking grass, not compared to the other choices.

Like other warm-season grasses, bahiagrass is aggressive and can choke out weeds and other grasses. It's shade-tolerant and not fussy about its soil. Sandy, clayey, infertile, dry—basically lousy soil is more than okay as far as bahiagrass is concerned.

Bahiagrass spreads via short rhizomes, which results in turf that, while providing good cover, is also fairly open. It continually forms seed heads during its peak growing season. Keeping this grass looking neat means lopping off those heads with frequent mowing.

If your yard has erosion problems, bahiagrass can help keep things in place, as its roots can grow up to eight feet deep. Those long roots are also super efficient at finding whatever moisture might be lurking in the soil around them, which also makes bahiagrass a good choice if irrigation is spotty or unavailable. That said, bahiagrass grows best when watered regularly during hot summer months.

Why I'd tell you to plant it.

It requires little to no irrigation. It's a grass to put down if all you want or need is ground cover. Remember, the key here is "all you want," because that's all it is.

Why I wouldn't.

Bahiagrass will not tolerate shade. It sets seed heads constantly, so you have to mow it to keep them from always sticking up. As a ground cover, bahiagrass is about one step up from weeds. Saying it could ever look "good" is like comparing my golf game to Tiger Woods's; no matter how much I practice or how hard I try, my game will always pale in comparison to his. So does bahiagrass when compared to just about every other turfgrass.

ZOYSIAGRASS'S CREEPY COUSIN

Centipedegrass is a grass that I actually kind of put akin to fine fescue, not so much for its adaptability but more because if you try to make this grass grow it will probably stop growing. With a fine fescue lawn, if you put lots of water and fertilizer on it, it turns into an annual bluegrass lawn. This one's in the same boat; if you start fertilizing this grass like you would bermudagrass or zoysiagrass, you might kill it. This is one of the reasons why it's called lazyman's grass: it will stay kind of green without a lot of care. It won't give you the lush green turf that will host the neighborhood picnic or a track meet, but it is a grass that you can look out at and know that it's not going to die. Bottom line, it's a pretty hardy grass.

Centipedegrass, which was introduced to the United States in 1916, is another Frank Meyer discovery. Unfortunately, while the seed made it to the United States, Meyer didn't accompany his find. Mystery shrouds his death to this day. What is known is that he was collecting seed in China's Hunan province. When his steamer returned to port after his expedition was over, his luggage and the seeds he collected were on it. Meyer, however, was nowhere to be found.

Centipedegrass, like zoysiagrass, is a slow-growing creeper. It has short, upward-growing stems that, when coupled with its creeping growing form, make it resemble a centipede—hence its name.

Like zoysiagrass, centipedegrass is a slow grower. Unlike zoysiagrass, it has shallow roots, which makes it a poor choice for high-traffic lawns and increases its watering needs. It's fairly easy to establish via seed or sod, and it isn't too picky about soil conditions. It's not as aggressive as zoysiagrass or bermudagrass. It is very cold-sensitive. Instead of going dormant, it will die in subfreezing temperatures. A light freeze will turn it brown, but it will green up as soon as temperatures rise.

Why I'd tell you to plant it.

Centipedegrass is a top choice for low-maintenance lawns, albeit for ones that are more for looks than use. It doesn't grow very tall, doesn't need much mowing, and will tolerate poor and acidic soils. It also doesn't need much fertilizer—feeding more than once a year can actually harm this grass. If benign neglect pretty much sums up your approach to lawn care, this grass is for you. It is better looking than bahiagrass, if that means anything.

Why I wouldn't.

This grass is a slow grower with shallow roots, which makes it a poor choice for high-activity lawns, as it doesn't recover quickly from abuse. It doesn't tolerate cold and might die altogether if frozen. It needs plenty of water in general and doesn't tolerate drought conditions well.

AT HOME ON THE RANGE

Buffalograss is, for most, an acquired taste. Buffalo herds love it. Depending on where you live, you might want to learn to love it too, especially if you're in or near one of the states where buffalo still roam. In fact, it might be the only practical choice to grow where you are, especially if you're living in a part of the United States where drought is common and it's windy. That said, this grass is such an acquired taste that having it in your yard is best when doing so makes you one of the pack in your neighborhood, not the Lone Ranger.

This tough-as-nails plant is the only native North American grass in wide use as turfgrass. Since it's a citizen of the plains, where temperatures can fluctuate sixty degrees in a matter of minutes and rain might be nonexistent for months, it can survive conditions—harsh temperatures, high winds, compacted soil—that would make other grasses whimper. You name it, buffalograss will stand up to it.

For being such a little toughie, buffalograss has a fine, almost hairlike texture. The leaves on some cultivars are fairly curly, and none of them grow all that tall—often less than ten inches for an entire growing season—which makes buffalograss a good choice for low-maintenance lawns. In fact, you don't even have to mow it, although doing so makes it look more like other turf.

Buffalograss spreads via stolons. It's unique in that it has both male and female plants, and each produces its own distinctive seed. Seeds on the male plants ride high; they're near the base on female plants. The high-flying male seeds can make buffalograss look a little shaggy, but neater-looking, all-female cultivars are available. So too are cultivars that produce more nodes on their stolons, which makes for a thicker, denser turf.

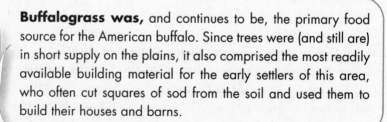

Buffalograss was, and continues to be, the primary food source for the American buffalo. Since trees were (and still are) in short supply on the plains, it also comprised the most readily available building material for the early settlers of this area, who often cut squares of sod from the soil and used them to build their houses and barns.

Once established, buffalograss can grow in areas that receive as little as ten inches of moisture a year. Compared with grasses that need an inch or so of water a week, this puts buffalograss at rock bottom when it comes to irrigation requirements. Newly established buffalograss lawns, however, need just as much water as others do, and buffalograss will do better in general when it's not gasping for moisture.

Why I'd tell you to plant it.

Buffalograss will live where other grasses won't. Once established, it needs significantly less water and maintenance than almost all other grasses. It doesn't necessarily have to be mowed, but it looks better when it is. It doesn't need much fertilizer—in dry climates, feeding once in the spring and once again in the summer will do it.

Why I wouldn't.

This grass is slow to green up in the spring—some two to three weeks later than Kentucky bluegrass. It doesn't tolerate shade or sandy soil well. Newer, improved cultivars can't be established by seeding, which makes them more expensive. Seeds are very slow to germinate if not pretreated with potassium nitrate, which softens the tough skins, or burrs, that cover them. If you want a green lawn, buffalograss might not be for you. Most cultivars are grayish green in color, although newer varieties with deeper, greener color are becoming available. If you live in a humid area with lots of heat and moisture, this grass is definitely not for you. If you're not in buffalograss country, don't feel like you have to introduce this turf. It's best in your lawn when everyone else has it in theirs.

BUFFALO'S BUDDY

When it's at home on the prairie, buffalograss is often found growing alongside its good buddy, blue grama. The two make such a great couple that they're also sometimes planted together in lawns.

Also beginning to garner some attention for turfgrass use on its own, blue grama is similar in texture, color, and growing style to buffalograss but it germinates faster and greens up faster in the spring. It can survive in conditions that even buffalograss finds difficult, including extreme cold. Temperatures down to -40°F won't kill it. Neither will drought or high temperatures.

Blue grama has distinctive flowers—they look like little crescent moons—on stems that can grow as high as eighteen inches. While this grass needs even less mowing than buffalograss does, and can be left to grow on for a more natural look, if you want it to look like turf, you'll have to mow it.

Why I'd tell you to plant it.

Blue grama will grow where others won't and will tolerate sandy, al-kaline soils better than others will. It's even more drought-tolerant than buffalograss is.

Why I wouldn't.

Like buffalograss, blue grama is a bunchgrass and can look thin and anemic until it's well established. And, again like buffalograss, it's not a good choice if you want a green lawn. Nor is it a good choice in warm, humid areas with lots of rainfall.

Hopefully by now you've got the idea that there are choices with re-gards to grass. There might be a lot of choices or not very many, de-pending on where you live, but there's always a choice.

If you're convinced that you have the right grass in your lawn, you can skip ahead to part three, where you'll learn the right way to take care of it. If you need to start a new lawn or renovate an existing one, the next couple of chapters are for you.

CHAPTER 4

Finding Your Turfgrass Mate

*Want to ensure a love affair with your lawn? Choosing the right
grass by knowing your zone is a great way to start.*

What we're talking about now is being able to identify the grass you
should grow, based on where you live. You'll find out shortly that it's not
rocket science, and that it's based on two environmental factors—
temperature and humidity.

Just about every grass will grow where it's put, at least for a while,
based on temperature. I can plant St. Augustinegrass in Syracuse, New
York, in July and it will grow, but it won't be around next July because it's
going to die in the winter. I can plant perennial ryegrass in southern Al-
abama in November, but it won't be around the next November because
it gets too hot during the summer; heat and humidity will knock it out.

What you want is a grass that will act more like a perennial, not
like an annual that you have to replant every year. The key is adaptation. Various species and varieties have adapted to the specific growing
conditions in certain areas better than others. Even if they don't receive the best care, these grasses stand a far better chance of doing well
and providing the kind of turf you're after—lush, weed-free, disease-free,
and so on—than ones that aren't as well adapted.

IN THE ZONE

In the plant world, we call the various areas in which things grow zones. Hang around grass and other outdoor plants long enough and you'll see lots of different charts showing what can grow where. There's a bunch of charts for the continental United States alone. There are even charts that will give you a macro look at the world's growing zones should you be interested in knowing the kinds of grasses that grow in places like, say, St. Petersburg or Buenos Aires.

All of them are based on two factors—temperature and moisture—and for good reason, as these two factors are what govern how well (or how poorly) grasses adapt to various areas.

Warm-season grasses, for example, grow best when temperatures are between 80°F and 95°F. As such, their use is limited by how well (or poorly) they handle cold weather. Some warm-season grasses, such as zoysiagrass and common bermudagrass, tolerate cold temperatures pretty well. The key word here is "tolerate." Sure, they can survive the cold, but they only look attractive for a short time when grown in cooler areas. They need warmth to grow well and look their best.

Other warm-season grasses, like St. Augustinegrass, centipedegrass, and bahiagrass, don't even make it out of the batter's box when it comes to cold weather. They simply don't tolerate it, which limits their use to warm climates in the South.

Cool-season grasses grow best when temperatures are between 60°F and 75°F. But high temperatures are just one of their limiting factors. Humidity levels are also part of the equation. These grasses will do okay when facing heat alone—look at the climate chart below, and you'll see how well cool-season grasses can persist and adapt in the arid western part of the United States. They need irrigation to survive in these areas, of course, but the low humidity in this region is what helps them adapt.

In the eastern United States, where relative humidity levels are higher, cool-season grasses quickly run into a wall of trouble, as the combination of heat and humidity delivers them a one-two punch. Irrigation and top-notch cultural practices can manipulate their ability to adapt to a certain extent, but at the end of the day Mother Nature rules.

Can you grow a grass that's not particularly well suited to your

 **Something** to keep in mind when choosing grass: All grasses are going to go through periods of stress. But we have more control over heat stress than cold stress because we can always water and cool things off. It's very hard to heat frozen turf.

area? Sure. As an example, if you grew up in the South and loved your bermudagrass lawn, but you now live in, say, central Nebraska, you could plant bermudagrass. No one's going to stop you, although you might get some funny looks when you go looking for bermudagrass seed at your local garden store.

At best, the plants will survive, but survival will take more work, more resources, more time, more, well, everything. Plus, since bermudagrass is a warm-season grass, and it needs heat to make it green up, it will only look good during the hottest summer months. During the rest of the growing season it will look brown and unattractive, while other grasses—the cool-season grasses that are better adapted for your area—will look green and lush.

At worst, it won't survive, and you'll be back where you started, having to make a decision about the kind of grass you should plant. And there's no telling what your neighbors might think of you.

"Can grow" can be very different from "will grow." As an example, zoysiagrass will survive utterly cold conditions, which means it will grow as far north as, say, Minnesota. Does this mean you should plant it in St. Paul? No matter how appealing you find its merits—rapid spreading, heat and drought tolerance, low maintenance—probably not. It's a warm-season grass and will grow best in warmer climates. In Minnesota—heck, for that matter, in any cooler climate—it will be, like other warm-season grasses, slow to green up in the spring and it will turn brown as soon as temperatures start to cool off in the fall. It also won't spread as robustly as it would in warmer climates, which means you'll end up with weedy, sparse turf.

Choosing a grass that handles cold weather better, even if you have to trade off some of zoysiagrass's positive traits for some that aren't as attractive, would be a very, very good idea.

MAPPING THINGS OUT

All plant adaptation zone maps have boundary lines. These are best guesses or approximations; they're not carved in stone. You won't see highway road signs saying, "Warm humid zone; centipedegrass does well here," or "Arid zone; don't even think about planting St. Augustinegrass here."

As such, consider the zone information that follows as a general guideline. It's based on solid research, but it's not 100 percent infallible. There might be certain conditions in your specific location—we call this a microclimate—that don't line up with the general recommendations for your zone. (You can even have more than one microclimate in one yard. Shade is often the determining factor here; when it is, growing a blend of different grass varieties or a mixture of different grass types is pretty much the only way you'll ever get decent turf across your entire yard.) If so, ask the experts where you live—county extension agents, master gardeners, even the folks at your local nursery or garden store. Local advice can be the best advice, especially if you're living in an area where several grasses compete for the "best grass" award.

The map here isn't the most complicated, nor is it the simplest one out there. That said, I've used it, or variations of it, in my work and my turf sciences classes for some time now, and it's the best one I've found yet.

While it might seem odd to have the wrong type of grass in a lawn, it can happen. A previous home owner could have made a poor choice, or climate conditions might have changed enough to render a grass that was once a good choice not a good one now. Maybe you inherited a house with an older lawn that's full of grasses (like redtop or clover) that aren't even recommended for planting any longer. Or a microclimate might have developed where one didn't exist before. If previous owners planted a lot of trees, for example, and they're now mature, your yard could be substantially shadier than it once was, and the Kentucky bluegrass that was planted years ago might be struggling to survive.

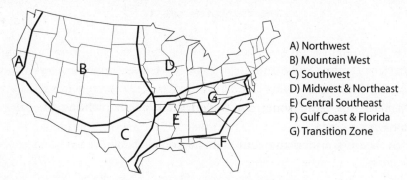

A) Northwest
B) Mountain West
C) Southwest
D) Midwest & Northeast
E) Central Southeast
F) Gulf Coast & Florida
G) Transition Zone

Turfgrass growing zones in the United States

Let's take a closer look at what the various zones are all about, and at the grasses that do the best in each. I'm not going to go into great detail on weather conditions—you don't need me to tell you what the weather's like where you live. When it comes to grasses, the best choices are listed first.

NORTHWEST

Cool-season grasses love the cool, humid temperatures and plentiful moisture in this region, and are the dominant choice here. A couple of warm-season grasses are possible choices for this zone's warmer areas.

Grass Selections

- perennial ryegrass, but might need replanting if ground wears bare from traffic
- creeping red fescue—good for dry, shady conditions
- Kentucky bluegrass—not good for extremely cloudy areas
- Supina bluegrass—good for moist, shady conditions
- tall fescue
- zoysiagrass
- bermudagrass

MOUNTAIN WEST

Temperatures in this large zone can fluctuate wildly, and precipitation ranges from low to moderate. Drought conditions and watering restrictions are common.

While temperatures can be high, humidity is low, which makes this zone a good one for cool-season grasses if irrigation is available. If it isn't, warm-season native grasses are the better bet.

Grass Selections

- Kentucky bluegrass
- perennial ryegrass
- tall and fine fescues—all are good choices for shady areas
- buffalograss—widely used in the warmer parts of this region, especially Nebraska, Colorado, the Dakotas, and Kansas, where irrigation is spotty or nonexistent
- blue grama—an alternative to buffalograss in colder areas with little to no irrigation

SOUTHWEST

Cool-season grasses are mostly a no-no in the land of high temperatures, low rainfall, and low humidity. Don't even think about using any of them here for anything other than overseeding dormant warm-season grasses over the winter. They won't survive. The exception to this rule is the high desert in New Mexico and Arizona, where cool-season grasses can survive if irrigated.

Most if not all of the warm-season grasses, if irrigated, are possible choices for this zone.

Grass Selections

- bermudagrass—the most popular choice
- buffalograss—can be used in the far northern reaches of this region

- zoysiagrass
- annual and perennial ryegrass—for winter overseeding
- Kentucky bluegrass for high-desert lawns

MIDWEST AND NORTHEAST

Grouping these regions together might seem odd, as they don't seem all that alike on paper, but they're united by similar climate conditions—high humidity, coolish temperatures, and abundant rainfall. Cool- and warm-season grasses are both possibilities here.

Grass Selections

- Kentucky bluegrass, alone or in a mixture with the following two grasses
- perennial ryegrass
- creeping red, hard, and chewings fescue—good for low-maintenance and/or dry, shady conditions
- tall fescue—by far the best choice in the southern part of the Midwest zone
- Supina bluegrass—for wet, shady conditions
- rough bluegrass
- bermudagrass—best in the southern parts of this zone
- zoysiagrass—a possibility for the southern part of this zone

CENTRAL SOUTHEAST

Things can get mighty steamy in this part of the United States. Grasses adapted to this area groove on its warm temperatures, good precipitation levels, and high humidity.

Grass Selections

- bermudagrass
- tall fescue—a good choice in shady areas with high temperatures

- zoysiagrass
- annual and perennial ryegrass—for overseeding during the winter

GULF COAST AND FLORIDA

This area is as tropical as things get in the United States. High temperatures, high humidity, and abundant precipitation mean that warm-season grasses rule the roots.

Grass Selections

- bahiagrass—for low-maintenance areas
- common and hybrid bermudagrass—a good, region-wide choice
- centipedegrass—best where abundant rainfall, more than forty inches per year, is the norm
- St. Augustinegrass—a perennial favorite for lawn choices along the Gulf Coast, it beats bermudagrasses hands down and retains its color when temperatures and rainfall back off in the fall.
- zoysiagrass—best for the northern reaches of this region
- seashore paspalum—you won't find more about this grass in this book, as it's not widely grown; it's not a bad choice for coastal lawns, however, as it tolerates salty water and can be irrigated with nonpotable water.
- annual ryegrass—for overseeding during the winter
- bermudagrass—will require the most maintenance, but it's the one grass most likely to survive all conditions in this region.

THE TRANSITION ZONE (A.K.A. THE ZONE FROM HELL)

Across the middle of the United States is an area where getting grass to grow well is, to put it nicely, a challenge. I call it the zone from hell. If you live here, you know why. Summers are too hot and humid for growing cool-season grasses without some trial and tribulation. Switch to

Some people call the transition zone a place where everything will grow . . . for a while.

warm-season grasses, and every few years winter temperatures will dip low enough to kill them; the long-awaited green-up of your cherished bermudagrass in the spring simply won't happen, and you'll have to start all over again with something else.

At the widest point of this zone there is enough fluctuation in humidity levels to challenge just about all cool-season grasses. Remember, when you're hot and sticky, cool-season grasses are, too. Their warm-blooded kin, on the other hand, are loving life.

If you live in this zone, your grass choices are, simply put, limited, especially if you want to play things safe, which here means not having to replant your lawn every couple of seasons or so. But things can get dicey even with the safest choices, and you can find yourself in this situation regardless. Remember, this is the zone from hell.

Grass selections for this zone, for the obvious reasons, are very much a hit-or-miss proposition. What grows well for you might not do as well for your cousins a couple of counties over. Getting some advice from local experts can be a very good idea, but again, keep in mind that the conditions in this region typically don't support long-term success.

Grass Selections

- tall fescue—a good choice for areas with lower annual precipitation, does well in the central and northern parts of this zone
- zoysiagrass—the best-adapted warm-season grass for this region
- common bermudagrass—used in the southern reaches of this zone
- Kentucky bluegrass—widely used in northern areas of this zone
- perennial ryegrass—good for the northern part of this zone

RATING THE GRASSES

So, you've read the grass descriptions in chapters 2 and 3, and you've gone through the zones here. Lots of grass information is now floating about in your head, but it's all in bits and pieces. Zoysiagrass, okay, it's good for this, this and this, but lousy when it comes to this, this, and this. St. Augustinegrass, hmm . . . I think it's a good choice if . . .

I put together the following lists to help you sort things out. This list is based on my three favorite words for the turfgrass world—science, sweat, and savvy. I always tell my students that in order to be good turfgrass managers they need a little bit of science, they need to work at it (that's the sweat part), and they need a little bit of street smarts. Nothing's automatic, you have to learn how to adjust.

What I'm giving them (and you) aren't rules, they're guidelines. Nothing's set in stone in the natural world; there are no hard-and-fast guidelines. I can give you (and them) rules for *establishing* turfgrass because these rules are very simple. But once the grass is up and growing, I have to give you guidelines because lawns are like children—no two are exactly the same and they start to develop personalities. Nothing fits all people, just like nothing fits all growing situations. You'll have to adjust for each kid . . . er, lawn. The beauty is that you have this book to continually refer back to.

These lists are based on my experiences (as well as those of my colleagues) and years of testing and observation. They rank the grasses on their various attributes—how they stand up to wear, how prone they are to developing various diseases, how they do with heat and cold, and so on. If you have to choose a grass to plant, what's here can help you make your selection. It can also help you understand why the grass you currently have isn't working, if it's not, and, again, help you choose a worthy replacement.

Like the zones, this information isn't carved in stone. There could be improved varieties of certain grasses that would elevate them on some lists. Microclimate conditions within zones can also affect how well certain grasses compare with others.

You'll find most but not all of the grasses in the preceding chapters here. Annual ryegrass isn't ranked, as it's simply not a good choice for anything other than winter overseeding. Nor will you find bentgrasses, as, again, I don't think they're appropriate for anything other than golf courses and other closely cropped sports fields.

Grasses that are at or near the same level are grouped together in each category.

Heat Tolerance (ranked from high to low)
- zoysiagrass, hybrid bermudagrass, common bermudagrass, buffalograss, centipedegrass, St. Augustinegrass, bahiagrass
- tall fescue
- Kentucky bluegrass
- perennial ryegrass
- red fescue
- Supina bluegrass

Cold Tolerance (ranked from high to low)
- Kentucky bluegrass
- Supina bluegrass
- rough bluegrass
- fine-leafed fescues
- perennial ryegrass
- tall fescue
- buffalograss, blue grama
- zoysiagrass
- common bermudagrass, hybrid bermudagrass
- bahiagrass, centipedegrass
- St. Augustinegrass

Drought Tolerance (ranked high to low)
- buffalograss, blue grama
- common bermudagrass
- hybrid bermudagrass
- zoysiagrass
- bahiagrass, St. Augustinegrass
- tall fescue, creeping red fescue
- Kentucky bluegrass, perennial ryegrass
- Supina bluegrass
- rough bluegrass
- centipedegrass

Shade Tolerance (ranked high to low)
- creeping red fescue, St. Augustinegrass
- Supina bluegrass
- rough bluegrass
- zoysiagrass
- tall fescue
- perennial ryegrass
- centipedegrass, bahiagrass
- buffalograss
- Kentucky bluegrass
- common bermudagrass
- hybrid bermudagrass

Mowing Height Adaptation (highest to lowest cut)
- tall fescue, buffalograss, blue grama
- creeping red fescue, Kentucky bluegrass, perennial ryegrass, St. Augustinegrass, bahiagrass, centipedegrass
- common bermudagrass, zoysiagrass
- hybrid bermudagrass

Wear Resistance (ranked high to low)
- zoysiagrass
- common bermudagrass
- hybrid bermudagrass
- tall fescue
- buffalograss
- bahiagrass
- perennial ryegrass
- Kentucky bluegrass
- creeping red fescue
- St. Augustinegrass
- centipedegrass
- Supina bluegrass
- rough bluegrass

Establishment Rate (ranked fast to slow, assuming ideal growing conditions)
- perennial ryegrass
- common bermudagrass

* hybrid bermudagrass
* St. Augustinegrass
* centipedegrass
* Supina bluegrass
* rough bluegrass
* creeping red fescue
* Kentucky bluegrass
* tall fescue
* bahiagrass
* zoysiagrass
* buffalograss

Recovery from Severe Injury (complete to partial)
* common bermudagrass
* hybrid bermudagrass
* zoysiagrass
* Kentucky bluegrass
* St. Augustinegrass
* centipedegrass
* bahiagrass
* Supina bluegrass
* buffalograss
* creeping red fescue
* tall fescue
* perennial ryegrass

Remember, there's no such thing as one right and perfect grass. If there were, you wouldn't be reading this book, as it and all others like it would be unnecessary. But there are some grasses that will resonate with you, and more important, the conditions where you live, better than others. They're not quite soul mate grasses, but they're the next best thing.

Finding your grass match is more than worth your time and effort. Think of it as a marriage of sorts. The more time you put in on the front end getting to know your intended mate, the better things will go in the long run.

PART TWO

Establishing a Lawn

CHAPTER 5

Building the Base Camp

Establishing a lawn is a lot like building a house—without a good foundation, the chances of success dwindle. For lawns, soil is the foundation, so it's imperative that things are good on the ground level before construction starts.

Most of us, most of the time, have to deal with the back end of lawns. Someone else established them, we inherit them, and our efforts focus on continuing what's right about them or troubleshooting what's wrong.

In most of my dealings with athletic fields around the world, the back-end scenario is, unfortunately, all too familiar. Only once in a blue moon do I get to begin at the beginning (and this does ensure a much smoother field, I can assure you). So even though inheriting an existing lawn is the more likely scenario, there might come a time when you get the chance to start a lawn from scratch: a true, virgin lawn, probably surrounding your newly built home.

Your response, if you're like most people, will probably be one of the following:

- Excitement!!!!!! All that virgin dirt, just waiting for little grasslets to populate it. Your mind fills with visions of expansive greenness every time you visit the job site. You can't wait to buy grass seed or place your sod order at the local farm.

- Fear! Body-numbing, knee-crumbling dread, bordering on panic and/or horror. The mere thought of trying to carve out an elegant lawn from what might be a mass of mud is enough to send you to the phone book in search of someone else to do the dirty work for you. And it is, decidedly, dirty work. Hard, too. At least parts of it.

If you're in the first category, hold your horses, bucko. You can't just throw down seed or roll out sod. It's a nice, utopian thought, but it simply doesn't work. No how, no way.

If you're in the second category, know that you have lots of company. You and lots of others like you drive a very healthy landscaping industry in this country. For many people, creating a lawn from scratch is simply not in their realm of reality. It calls for equipment that they wouldn't own for any other reason, muscles they wouldn't develop for any other reason either, and time they don't have.

No one's going to think any less of you for calling in the experts to do it all, and, depending on various things like the size of your lot and its topography, doing so might be a very good idea. But here's the deal. Apart from the heavy-duty moving around soil part, which is almost always best left to people who do this sort of thing for a living, lots of what goes into building the base camp for new lawns are things that you can do, either by yourself or with some help.

No matter what category you're in—you want to do it, you have to do it, or you're just going to supervise—it helps to know what goes into creating the ground floor of a great lawn. It also comes in handy should you need to start a lawn over from scratch, as many of the steps are similar.

What follows are best practices gleaned from the years I've spent working with playing fields, golf courses, and lawns. No two projects are the same, of course, but I can assure you there is a tried-and-true formula or sequence that needs to be followed no matter what. Leave out or reverse a step in the process and, well, let's just say that this is one of the few lawn-care areas where there is a pretty solid formula to follow. You'll be much better off not deviating from it, as doing so vastly increases the potential for setbacks and even failure down the road.

I like to use the analogy of brewing a cup of coffee when talking about preparing a site for planting. If you skip a step or do them out of order, you won't end up with coffee despite your best intentions and efforts.

A ROCK-SOLID BEGINNING

To me, establishing a lawn is a lot like building a house. You simply have to have a rock-solid foundation no matter what you're doing. Without it, things can look good for a while, maybe even a long time, but they'll eventually crumble.

Thanks to centuries of house builders and site preparers who have gone before us, building rock-solid foundations for houses and lawns isn't guesswork. There are steps to follow. Good, solid steps, ones that have withstood the test of time. While they aren't technically carved in stone, they might as well be because they just about have to be followed in the order in which they appear. Mix things up, or skip a step, and, well, let's just say that you do so at your own risk.

ESTABLISHING THE SUBGRADE

Also known as rough grading, this step is one that builders typically do on new construction projects. It works the subsoil—the layer that's under the topsoil—and creates the basic contours of your yard, and it requires things like Bobcats and small tractors to move soil around. As such, of all the steps, it's the one that's best left to the experts unless you really know what you're doing and you have the manpower and the equipment to execute it.

A rough grade should leave the site relatively smooth and primed for topsoil application, which, hopefully, the builder thoughtfully removed and stockpiled to one side prior to rolling a whole bunch of heavy equipment over it. (If not, you might have to bring in some new

Flat land or ground that slopes toward the house is the culprit behind most foundation damage. If you're doing any site prep work yourself, you absolutely have to get this part right.

stuff.) I'm not talking flat as a pancake, unless that's what your site is all about to begin with. What I am talking about is a smooth surface without high and low spots that will do things like collect water and disrupt an even glide of mower over turf.

Even if the site seems flat, the soil around the foundation of your house must slope slightly away from it. This will prevent water from flowing toward your house and accumulating around its foundation, which can cause huge problems for yard and house alike. Look around your yard for places where excess water can go—curb and street, woods, ditch, neighbor's yard (a little geek humor there, not advisable). Remember, water flows from smaller bodies to larger ones; streams to oceans, in reality. If the process is disrupted you get water backup and lakes, and I doubt this is anyone's idea of a good time, as grass has no chance in a lake. The subgrade stage is the least expensive and most important time to take care of drainage issues. Even if you're not doing the subgrade yourself, go out and inspect the work. It is worth your time.

The soil around your house should ideally be at no less than a 2 percent grade. This equates to a one-foot drop in elevation for every fifty feet of distance. Measuring it is pretty easy. All you need is a tape measure, a level, some string, and two things to tie the string to. Plant stakes or something similar will work. Here's what you'll do:

1. Sink one stake into the ground right next to your house. Tie the string to it at ground level.
2. Pull the string straight out from where it's tied and tie it to the second stake, which you've placed fifty feet away (or twenty-five if your lawn is smaller). Make sure it's taut, and that you've tied both ends at the same height.

3. Using the level, check to see if the string is level and adjust accordingly.

4. On the second stake, measure the distance from where the string is tied to the ground.

If the distance between the string and the ground is one foot or more (or six inches, if your second stake is at twenty-five feet), you can stop, the slope is fine. If it's less, you'll have to move some dirt around. If it's pretty close to the right slope, you won't have to move much dirt and you can probably do it yourself. Here's what you'll need:

- Wheelbarrow, for moving dirt.
- Shovel, for digging and off-loading dirt from wheelbarrow.
- Yard or landscape rake. One with a three-foot head will work well. If your job is of any size get a high-quality rake from a landscaping supply store and your tail will be waggin'.
- Gloves. Leather is best for cushioning your hands.

Move the dirt from high spots to low spots. Push the dirt toward the foundation with the back of the rake, and then pull it away from the foundation with the tines. Use the string and stakes to check your work as you go.

If you have to do any digging, and I mean any, even just a couple of inches below ground, call your utility companies and have them mark

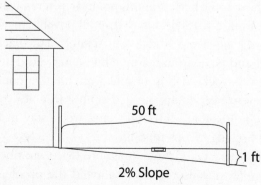

Soil should slope away from your home at a rate of one foot to every fifty feet.

If you need to hire site preparation help, start early. Landscapers and irrigation installers book up months ahead, especially as good construction weather approaches (the best ones are backed up the most, by the way). Check references. Ask for an estimate of costs, materials that will be used, and completion dates. The best contractors will draw up a plan so you can see what's going on, especially if they're handling the whole show. They should also provide a detailed breakdown on costs and materials.

all underground lines. *Do not* assume anything here; the consequences aren't worth it.

Remove all construction debris. Get rid of everything that's not soil—pieces of wood, nails, wallboard, cement, gravel, bricks, you name it. Rocks, too. Don't think for a minute that covering them with grass puts an end to them. They'll come up for air and surface in your lawn at some point, and you'll then hit them with your lawn mower blade. The result: a nicked or broken blade, which you'll have to replace. Remove the rocks at the beginning.

This is also the time for installing an in-ground irrigation system and/or drain tile if your location calls for it.

If your builder removed the existing topsoil, or you're bringing in new topsoil, now's the time to put it in place. It should be spread to a depth of four to six inches and it should follow the established contours of your yard as much as possible—you still have some work to do on it, so it doesn't have to be perfect at this point. If you're buying topsoil, be sure to get it from a trusted source. If at all possible meet the truck at your lot. Buy the guy a cup of coffee, then jump in the back of the truck with a shovel and poke around a little bit. What you don't want to see are lots of weeds, rocks, debris, or junk from another construction site. You can't prevent everything, but if there are troubles you'll see them pretty quick. Truth is, though, most guys won't stay in business very long if they're selling crappy topsoil.

This is another one of those "measure twice, cut once" situations. It's hard to take topsoil off, easier to avoid the problem in the first place.

PUT YOUR SOIL TO THE TEST

I personally don't like to guess about what's in the soil, but soil tests aren't mandatory. That said, if you are going to do one, do it before you start the project. Doing it after you establish the grass won't do you any good; the cow is already out of the barn.

Soil is the foundation of lawns, so things have to be right on the ground level before the first seed hits it. This means putting the soil on your homesite through its paces by testing it, or, better put, having it tested, as the information you really need you can't get on your own.

If your soil looks good, skipping this stage can be tempting. But remember the cup of coffee analogy. Enough said.

Soil is tested to determine two things: its physical composition and its chemical composition.

On the Physical Side

You'll often hear soil described as clayey, loamy, or sandy. These terms refer to the size of the solids in the soil—kind of. Loam is actually the term for soil that contains a mixture of clay, sand, and silt. Somehow or other, in general layperson discussions, silt got lost in the shuffle and loam took its place. The correct terms are "clayey," "silty," or "sandy."

The solids in soil—there's water and air too, of course—consist of organic and inorganic particles ranging in size from microscopic to fairly large. But "fairly large" is a relative term here. Sand, for example, has the largest particles, measuring from 2 millimeters on the large side—about half the size of a pencil lead—to 0.05 millimeters on the small end of the scale. It feels gritty because the particles are so large. (Anything bigger than 2 millimeters, by the way, we simply call gravel or rocks.) Silt ranges from 0.05 millimeters to .002 millimeters in diameter and has a soft, floury texture; clay is less than 0.002 millimeters in size and feels sticky when wet.

> **"Soil texture"** refers to the proportion of sand, silt, and clay in the soil. Depending on the proportions, soil can be classified as clay, silt, sand, or loam, or as sandy clay, silty clay, sandy clay loam, clay loam, silty clay loam, loamy sand, sandy loam, or silty loam.

No patch of dirt contains only one type of solid, no matter what you think or have been told. Soil tests measure the percentages of each of these components.

Sandy soil contains mostly large mineral particles and lots of large pore space between the particles. It's great at letting water and nutrients flow through it, which means that sogginess is rarely a problem. Sandy soil, however, is typically low in the nutrients grass needs to grow well, because it doesn't hold anything in place for very long.

Clayey soil is just the opposite. It contains lots of fine mineral particles that do a great job of sticking together, especially when water's around. This means they also do a great job of retaining nutrients, but the lack of space between the particles makes it tough for plant roots to

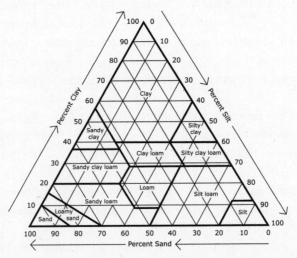

Soil consists of sand, silt, and clay. This triangle illustrates how the percentages of each component create different soil textures.

dig in and get to those nutrients. Standing water is often a problem with clayey soil, as it is so dense. When it's dry, it can feel more like cement than soil.

Silty soil holds more moisture than sand but less than clay. It can have drainage problems similar to clay, but it typically doesn't get water-logged.

The best soil is about 10–20 percent clay with the rest split between sand and silt. This is loamy soil, and it's the best stuff you could ask for. It's brown and crumbly and fluffy enough to be well oxygenated but firm enough to hold water and nutrients where eager plant roots can get to them. Loamy soil can also contain a good dose of organic matter—bits and pieces of plant detritus, microorganisms, and so on—but it doesn't always.

You can get an idea of your soil's physical composition by grabbing a handful and squeezing it hard enough to form a ball. Make sure it's moist before you grab; dry soil won't tell you anything. Sandy soil, because there's not much there to hold it together, typically won't form a mass of any sort. It will crumble and fall apart even when it's really wet. Clayey soil will easily form a ball when moist. If it's wet, it will feel more like slime than anything else and will literally ooze through your fingers.

If you're lucky, the ball of soil in your hand will hold together nicely with just medium pressure and will fall apart fairly easily if you start messing with it. Then you've hit—sorry for the pun—pay dirt. You have a loamy soil. Do a small dance; it's a happy time for you.

But don't celebrate too long. The ball test can tell you some of what you need to know about your soil's physical makeup, but when it comes to doing the right thing for your grass, you need to know the soil's chemical composition, too.

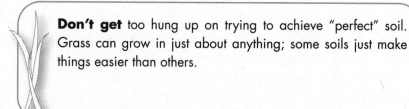

Don't get too hung up on trying to achieve "perfect" soil. Grass can grow in just about anything; some soils just make things easier than others.

Getting Serious About Soil Chemistry

There are basic soil chemistry tests, and there are tests that go beyond the basics. Basic chemistry tests you can do yourself with a kit from any lawn and garden store. They'll tell you what your soil's pH level is, but usually not much more than this. It's good to know pH levels, as they can affect plant growth by making certain nutrients less available to roots. The level can also be too high or too low for the kind of grass you want to grow. If it is, you'll have to change it by adding something to the soil, which I'll discuss in more detail later.

Beyond-the-basics chemistry tests go way beyond anything you can do at home. They measure pH plus the levels of the most important plant nutrients—phosphorous, potassium, calcium, and magnesium. (But not nitrogen. The level of this nutrient in the soil changes so quickly that testing it won't tell you anything more than what its level was at the moment the test was done.)

There are also beyond-the-basics physical soil tests, which will tell you a lot more about your soil's texture. These aren't essential, but they're a good idea if you suspect soil layering—fine-textured soils layered over coarser-textured soils—which happens a lot with new construction. Soil in layers (fine over coarse) will trap water and cause drainage problems, which you definitely don't want.

Many county extension agencies offer soil-testing services for a small fee, and there are companies that do so as well, usually for larger fees. Timing is important here. If possible, plan to test at least one month prior to when you want to seed or sod. This will allow ample

The pH number represents the measure of the concentration of hydrogen ions in a solution. It's a pretty big deal for living things because those hydrogen ions are positively charged and they alter the charge environment of other molecules around them. Or, in English, they make other molecules more or less accessible. Pure water has a pH of 7, which is considered neutral. Anything below 7 is acidic (think vinegar, which has a pH of 2); anything above 7 is alkaline (think baking soda, which has a pH of 9).

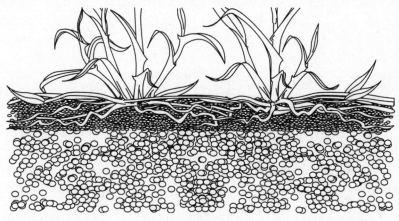

Soil layering in topsoil creates incompatible layers that can disrupt water flow.

time for test results to get back to you and will give you enough time to work your soil based on their recommendations.

Taking the Tests

Your test kit should come with instructions on how the agency or company wants the samples collected. They can vary a bit, but they'll all require sampling the topsoil from various parts of your yard, as content and texture can change quite a lot across a site. Just follow orders.

Be sure to pull samples from any parts of your yard that are potential problem areas, like shady spots. Also be sure to sample the soil around your house's foundation. If it's soil that the builder pulled up when he excavated the site, it's probably lacking nutrients. If there's a problem here, it's better solved before you put grass over it, not after.

Putting Results into Place

When you get the test results back, look at the soil's pH level first. Ideally, you'll see a figure between 6.0 and 7.5. Since most turfgrasses do well with pH levels between 6.5 and 7, you'll be golden. A number higher or lower, however, isn't necessarily cause for concern, as most grasses can handle pH levels from 5 to 8 without a whole lot of trouble.

The test results might come with a recommendation to change the pH level by adding lime if it's too low (acidic) or applying sulfur if it's too high (alkaline), but truth is it's difficult to significantly change pH levels and most of the time you really don't have to. My advice, just keep an eye on how things are growing after you seed or sod. If you are fertilizing at recommended rates but you're not seeing good green-up and growth, you might have a pH problem and you might have to fertilize more often, as nutrients might not be as available to the plants.

Chemical test results will also detail the soil's ability to hold nutrients—in other words, how the soil will respond to fertilizing. The technical term is "cation exchange capacity," or CEC. If CEC is below 5, you'll have to add some fertilizer to the soil before you plant. Again, the testing facility should recommend how much.

You'll also see potassium and phosphorous levels. These minerals are two of the three—nitrogen is the other—most important plant nutrients. If the soil test shows a significant phosphorous or potassium deficiency, add fertilizer that's high in one or both of these ingredients. If not, just put down a good starter fertilizer before you plant.

Don't do any of this yet, however. If you did, you'd be working out of sequence. Remember that cup of coffee?

If you have soil pH between 5.5 and 8, you don't have a pH problem. And the truth of the matter is that trying to alter pH isn't that easy, because there's usually a fairly strong external factor that's driving the pH, particularly moisture. (Rainfall amounts have a big effect on pH levels. Soil east of the Mississippi, where moisture is more abundant, tends to be on the acidic side. West of the Mississippi, you can almost count on alkaline soil.) If the pH is really out of whack, add lime to raise it or sulfur to lower it. You can get a good sense of your soil's pH just by walking into a lawn and garden store; if you see a big pile of lime, you're probably in an area where soil pH is low. If the store doesn't stock it, you live in an area where acidity isn't a problem.

WHACKING DOWN WEEDS

If work has been completed at the site for a while, you'll probably have some weeds to contend with. Start off with a clean slate by applying a nonselective herbicide (see chapter 12 for more on what to use) about two weeks before you go to the next step. This will eliminate anything currently growing. You may need to apply it twice, spacing the applications twenty days apart, to control weeds with deep-growing rhizomes.

SAYING AMEN TO SOIL AMENDMENTS

If you did a physical soil test and you came up with sandy or clayey soil, now's the time to change its texture into soil that will better support good grass growth. Adding sand to clay or clay to sand might seem logical here, but it's not, as both approaches typically result in something that looks more like concrete than soil. Adding some sort of organic matter is the better approach. Actually, the only approach.

Organic soil amendments run the gamut from hay to grass clippings to compost. All will do good things for your soil's texture and your future lawn by improving the soil's ability to retain water and nutrients, but some are definitely better than others. Wood chips or sawdust might be plentiful and cheap where you are, which would make them a good choice from a cost perspective. Both products can bind nitrogen in the soil, however, and make it less available to plants. If you use them, you might have to apply a nitrogen fertilizer at the same time, which could erase what you saved by using them. Sphagnum peat can be a good choice for sandy soil, or if pH levels are low, as it will bump them up.

Soil texture doesn't determine which amendment to use, as all amendments can improve soil composition. In sandy soil, for example, amendments will decrease the space between particles. In finer-textured soils, they'll increase it.

Compost is my top pick. It not only improves soil texture and composition, but also adds some nice nutrients to it. It's pretty easy to find these days. Lawn and garden centers carry it; some cities make it as part of their recycling programs.

There are also inorganic amendments, like vermiculite, perlite, pea gravel, tire chunks, and so on. My take on these: Why bother? All they do is change soil texture; they do nothing to enhance the soil's nutrient content. Why not use something that does both?

Be prepared for lots of mixing and digging if you have to add soil amendments. You can't just dump the stuff on and call it a day. It has to be mixed thoroughly with the existing soil or it's next to worthless. If it ends up layered in any way, those layers may grab water and nutrients and keep them in place. Not exactly what you're after. Instead, turn it under the topsoil and mix it in very well with a rototiller, which is something you might own if you're also a gardener. If not, rent one.

Don't overwork the soil. You want to create smooth-textured, well-aerated dirt, which your turfgrass will love. Working it too much can

If you decide to use compost, be careful about where you get it from. Not too long ago, one of my colleagues (not a lawn geek) wanted to establish a new lawn at his new home and decided to use cow manure compost. Problem was, when the compost was delivered it didn't look like it had been away from the cow for that long. My colleague and his buddies went ahead and put it down anyway, figuring it had to be okay since, after all, it was compost and it would keep breaking down. Oh, they were right about that—but as it did it would also release ammonia gases high enough to choke off any possibility of life-forms taking root underneath it. If the compost had been six months older it would have been fine. As it was, they had to remove it and start over again.

If you're not familiar with the source, check it out first. Compost that's ready to use should smell rich and musty, not like it just came out of the north forty.

take all the air out of it. The result: compacted soil, which your grass will hate. Remember, you can always work it some more, but you can't subtract your efforts. Work the soil once, then grab a handful and do another ball test. The soil should form a ball under light pressure yet break apart fairly easily.

If you need to change soil pH by adding lime or sulfur, this is a good time to do it. Working everything in at the same time will save you time and prevent overworked soil. This is also the time to add fertilizer to balance significantly low phosphorous and potassium levels, if necessary. The soil test should tell you how much to add.

FINISHING THE GRADE

You appreciate a wrinkle-free bed, right? So does grass, and finish grading is what you do to make its bed as smooth as it can be. Not flat, remember. Smooth.

Check the site over and make any necessary corrections and changes. Pluck any stones or weeds that might have cropped up. If you had to till in soil amendments, make sure the topsoil still matches the contours of the ground. If low spots developed, smooth them out by raking or moving soil around as needed. Check the grade around your house one last time. A good rain, which will expose high and low areas, is the best thing that can happen during this process. If there isn't one in the forecast, water things down yourself if you can.

If you're going to seed the site, it should be even to one half inch below hard surfaces, like the driveway, when you're done. If you're sodding, give yourself one inch to allow for the thickness of the sod layer.

Don't mess up your soil's structure by working it when it's too wet or too dry. Do a squeeze test first. If water squishes out, go fishing for a day. If it crumbles under pressure, water things down first.

START 'EM OFF RIGHT

Finally, spread a starter fertilizer following the label's recommended rate (see chapter 9 for how). *Be sure to use a starter fertilizer*; it will have more phosphorous and more soluble nitrogen. Both are important for starting baby grass plants off right. Finally, smooth the surface with one last raking.

Whew! You're done. Your site is primed and ready for planting.

CHAPTER 6

Putting Down Roots

Seeds, sod, plugs, sprigs . . . there's more than one way to start a lawn from scratch or spruce up an existing one. Here's the skinny on each approach and how to know which one's right for you and your lawn.

To me, establishing a new lawn is a lot like bringing home a newborn. Baby grasses are like baby humans; they're defenseless and lots of things can happen to them (and happen pretty quickly) if you're not right there to prevent them from happening. For this reason, there isn't a whole lot of leeway in dealing with either type of infant. Instead, there are pretty solid guidelines. Absolutes, even. Follow them, and your lawn (and your kids) will make it to the terrible twos.

GOING FOR THE GREEN

Scattering seed or laying down sod is usually a heck of a lot easier than preparing the site where it will grow. In fact, this is a lawn-care area that just about anyone can do. That is, if (have you noticed there's almost always an if?) you take the time to do it right and you have the right tools.

The right tools part is pretty easy. You won't need many, and while most of them aren't things you'll want to have on hand unless you do a lot of this stuff, they're easy to find and cheap to rent. The doing it right part

Every year, turf tenders in the United States—amateurs and professionals—spend an estimated $750 million on turfgrass seed. Sod expenditures are even higher, with recent estimates putting them at more than $1 billion annually. No matter how you cut it, that's a lot of little green plants.

is also pretty easy. Like other facets of turf care, there's a well-established approach to follow for both methods, and doing so will go a long way toward success.

If you decide to rewrite the rules and wing it on your own, chances are still relatively good that you'll end up with a lawn, or something that looks somewhat to a lot like a lawn, which might be just fine in your book. If you're interested in having a great lawn, a good thick stand of grass for people to congregate on and kids to play on, and you don't want that great lawn to be years in the making, you'll follow the rules—which, by the way, will also save you from spending more time or money than you should.

Another thing to keep in mind: it doesn't matter if you're the greatest turf manager in the history of turf or just starting out. Either way, the following two rules apply: Rule #1—Grass dies and the reasons are numerous. Sometimes you're the reason, but not always. Rule #2— Even the best of intentions and preparations can't change Rule #1. Taking these two rules to heart, it's a good idea to know how to do this stuff even if you're not working on a virgin site. You can perk up a sad-looking lawn in a hurry by filling in bald spots with a fast-growing seed or laying in a few strips of sod. Consider both good first-aid practices for your turf; Band-Aids well worth adding to your lawn geek arsenal.

CULTIVAR CONSIDERATIONS

First up about putting down roots is deciding which grass to grow. If you haven't already done so, go to chapter 4 and figure out what growing zone you're in. Then turn to chapter 2 or 3—your zone will determine which chapter unless you live in the transition zone, a.k.a. the zone from hell, in which case both cool-season and warm-season grasses

Run your selection past a local turfgrass expert if you're at all concerned about how well your choice actually performs in your area. What looks good on a list might not be the best choice for your spot of green.

might be in the running—and go through the grass descriptions. You should come up with a fairly concise list of options. You can narrow them down further by thinking about the following:

- What do you want your lawn to look like? Do you like a manicured, thick turf, or something a little more casual?
- How will you use your lawn? If you have small kids and/or pets, or you want to make your yard the in spot for outdoor parties, you'll want to stay away from delicate turfgrasses and choose something that stands up to wear and tear and reestablishes quickly when injured.
- Are there any special concerns about the site—shade, slopes, blazing sun, and so on—to factor in? How about watering restrictions?
- How much time do you want to spend tending your turf? While solid cultural practices can lessen your turf-time commitment, some grasses simply demand more attention than others.

It's also not a bad idea to take a gander at what your neighbors are growing. If you're living in a fairly homogeneous neighborhood, you might not want your lawn to stick out like a sore thumb. Planting a rugged grass like buffalograss when everyone else is growing Kentucky bluegrass would make it do exactly that.

Made in the Shade

Of the variables mentioned above, shade is the one that tops the list for most home owners. All grasses need sunshine—photosynthesis grinds to a halt without it—but some grasses definitely do better with less of it than others.

Here's what I recommend for shady lawns:

- In cool-season areas, Supina or rough bluegrass are good choices for shady lawns that get a decent amount of moisture. Supina is the superior choice, as it has the best shade tolerance under high-traffic conditions, but it can be hard to find. If necessary, check the Resources appendix for a wholesale source. Although it's expensive, you can bring down the cost by mixing it with another grass, maybe perennial ryegrass, at a one-to-ten ratio during seeding. Everything will germinate and you'll have adequate ground cover, but the perennial ryegrass will die after six months or so. The Supina will not and it will begin to creep and fill in. Keep in mind, though, that this grass is stoloniferous, so make sure you want it, because once you plant it, getting rid of it is next to impossible.
- For lawns in drier climates, fine-leaf fescues, including creeping red fescue, chewings fescue, sheep fescue, and hard fescue, are good choices.
- In warm-season areas, St. Augustinegrass performs best in partially shaded areas in the deep South and along southern coasts.
- In the transition zone, tall fescue and zoysiagrass will both work and are both good choices. If it were me, however, I'd prefer tall fescue because it will stay green over the winter (zoysiagrass, being a warm-season grass, will go dormant and turn brown when temperatures get too cold for it). If you go with zoysiagrass, Diamond and Royal, both newer varieties, have shown excellent shade tolerance.

Finally, seeding or sodding in early spring or fall, before trees leaf out or after they're done shedding them, will give you the best results. Seeding when trees are leafed out basically ensures you will come in third place in a two-horse race because you're asking grass to grow without sunshine. (Don't think fertilizer is going to help here because it actually hurts; it has to be combined with sunshine to get any growth at all.) Remember, grass needs sun to build its food (carbohydrate) stores. Planting when trees are bare maximizes its grow-in time; long before you're even thinking about mowing, that grass is absorbing sunshine and storing the carbs it needs to survive shady periods during the summer.

This is harder to do for warm-season grasses. They don't like to grow in the fall and winter, when leaves are off the trees, because it's not warm enough for them. That's why if you go down south and into heavily treed areas you won't see much grass, with the exception of tall fescues, which have better heat tolerance, do better in the shade, and grow during winter months.

Blends and Mixes Versus Monostands

These days, most cool-season grass seed comes as mixtures or blends. Blends combine several cultivars of the same species; mixtures combine seeds from different species. You can also buy seed for just one type of grass. This is called single-stand, monoculture, or monostand.

Single-stand cool-season lawns used to be fairly common, but you don't see them very often anymore and I don't recommend them anyway. Should you choose a seed that, for some reason, doesn't do well after it's planted—say it falls prey to a turf disease or conditions simply aren't right for growing it—you could end up with a field of nothing.

You'll almost always get better results with a seed mix, as the strengths of some of the seeds will mask the weaknesses of the others. If growing conditions don't favor one type of grass, the others will carry on. As an example, slower-growing species like Kentucky bluegrass are often combined with faster-germinating perennial ryegrass, which, since it's up and out of the ground so quickly, guards against erosion and delivers some green while the Kentucky bluegrass is working at it.

How do you choose between mixtures and blends? Start with the type of grass you want to grow and look for products that lead with it. Also keep in mind that blends, since they're composed of grasses from the

Seed mixtures and blends, since they contain a diverse selection of grass plants, almost always yield the best lawns. They're cool, calm, and collected about adapting to the various conditions they might encounter in their new home, and they take things like insect attacks and disease problems in stride.

same species, typically yield lawns that are more uniform in color and texture. The grasses in seed mixes will vary a bit in color and texture, as they come from different species, but they're selected to complement each other when they're growing, and they'll look just fine together.

In reality, when you go to the store and pick out a seed mixture for your lawn, it will usually contain two or more varieties of each species, thereby making it a blend as well. So, for example, your typical bag of a perennial ryegrass and Kentucky bluegrass mix will contain a few varieties of each. It's an easy insurance policy. The point is, you'll rarely have to go to a seed store and say, "Gee, I have to buy three different types of seed." The work's already been done for you.

Know that you aren't going to find monostands at retail stores. If you desperately need one, you'll have to look for it on the Web or at a seed supply store. Your typical big-box retailer just won't have it.

If you want to get really geeky about the grass selection process, there's a Web site that will help you do it. Go to www.ntep.org. This is the home page of the National Turfgrass Evaluation Program, and it's lawn geek heaven, take my word for it. If you're wondering how well a specific cultivar is adapted to where you live, the NTEP has the answer.

Most warm-season grasses are monostands, which makes the decision process much easier.

SEED IT OR SOD IT?

Seed or sod, seed or sod . . . this decision is typically really easy or really tough, without much gray area in between. If you have to establish an entire yard and your funds are limited, you might not have much choice; it's seed for you. But seed might be the way to go for other rea-

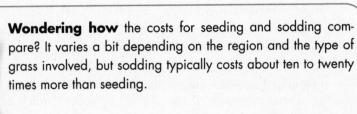

Wondering how the costs for seeding and sodding compare? It varies a bit depending on the region and the type of grass involved, but sodding typically costs about ten to twenty times more than seeding.

sons. The grass you want might not be available as sod, or it might be beyond your budget.

If you have a choice, know that both approaches have their advantages and disadvantages. Here's how they stack up:

Seed	**Sod**
inexpensive	expensive
takes time for seeds to sprout	instant lawn
more species and cultivar choices	limited to what's being cultivated by local farms
compatible with all soils	potential for soil incompatibility, soil layering
planting times limited	plant anytime, weather permitting
not good choice on slopes, seed can run off	fewer erosion problems, might be the most cost-effective way to get grass to grow on slopes
can dry out quickly	won't dry out as quickly
greater chance of weeds	fewer weeds (if high-quality sod)
no heavy lifting required	more labor intensive; sod is heavy

MORE OPTIONS

Most people start their lawns either by seeding or sodding, but these aren't the only options. Hydroseeding, which combines seed, water, fertilizer, and fiber mulch into a slurry sprayed onto the prepared seedbed, is another one, although you can't do it yourself, as the requisite equipment isn't available for home use. But it can be an approach worth considering, as its advantages and disadvantages (and costs) put it somewhat in the middle of seeding and sodding.

I think hydroseeding's a great choice if you have to seed a large area. It combines a number of seeding steps into one and gets the job done fast. The combination of mulch and seed delivers quick, high germination. It's also an excellent approach for steep and/or hilly sites, as

The wet fiber mulch in hydroseed helps the seeds stay in place, keeps them moist, and protects them from wind and erosion. The mulch slowly decomposes as the seeds germinate.

the slurry will stay in place and keep the topsoil under it in place as well.

The downsides to hydroseeding? Grass and/or fertilizer choices can be limited. An inexperienced applicator might put too much down in one spot and not enough in another (if so, the results will be rather apparent). And seed-to-soil contact can be less than optimal. You can improve the chances of seed meeting soil by hydromulching—having the seed put down first, then capping things off with the mulch slurry. This is by far my preferred approach.

One of my great friends, the late Dr. George Hamilton of Penn State University, was big into making grass establishment easier. He knew that mulching was a good idea. He also knew that expecting home owners to have slurry machines at their disposal wasn't going to happen, so he invented PennMulch. What George did was to somehow shrink the mulch down to small, easily spreadable pellets that expanded when watered and began to act just like the fiber mulch you love so much. This meant you could buy bags of this stuff and wait until you needed it. My teaching lab at Michigan State University was one of his testing grounds. His product worked so well, within a year there were two other competitive products on the market. You have lots of flexibility in the establishment process—specifically, you can seed and mulch in separate steps.

Putting down less than a complete blanket of sod, another fairly common alternative, offers the benefits of sodding—to a certain extent, anyway—at a considerably lower cost. You can plant sprigs, which are pieces of grass with roots attached but sans soil; or plugs, which are two-to-four-inch squares or rounds of sod. Strip sodding—laying sod with spaces between the strips—is another option. As the grass in the strips or plugs takes root, it spreads and fills in the gaps. These alternatives work best with grasses that spread more aggressively.

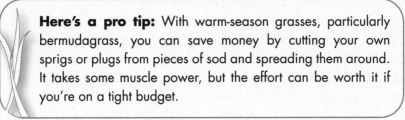

Here's a pro tip: With warm-season grasses, particularly bermudagrass, you can save money by cutting your own sprigs or plugs from pieces of sod and spreading them around. It takes some muscle power, but the effort can be worth it if you're on a tight budget.

Many warm-season grasses are established by sprigging or plugging, and they might be the only options if you want to grow certain varieties. All three approaches are less expensive than all-out sodding; none are as foolproof, as they don't cover every inch of the site and they can dry out faster than sod does. They also take more time than sodding does, and the turf will take longer to fill in (in most cases up to a year or so, but it can be as long as two seasons). Bermudagrass is the exception; even when sprigged it can deliver a full lawn in around a hundred days.

One strong advantage to sprigging is the ability to use any type of preemergence herbicide to control crabgrass seeds from germinating. Most preemergents are intended for established lawns and the herbicide prevents all seeds from germinating. This is a nonfactor if you are sprigging or sodding, for that matter, as the sprig (and the sod) is technically a mature plant.

If you're still pondering seeding versus sodding, the grass of your dreams is available either way, and price isn't a consideration, just do what works best for you. If you don't want to spend lots of time coddling a new lawn for the next few weeks, opt for sod. If the thought of seeing your hard-earned wages executed as sod is keeping you up nights, obviously you need to seed. You can do it all in one shot after the ground is prepped if you hydroseed, but putting down the seed first and then the mulch is my preferred method—it gives you more control over the process and you don't need special equipment to do it.

SEEDING SUCCESS

Seeding is how all turfgrass is established—if not by you, then by a turf farmer. The big difference between you and the farmer is that the farmer does it for a living and has all the steps down pat. The key to success for you, then, is doing it like the farmers do.

Here are their keys to success. Let them be yours, too.

Measuring Up

Figuring out how much seed you'll need for your new lawn is pretty easy. Seed is sold by the pound, and application rates are factored by pounds per thousand square feet. If you know the measurements on your lot and your house, simply subtract the house from the lot, along with other hard spaces like pathways and driveways. If they're not linear, guesstimate them. You shouldn't be far off unless they're huge.

If you need to measure, have someone help you run a tape measure along your lawn's length and width. Multiply these figures for total square footage.

Making a Quality Choice

All grass seed producers are required, by law, to analyze the content of their seed mixes and to display the results of that analysis on their products. Knowing how to read those results is your ticket to choosing the right stuff.

Let's say your research has led you to a bluegrass-ryegrass-fescue blend. Here's what you might find on a typical label:

1. Brand name, if buying branded seed or seed mix.
2. Weight. This is the net weight of the bag.
3. Amount of seed, expressed as percentages. Our sample bag contains two Kentucky bluegrass cultivars, two perennial ryegrass cultivars, a tall fescue cultivar, and a fine fescue cultivar. You may or may not see specific cultivar names on seed bags; if you're after a particular one, be sure to look for it. Don't assume you're getting it. Notice that the numbers don't add up to 100 percent. That's because bags of seed contain other things besides seed.

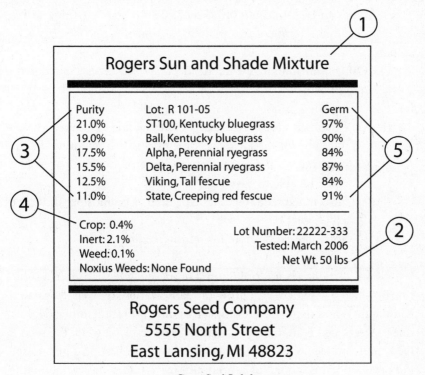

Grass Seed Label

4. Other ingredients. These are the "other things." Plants don't grow in vacuums. Seeds are always accompanied by some of the stuff that accompanies their mother plants in the field. These substances are listed as other crop seed, inert matter (read dirt and other debris), weed seed, and noxious weeds, again by percentages. Yes, all grass seed contains some weed seeds, there's no way to get around it. The noxious weed percentage, however, should be zero, because you definitely don't want these in your yard. These percentages and the seed percentages should total 100 percent.

5. Germination rate. Also expressed as a percentage for each grass. This represents the number of seeds that germinated when the seed was tested. If the rate is 85 percent, eighty-five out of a hundred seeds germinated. Germination percentages go down as seed age goes up, which is why you'll also see test

dates and sell-by dates on seed bags. Don't buy anything with a germination rate of less than 80 percent.

Other information included on grass seed labels (but not required by law):

- Coverage area. This can be misleading, as the coverage might be for the lowest seeding rate, which might not be the best rate, so consider it an estimate of how much ground you'll be able to cover.
- How much seed to plant, expressed as pounds per thousand square feet.
- Spreader calibration, for setting seeding rate.

Good seed comes at a premium, and deservedly so, as it is a superior product. Two farms can grow the same variety of, well, let's call it Midnight. When the fields are inspected, one passes; the other doesn't, due to weed seed contamination that can't be resolved when the seed is harvested and cleaned. The farmer who owns the first field gets to sell the product of his labors for a premium price under the variety name Midnight. The seed from the second guy's fields will also be sold, but labeled as "grass seed" and in the bargain bin.

My advice, buy the premium stuff. Don't even think about the other stuff. Years of helping home owners who cheaped out and got what they paid for are behind this advice. Plus, most seed isn't all that expensive to begin with. We're only talking about two to four dollars per thousand square feet here. Buy cheap seed, and you'll spend anything you think you saved on controlling the weeds that came along with the seed.

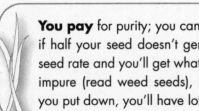

You pay for purity; you can adjust for germination. In theory, if half your seed doesn't germinate, all you do is double the seed rate and you'll get what you need, but if half your seed is impure (read weed seeds), it doesn't matter how much seed you put down, you'll have lots of weeds.

Focus on the weed seed percentage and the purity of the seed. You can't adjust for either of them when you're seeding. Technically, if the germination percentage is low you can adjust for it by simply bumping up the application rate accordingly.

Give Them a Good Foundation

If you have any questions about this, go back to chapter 5. The emphasis on site preparation might seem picky, but I guarantee you that the more time you spend making the seedbed as good as it can be, the better your chances of getting a good-looking stand of grass to grow on it.

Time It Right

Seeding is kind of like fishing. The fishing part is always good. The catching part can be another story. Like trying to snag bass and walleye, there are definitely good, better, and best times for planting seed.

Your goal here is to give those seeds the best start possible, which means putting them down when growing conditions are most favorable. Spring and early fall are best for cool-season grasses. Late spring to early summer is best for warm-season grasses. Your chances for success will be better the earlier in the seasonal window you seed. You want to give the seeds ample time to get going before conditions turn against them. As the days in the window march by, success rates drop. Not a lot, but they do.

Kill the Weeds

Remember, establishing grass is like taking care of a baby. In the beginning both need a lot of attention and can't fend for themselves very well, so you have to take up the sword for them.

As mentioned, soil always contains some weed seeds. When you start prepping it for seeding what you want to grow, the weed seeds will pop to the surface, where they can take full advantage of your work and happily sprout away. They'll also compete with the baby grass plants for nutrients and water, and those baby plants will be at a decided disadvantage.

No matter where you are, if you're seeding in the spring, you'll have to deal with annual grassy weeds like crabgrass. If you don't, the crabgrass will compete with your poor immature turfgrass, and believe me, it will win the battle; it's genetically programmed to come on like the Hulk during spring and summer. If you seed in the fall, the summer annual weeds are not an issue, and neither is the need for preemergence herbicide.

Assume crabgrass seed is in your soil in abundance; bare soil is the one instance when crabgrass has full run at the refrigerator. When soil is bare a preemergence herbicide called siduron is the only one you should use. No, scratch that, *can* use. Here's why: It's the only herbicide that will kill crabgrass weed seeds but will let grass seeds survive. Other preemergence herbicides will prevent weedy grasses from germinating, but they're nonselective products, which means they'll stop all seeds in their tracks, including grass seeds. Not exactly what you want, right?

Put it down with starter fertilizer, or buy starter fertilizer premixed with siduron. It can be a little pricey and you may even hear someone say they can't get it or never heard of it. Just smile and go to the next store; it's out there.

If for some reason you can't put down siduron when you're planting, wait thirty days (your grass will have germinated by then) and apply dithiopyr (brand name Dimension). It will kill small emerging crabgrass plants and keep future crabgrass seeds from germinating. Be sure to wait the thirty days after planting to ensure that your grass seeds have germinated and won't succumb to the herbicide.

Warm-season grasses (and cool-season, for that matter) established from sod, sprigs, or plugs are plants, not seeds, and aren't affected by preemergence herbicides. Any preemergence herbicide is fine when planting them.

If you put down the preemergence herbicide you'll enjoy watching the grass grow instead of watching the weeds grow.

Spread the Seed

Even, uniform seed application will give you an even, uniform lawn. You won't accomplish this by grabbing a bag of grass seed and scattering it by hand, but you will accomplish this with a spreader. You can rent one, but it's a good thing to have on hand, as you can also use it to apply fertilizer.

Spreaders come in three basic configurations: hand spreaders, which, you guessed it, are operated by hand; drop spreaders, which roll along the ground and drop seed through their bottoms; and rotary spreaders, which also travel along the ground but apply seed in circles instead of straight lines. There's also a new hybrid spreader that lets you choose between drop and rotary application. (See chapter 9 for more information on choosing your spreader.)

All come with controls for setting the seeding rate, which you'll determine by checking the seed package—it will vary somewhat depending on the type of seed you buy.

A seeding rate of ten to fifteen seeds per square inch is fairly standard. It might not look like enough, but trust me, it is. Resist the temptation to overseed. More is not better here. Drop those seeds too close together and the poor baby plants will have to fight among themselves for every little bit of nutrition and moisture. Most of them will fail and you'll end up with thin turf.

The secret to good, even coverage is to hit every part of your soon-to-be yard with the right amount of seed, no more and no less. The best way is to divide the seeding rate in half and apply the seeds in two directions—north to south, then east to west. Do this, and you'll drop the chance of missing any areas to around zero. This is an especially

Stick to the seeding rate recommended for the grass type or mixture you bought. And don't panic when the initial growth looks sparse. It won't look like enough, but it is. Remember, grasses spread, and they need ample space to spread right. Crowd them by planting too closely and you'll actually end up with thinner turf.

> **Good seed-to-soil** contact is the one big advantage to seeding and mulching separately.

good approach when applying bunchgrass seed, as these grasses don't spread well. Seeding in two directions is a must with these.

If you're planting tall fescue, go three ways and apply it diagonally as well. You'll have the best tall fescue lawn in town.

Smooth Them Out

Seeds suck up water from the soil, so the better contact they make with it, the better their chances of developing into healthy grass plants. Make sure you get good seed-to-soil contact by slightly pushing the little guys into the ground. The back of a lawn rake works well on small areas. For larger areas, rent a weighted roller and run it over the seeds empty; that is, don't fill it with water. You want to push the seeds into the soil so they're just barely covered, to about a depth of a quarter inch or so. Less is fine. More is not.

Swaddle Them

After you've taken the time and trouble to pick the right seed, prepare the seedbed, and put the seed down right; leaving it vulnerable to all the things that can prevent it from turning into a yard is the last thing you want to do. Placing a protective layer of an organic substance—mulch—over your grass seeds keeps them safe from the elements, number one being a thunderstorm. It will help them germinate at or close to the rate on the bag, keep them moist so they'll germinate faster, and help them stay where you put them. Lots of substances can be used as mulch; compost and straw are inexpensive and usually readily available. PennMulch and similar products are another terrific option.

If you decide on straw, be sure you buy straw, not alfalfa hay, or else you'll soon find your yard growing hay. Buy one bale per four hundred square feet. Spread it out evenly and not too thickly; if you can't see the soil beneath it, the seeds can't see the sun. I won't kid you about straw: it came from a field and likely brought along a few weed seeds that may or may not have to be dealt with as your lawn fills in. More on this later. The other thing to know about straw is that it will break down and you will not even know it was there. The less there is on the ground, the faster it breaks down (this is another case when less is more). If you did spread it too thick and you feel it's keeping the grass from growing, you can get out there with a rake and pull it off (just be careful you don't pull up too many grass plants with it). Better yet, don't put a lot on in the first place. And don't use peat mulch. It looks nice, but it's greedy and it will grab all the water and nutrients it can for itself.

Do you absolutely have to use mulch if you got good seed-to-soil contact? No; as my grandpa used to say, you don't have to do anything except die and pay taxes. But if you don't have the ability to water faithfully (read automatic irrigation), you're on a slope or droughty soil, or at the end of a seeding window or completely out of one, for that matter, which means temperatures aren't real conducive to success, the proper mulch is a good friend. It's going to provide a longer-lasting, more favorable environment for germination.

Stay Off Them

Depending on the type of grass you planted, it can take anywhere from three to twenty-eight days before grass plants appear. Any activity where seeds are incubating can impede their progress and create a lumpy, bumpy lawn. Wet soil is unstable soil. Footprints and other disturbances show up real easily in newly seeded areas, and they don't go away.

Give your new lawn the best chance for success by keeping seeded areas off limits. Put up signs. If area boundaries aren't obvious, mark them with stakes and run string or warning tape between the stakes.

Want to know how long before you'll see any action out of your seeds? Check the following chart for germination rates.

Grass	Days to Germination
perennial ryegrass	3–7
annual ryegrass	3–8
fine fescues	7–14
buffalograss	7–14
tall fescue	7–14
bermudagrass	7–15
centipedegrass	7–15
bahiagrass	8–15
Kentucky bluegrass	14–28

Water Them

Now that you have the seed down in place, you may actually start to feel a little panicky. Your palms might start sweating. You've got the newborn home, but now what do you do with it? Remember the baby analogy. If you're a first-time grass parent, you might be surprised at how watering, fertilizing, and mowing matches up with feeding, bathing, and changing diapers. You must be consistent about providing all three, but the most important is feeding. Provide water and for the most part things will take care of themselves.

Assuming good growing conditions (temperature), grass seeds will begin to germinate as soon as water hits them. Sunlight isn't even a factor at this point. They'll stop growing if they dry out, and, if this happens, they're dead in the water. They won't start up again no matter how much moisture you give them. Why? Each seed only has enough food to support one full germination process, nonstop. This means that once you start watering them, you have to keep at it until they develop leaves and roots. (Conversely, since water is the key to germination, seeds can lie on dry ground for some time without worries, except for birds plucking them off.)

All you have to do is keep the soil surface wet. The seeds only take water from the soil's top layer. Plan on watering daily, and even twice a day if conditions call for it (like very low humidity or dry, windy weather, both of which are most likely to show up at the end of a planting window, which is why mulching is important). About one-tenth of an inch of water per application, at the most, should be enough to wet the seeds and moisten the soil. Anything more than this and you run the risk of running the seeds off the site.

Continue watering at least once daily or as often as necessary (the weather will play a big role in this) until the grass reaches about one inch. How much is necessary depends on whether it is hot and dry or if it is cloudy, or if you have mulched or if your soil is prone to easily drying out. The possibilities are endless; your abilities to go on autopilot at this point are about the same as when you have a newborn in your house. You can't.

When the grass gets to around one inch, their leaves and roots can support them, and they'll be able to pull water from deeper in the soil. At this point you can begin to drop your watering schedule back to once every other day. If the grass is doing well, increase the time between watering to two or three days. But at all times remember the newborn and how things can rapidly change.

Feed Them

Baby grass plants are hungry little buggers, and they'll use up the starter fertilizer you put down about a month after they start growing. To keep them happy, apply a half pound to a pound of nitrogen fertilizer per thousand square feet at the one-month mark and the same amount in another twenty to thirty days.

Control the Weeds

Ideally, you applied a preemergent containing siduron before you seeded. Don't use any other herbicides on newly seeded areas. Remember, doing so will keep crabgrass seeds from germinating, but you'll also stop the grass seeds in their tracks. Wait until you've mowed two or three times, and then apply a broadleaf or grassy weed herbicide as necessary. You'll know if it's necessary if you still see weeds after you start mowing. Some of the weeds that come up with the grass seedlings will not tolerate mowing and will go away without a fuss. Other weeds, mainly broadleaf weeds if you applied siduron, can be controlled at this point, but you can also choose to wait. You can have a very nice-looking lawn even with a few weeds and they may well disappear if you keep up

Simply following a good mowing program might be all you have to do to control weeds in your new lawn. Young weed plants typically succumb to mowing, and the ones that don't are pretty easy to pluck out by hand.

with your mowing, watering, and fertilizing. The key here is being willing to wait a year or two until the grass can outcompete the weeds. If you're not, and you don't like the weeds in your yard, go ahead and spray them.

If you didn't apply a preemergence herbicide, you'll have to battle the summer annual weeds, like crabgrass and foxtail, that sprout along with your new grass plants. A product like dithiopyr (Dimension) can work thirty days after germination, or you can also apply quinclorac (Drive). Turn to chapter 11 for more on how to do this.

Mow Them

Mowing is absolutely the best thing you can do to get your lawn to fill in. Not mowing or not mowing often enough will slow down or delay the grass's maturation process.

Don't let the blades on your baby grass plants get too long. When they reach three inches, the plants will be firmly rooted and any possibility of damaging the area by trudging across it with a mower should be past. Don't assume that longer is better—letting the grass go much beyond three inches won't help the roots any.

Remember, you never want to take off more than one-third of the grass blades when mowing. When mowing cool-season grasses for the first time, set your mower at three inches for optimum results. For warm-season grasses, set it at two inches.

OH, SOD IT!

Sodding can be a lot easier than seeding, but this doesn't mean you can just put things on autopilot. Sod may not be as vulnerable as a newborn, but you still have to take care of it to help it thrive. You just don't have to micromanage it.

As mentioned, sodding also includes sprigging, plugging, and stripping. You'll find guidelines for each approach here as well.

Prepare the Site

Don't skimp on soil prep. Sod needs a good foundation to grow on just like seeds do. Every minute you spend on this step means one less minute of worrying about whether your sod will take, and it will also translate into less wear and tear on your teeth and joints because you'll be gliding over a smooth surface, not clattering over a bunch of bumps that are only there because you got lazy. Level, grade, and fertilize just like you would for seeding. *Do not forget starter fertilizer!* Put it down before you put down the sod.

While you're out there, measure the area so you know how much sod to buy. Add an extra 5 percent or so to allow for cutting and shaping the sod to fit.

Select Your Sod

If possible, deal directly with the source—the farmer who grew the sod. This is the best way to ensure that the grass you're getting will grow where you live, as it's coming from climate and soil conditions similar to what's in your yard.

If you're buying already-harvested sod from a nursery or a garden center, unroll a couple of sections before plunking down your dough. You should see very little soil, which might come as a surprise, but properly cut sod should be mostly grass and roots. Ideally, what soil you do see should be similar in composition to what's already in your soon-to-be-lawn. Matching soil to soil will give the grass roots every opportunity to dig down deep and grow, and prevent drainage and disease issues in the future as well. The key is to have the soil from the sod be equal to or coarser in texture than the soil in your lawn. What to do if it isn't? Well, you can't change the soil in the sod, but you can merge the layers by cutting small holes through them, which I describe in more detail in chapter 10.

The sod should be cool to the touch and uniformly moist but not wet. Warm sod is sod that's been on the shelf (harvested) a little too long and it's starting to break down; the warmth indicates decomposition. What roots there are should be white and moist. Check for weeds, undesirable insects, and diseases; it should be virtually free of the first two and definitely free of the third. That said, a worm or two is a good thing. One weed, not a cause for panic.

Sod is measured from the bottom of the plant downward and typically cut one-quarter to one-half inch thick. Thinner sod is not only easier for farmers to ship, it's easier to handle and it will root faster. You'll have to water it more often while it's rooting into place, however, as it can't hold as much moisture as the thicker stuff.

Plan on selecting and ordering your sod about a week before you need it, and be ready to install it when it's delivered. This means that day. If you're dealing with a local grower, it should be absolutely fresh when delivered, as many growers will cut and deliver the sod on the same day. If they're willing to deliver sod pallets to different parts of your yard, opt for this. Your back and your labor force, which you'll hopefully have, will thank you later.

Lay It Down

It's best to lay sod immediately after you get it, when it's at its freshest and best. If you can't get to it right away, it will keep for up to two days, but only if you take care of it. If you have to wait for any reason, keep pallets cool by placing them in a shady spot. Leave the sod rolled up and keep the rolls moist by misting them with a hose-end sprayer.

The equipment list for laying sod is short and sweet. You'll need:

- a sharp knife (or two) to cut the sod. A utility knife will do.
- a wheelbarrow to haul it around.
- a water-filled roller to smush it down when it's in place. Rent this.
- a hose or sprinkler to water the sod as you place it.
- a board or piece of plywood. Stand or kneel on this instead of your new lawn, as you're working to minimize lumps in your dirt.
- If your site has slopes, add stakes to the list.

Here's how you'll lay the sod, step by step:

1. Choose your starting point. If possible, find a straight edge to work along. Driveways and sidewalks are good for this, but you can also make one yourself. Pick two spots somewhere in your yard—along property lines works well. Sink stakes into both spots, then tie a string between them. That's your starting line.

2. Moisten the soil. Remember, the sod's roots are cool and moist. Ideally, the soil they're going onto should be the same. Don't flood the soil; just apply a fine mist. And don't water the entire area at once. Hit the section you're going to work on first, then the next section, and so on.

3. Unroll the first piece of sod and place it against the straight edge. Unroll the next piece and place it right at the end of the first one. You want a tight fit from end to end. Don't try to fill bare spots between pieces by pulling on them; do it and you'll tear the sod and disrupt the even coverage you're after. Don't overlap the ends; you'll create a bumpy lawn. Keep going until you're done with the first row.

4. To start the next row, cut a piece of sod in half. Then continue as before. The ends of the sod won't line up with the previous row, and that's exactly what you want. End the row with the other half piece, a full piece, or another piece cut to fit. You should see a staggered, bricklike pattern when you're done with the second row. Be sure to have your plywood board at the ready if you have to kneel on bare soil. You don't want the ends of the pieces aligned in rows because, guess what, your new grass will end up looking like it was planted in rows, and you definitely don't want that. You also want to minimize areas where corners come together, as they dry out faster.

5. Keep going. Cut the pieces as necessary to fit the space. Small pieces are much more likely to dry out and die than large ones, so throw the little guys away and do the job with bigger pieces wherever possible. If there are hills or slopes, lay the sod horizontally across them and anchor the pieces with stakes at both ends to keep them in place.

Always work away from the sod as much as possible. It might look sturdy, but it's not. If you have to be on it, stand or kneel on the board or piece of plywood I told you to get. This will distribute your weight over a wider area and keep the sod in place better.

When you're done, fill the water roller about halfway and go over the sod in a diagonal pattern. This will eliminate spaces between the sod and the soil and maximize root-sod contact.

Walk carefully as you roll; the sod will come up fairly easily at this point, less so after you roll it. When you're done, check for strips that might have shifted and loose corners. Press them back into place.

Seams and corners on newly laid sod simply dry out faster than the rest of the strips. Here's a pro tip to help them stay moist: scatter a little soil on top of the seams. This is called topdressing, which simply means applying a layer of soil or other materials over the top of the existing grass or surface. It might be the last thing you want to do when you're hot and sweaty and exhausted after a day of laying sod, but putting down a little extra soil in these spots is more than worth the effort. You won't need much soil for this, probably not more than one cubic foot or so. Do it as you go and it is not as daunting a task.

In a way, topdressing is akin to caulking between joints of bricks, and it may remind you of such. It will also serve to re-mind you of how tight you actually got your sod pieces, and if you're sodding for the first time and they are a little looser than they should be, your grass will very much appreciate this spe-cial attention.

Water It

Water your new sod thoroughly. Really saturate it. Getting moisture into the soil beneath the sod is a must. Check penetration by lifting a corner on one piece. The sod should be wet through and the soil be-neath it should be damp. If it isn't, water again. When you're done, check it again. If it's not damp, water again.

Plan on watering every day, and maybe a couple of times a day, for the first week or so. Keeping the sod and the soil beneath it moist at this stage is imperative. Remember, edges and corners will dry out first, so pay particular attention to them. If you topdressed, they will not dry out as fast. Check rooting progress by pulling up a corner every couple of days or so. If all is well, you should feel a little resistance the first time you do this. The next time, more resistance. In about ten days, things should be pretty firmly in place. When they are, start skipping a day between watering. If the sod stays green, stick to this schedule. If not, keep watering every day for another couple of days, then try backing off again. Stick to an every-other-day schedule for about two weeks. On the third week, you should be able to increase the intervals.

Protect It

Every step you take on new sod, especially during the first week, can shift it out of place. Do what's necessary to minimize foot traffic until at least the second week. After three weeks or so, the sod should be firmly rooted and walkable. It's still tender, though, so take it easy.

Don't think sod won't move, because it definitely can. To drive this point home, I sometimes tell people about a certain athletic field I know about. The sod on it was moved slightly during the establishment process and left smallish gaps, maybe six inches or so, which went unnoticed as the grass grew and covered up the holes. When the field was mature enough to host athletic events, a player tripped over one of the holes and broke his arm.

I often get asked if rolling will help the lawn if some dang fool walked on it and shifted turf around enough to create holes. Not much is the answer, although it will help the economy because you rented a roller. If you want to fill in those holes, you can do it in one of two ways. You can take topdressing and fill them in (if you have to put down a lot of soil and you smother the grass, you can always reseed). Or you can core cultivate, then take a drag and drag those cores around your yard. The soil from the cores will fill in the low spots; loose soil always fills in holes. For more on what core cultivating is all about, turn to chapter 10.

Mow It

Again, you want to cut your new lawn when the blades are just over three inches long. Your sod, on the other hand, might be longer than this by the time you can walk on it safely. Remember, though, you never want to cut off more than one-third of the leaf. If your grass is four inches long, three inches is the lowest you want to go.

Feed It

Apply a fertilizer appropriate for your grass about a month after laying it down. Make this application part of your planned fertilization program. At this point, consider your sod established lawn, because that's what it is.

SPRIGGING AND PLUGGING ALONG

As mentioned, sprigging and plugging, along with stripping, are alternatives to full-coverage sodding. Their lower cost can make them extremely attractive, and in some cases they're the only way to start certain grasses.

As with seeding and sodding, site preparation is the key to success with these approaches. Treat newly planted areas with care, water them thoroughly, and hold off mowing until grass blades are at least three inches long.

Sprigging

Sprigging is how many warm-season grasses—bermudagrass, St. Augustinegrass, and zoysiagrass in particular—are established. Certain varieties of these grasses produce sterile seeds and must be started vegetatively.

Sprigging is not only the best way to get some of these varieties; it's also very economical. It's an efficient way to have a nice lawn, it's lots easier to care for and establish than seeding is, eliminates any soil-layering possibility, and is a lot cheaper. How do I know? I put myself through my second year of graduate school by sprigging people's lawns. Granted, it was warm in Arkansas, but I could start their lawns in June and by the time we got to the middle of August they had the best lawns in town.

If you're in bermudagrass land, sprigging is definitely a good option.

It also works with St. Augustinegrass, and you can do it with zoysia-grass, but the latter takes longer to grow into a lawn. The thing with zoysiagrass is, by the time you put down as many sprigs as you need, you begin to wonder why you didn't just sod.

You can order sprigs from nurseries or garden centers. They usually come in bushels; have your measurements ready and the store or nursery staff will know how much to order.

You'll plant your sprigs by:

- Furrowing. Dig shallow trenches spaced about twelve to eighteen inches apart. The closer they are, the better they'll fill in. Spread the sprigs across each furrow; make sure the tops of the sprigs face the sun. Fill in the furrows, but don't cover the sprigs all the way. Leave about two to three inches bare. Tamp or roll the soil over the sprigs to firm them into place.
- Spreading. Simply scatter the sprigs across the soil, and then poke them into the soil with a stick. Again, leave the tops exposed. Spread a thin soil layer over them (topdress), then tamp or roll as before.
- Poking. Use a tree planter (this is a long bar with a spade-type end used for making holes for planting small trees) to poke holes six to twelve inches apart. Drop the sprigs in, and then kick the soil over them. Tamp or roll as before.

Keeping sprigs moist is a must, as they're planted so close to the surface. Watering twice a day might be necessary. Don't leave this to chance; if sprigs look dry (you'll be able to tell because they'll turn color, a deep blue, purple, or brown instead of green), water them down.

Make sure you've put down a preemergence herbicide to battle annual grasses. The competition will be fierce.

> **By definition,** when you borrow grass from one spot to fill in another spot, you're plugging.

Plugging

Think of plugging as sodding on a smaller scale. You dig small holes about six to twelve inches apart and about two to three inches deep and insert the plugs. Tamp or roll as before.

Again, the closer you position the holes, the better the initial coverage will be. When the plugs are established, they'll spread and fill the bare ground around them.

Any spreading grass is a candidate for plugging; buffalograss, zoysiagrass, and St. Augustinegrass are often started this way.

You can buy precut plugs or cut your own from sod. A square yard of sod will yield 324 two-inch plugs, enough to cover about nine square yards of ground.

Strip Sodding

Strip sodding might seem an odd approach for establishing a new lawn, especially if you remember the warning about leaving gaps between pieces of sod, but it does work with spreading grasses. All you do is leave about six to ten inches between each piece of sod as you put them down. They'll eventually fill in.

This is a good approach with zoysiagrass because it's so expensive, but any spreading grass is a candidate for strip sodding.

Whether you seed, sod, sprig, or plug, follow the rules and remember to water, fertilize, and mow and you'll be a pro in no time and actually giving advice at the next barbecue. They'll be gathered around you like flies on cow patties. Trust me on this.

The next few chapters describe in more detail the major cultural practices—mowing, watering, fertilizing—and some other important practices, including cultivation and pest management. There are some rules ahead, but no absolutes. Your lawn is no longer an infant; it's developed its own personality and, like kids, there's no one-size-fits-all approach.

No two children are alike. Neither are any two lawns.

PART THREE

Maintaining a Lawn

CHAPTER 7

Making the Right Cut

Some 70 percent of the things that can go wrong with lawns are caused by mowing the wrong way, so it's pretty safe to say that many people—and you, most likely—have lots to learn when it comes to doing it right.

I can't tell you how many times people have asked me how they can get their lawns to look like the ones that the pros grow, and my answer is always the same. Mow it right! If I had a dollar for every time I've looked at a lawn that's struggling, only to find out that the owner's not mowing right, I'd be driving a Mercedes instead of a minivan.

Of everything you can do with and for your lawn, mowing it *right* is the thing that can and will make the biggest difference in its looks and health. In fact, if there's something wrong with your lawn, you can almost bet that a bad trim job either caused the problem—or, better put, problems, as turf tribulations almost never fly solo—or made it worse.

Great-looking lawns are the product of well-executed mowing programs more than anything else. This might seem too easy, simplistic even, but it's the gospel truth. What's more, if you have a healthy, well-established lawn, mowing it right might be the only thing you'll have to do on a regular basis to keep it that way. You'll still have to water and fertilize, and you'll have to keep an eye on things like weeds and thatch— the organic stuff that builds up between grass blades and the soil—but you won't have to spend anywhere near as much time or resources on them as the guy down the block who doesn't mow his lawn right.

Mowing incorrectly accounts for some 70 percent of lawn problems. Scalping, or mowing too short, is the worst of the bad practices.

Why this is so speaks to turfgrass's amazing ability to adapt to adversity. Have you ever come across the old saying "That which doesn't kill you makes you stronger"? When it comes to turfgrasses, nothing could be truer.

IT HURTS SO GOOD

When you lop off part of any living, growing thing, you hurt it, which means that mowing, in and of itself, is a painful process for grass. Not only do the open wounds that you inflict on the blades of your grass plants make it possible for insects and diseases to get in, but they bleed water from those cuts, which dehydrates them to a certain extent.

In response to the trauma, the plants withdraw from their environment, just like wild animals do when they retreat to their dens to lick their wounds. The grass plant version of wound licking means they stop sending roots into the ground, which, in turn, slows down their food production and storage. Water and nutrient absorption via roots also slows down. But it's just a momentary withdrawal, barely noticeable. When they recover, they come back better and stronger than before.

This pattern of growing, lopping, and recovering, repeated over and over again, is what makes cultivated grasses, and especially the ones used as turfgrasses, what they are. It's part of their heritage, and how they developed.

The big difference between turfgrasses and some old grass growing wild somewhere is their ability to adapt to being cut down to size on a fairly regular basis. Grazing animals were the first grass whackers. How we cut grass today, no matter how we do it—by hand, mower, Weedwacker, what have you—simply mimics those animals.

Don't let the fear of causing pain to your grass keep you from cutting it. Not lopping off the tops of those plants on a regular basis is worse than doing so. Frequent and proper mowing also encourages their lateral growth, which is what fills in your yard and creates the thick, lush turf that you're after.

The grasses that survive this cycle are truly the fittest of the fit. They're the ones we're proud to call turfgrasses.

WHO MAKES THE CUT?

At some point during your life as a lawn geek, you might decide to have a more arm's-length relationship with your turf and hire someone else to do the dirty work (or parts of it) for you, but at the beginning stages of geekdom, you can't. Or, better put, you shouldn't.

The time you'll spend getting to know all of your lawn's little quirks, exploring its nooks and crannies and what have you, is not only part of the lawn geek initiation process, it's what will put you above those who merely aspire to geekiness. Hands down, it's the best way to really understand what your lawn's all about. You'll know the areas that respond well to your love and attention, and those that turn a cold shoulder. You'll be able to spot problems a lot faster, and deal with them quicker. Beyond this, it can make for some decent attitude adjustment if you're in need of it. It's pretty hard to be mad at the world after you've communed with nature by being at the helm of a mower for a while.

If you're going to mow your yard yourself, you'll need the right equipment. Without it, you might as well hire a service.

Back in the day, and I'm talking centuries ago, scythes were the de rigueur mowing equipment. Well, pretty much the only mowing equipment if there weren't grazing animals around to do the job. If you've ever seen one of these tools, or handled one, you know how potentially lethal they can be. (Grass isn't the only thing they're good at whacking.) And you know how really hard it is to get a uniform cut out of them.

Fortunately, we and turf care have come a long way, baby. You can

Is hiring a lawn service the worst thing you can do? Not necessarily. If you can't take care of your lawn consistently, for whatever reason, having a service do it is better than doing what you can when you have the time. If you decide to have others do some (or all) of your lawn care, ask for references and scope out lawns they're already working on. Make sure you know exactly what they'll do. Some services just mow. Others offer just about everything necessary to keep lawns looking good—at a price, of course.

Okay, true confession time here. I don't mow my own grass, and I haven't for some time now. This doesn't mean I don't pay attention to what's going on in my yard, however. I set the mowing schedule and I remind them of the old one-third rule (probably not necessary; they do understand it by now, but I can't help myself). So, mowing isn't a necessary cross to bear in order to be a lawn geek. But you do have to understand what's going on and keep an eye on things, because whether you scalped it or somebody else did, you still need to know that it was scalped.

still scythe your yard, of course, and if your grass is so long that it whips around at about knee level when you walk through it, doing so might be your only option until you get things under control. That, or attacking it with an industrial-strength weed trimmer.

If you're like most folks, though, a lawn mower is the far better choice. Save the Weedwacker for what it was invented for—trimming grass around trees, sidewalk edges, garden areas, and whatnot. And forget about scything unless you're really serious about taking the Luddite approach to lawn care.

YOU AND YOUR LAWN MOWER

Of the pieces of lawn maintenance equipment you could and should own, your mower is the most important. It's also the piece of equipment you'll use the most, and, potentially, the one you'll spend the most money on.

You, your lawn, and your lawn mower should be a well-matched team. If you're currently using a mower that the previous owner left behind, you probably already know why it was. Or maybe your mower was fine for your old yard but it's not the best choice for where you are now. If you're more frustrated than not when you use it, and your frustrations aren't caused by fixable things, like tuning the engine or sharpening the blade, it's probably time to get a new one.

If you already own a mower and you're happy with it, skip this section. If you don't, or you know you need a new one (or you simply want a new one), read on.

First things first. A mower shouldn't be an impulse purchase. Do some research before you buy. Think about how you're going to use it. Preferably, do all of this before the growing season sets in so you're ready to go when your grass starts growing.

Our love affairs with our lawns translate into lots of mower choices. This can make the selection process a royal pain in the rear, especially since it's not the sort of thing you do very often. If you had to buy a mower every year, you'd probably keep up with all the neat things that are taking place in the mower business. You'd know about things like robotics and zero turning radii, and whatnot. But, since you don't, you'll have to rely on other sources for your information. Sources like the sales guy at the hardware or home improvement store. He might know what he's talking about. Then again, he might not. There also might be a special promotion going on, and he'll get a spiff if he sells you a certain brand or model of mower, which might override his usual sense of honesty and decency and make him recommend machines that might not be right for you or your lawn.

So, don't rely on the hardware guy. Or the big-box home store guy. Not entirely, anyway. Do your own research. Start here with the basics. Once you work through them, you should know what kind of mower you need. At the very least, you'll have a better idea of what you think it is. When you're at this point, you can use what you've learned to comparison shop any way you see fit—online, in stores, in advertising circulars, whatever.

You've got two basic choices when it comes to mowers: reel or rotary.

The Reel Deal

We have a guy named Edwin Budding to thank for the first commercially viable mechanical lawn mower. Budding, a textile engineer, understood the similarities between carpet fibers and grass, and he modified a device that cut the nap on carpets to do the same even trimming on grass plants.

Lots of modifications have been made to Budding's original machine over the years, but its basic approach to cutting grass hasn't changed. Think of it like running a big scissors over your lawn, because that's exactly what it is. The cutting mechanism has two parts—a sharp, horizontally mounted stationary bar called a bedknife and a revolving cylinder fitted with sharp blades. As you push the mower forward, the reel moves and the blades contact the bedknife, which is holding the grass blades at attention. The mower blades then shear the tops off the grass blades, making a sharp, clean cut.

Muscle power was the original moving force on reel mowers, and many are still powered by muscle alone. As such, using one can be great exercise. If you're not looking for that much of a workout, there are gas- and electric-powered reel mowers. They're heavier and more expensive, which kind of cancels out some of the reasons why you'd want to use a reel mower, but if you're after some of the other benefits they deliver, they can still be a good choice.

Manually powered reel mowers are environmentally friendly, which is another reason why their popularity has boomed of late. Because they're so light, they're easy to whip out and work with. Plus, you can cut your lawn just about any time you want and not bug your neighbors with the sound of a motor.

Reel mowers have lots of fans, and deservedly so. When the blades are sharp and adjusted correctly they make cleaner cuts than rotary mowers do, and the cuts heal faster, which keeps moisture in and diseases out. They can cut shorter than rotaries—they're used on every golf green, tee, and fairway, and many collegiate and professional sports fields, for this reason. They do a great job on many types of grasses, especially shorter varieties like bermudagrass and St. Augustinegrass. The shearing action also creates finer grass clippings. Many reel mower owners leave the clippings down for this reason (and I am always pro-clippings on the lawn), but you can also buy a basket attachment for the back of the mower to catch them.

Manual, gas, or electric reel mowers do have their drawbacks. The bedknife and reel have to come together correctly to cut properly. If they don't, they'll tear and bruise the tips of the grass blades. That said, adjusting the blades is relatively simple and easy if you know how. They don't do well on taller grasses or weeds, which can be a real problem if you get behind for whatever reason. You'll have to sharpen the blades periodically and the bedknife will need grinding every year or two. If either is nicked or compromised in some way, you'll have to sharpen or replace it. Compared to simply pulling off the rotary blade and replacing it, which can be accomplished in all of five minutes, including drinking coffee for three of them, maintaining a reel mower might be more than you bargained for.

If you have a small yard, say less than two thousand square feet of turf, and you don't want to spend a lot of money, you might enjoy using a push reel mower. If you decide to go this route, look for mowers that let you adjust mowing height, for the obvious reason. Also consider the width, which ranges from fourteen to twenty-four inches. The wider the reel, the faster you'll be done, but wider-reeled mowers can be tougher to maneuver.

You can buy a small, basic manual reel mower for under a hundred dollars. Gas- and electric-powered reel mowers cost from three hundred to fifteen hundred dollars. As reel widths and add-ons increase, so do prices.

The Spin on Rotaries

Rotary mowers hit the lawn-care market in the 1930s and are far and away the dominant machines today. Like reel mowers, the cutting mechanism on rotaries is also relatively simple. There's an engine that sits in a housing called a deck. A piece of metal called an engine shaft sticks down through the deck. A flat, horizontal blade is bolted to the bottom of the shaft. When you fire up the engine, the shaft rotates and the blade spins. The underside of the deck, which keeps the blade from coming into contact with things it shouldn't, like body parts, also acts like a vacuum chamber and lifts the grass up as it's being cut. Still, the blades on rotary mowers tend to bend the grass as they cut, even with the vacuuming action. For this reason, rotary mowers don't cut as cleanly as reel mowers do, but they're easier to maintain and easily the more popular choice, and they've come a long way in being able to provide a quality cut.

Rotary mowers come in three different configurations:

- Push. You provide the horsepower that moves these mowers along while the engine is turning the blade and doing the cutting. They're the most common rotary mowers and they work well on smaller lawns—one thousand to five thousand square feet—that are smooth and flat. Depending on engine size and other options, like push-button or pull starters, electric- or gas-powered, these mowers can cost anywhere from a hundred and fifty to seven hundred dollars or so.
- Self-propelled. These mowers have mechanisms that move them along without much help from you. They're a good choice for larger lawns between five thousand and twenty thousand square feet and smaller lawns that aren't flat. Prices on these mowers range from around two hundred to eight hundred dollars.
- Riding. If you have a large lawn—anything over twenty thousand square feet—a riding mower can make a lot of sense. Although these babies might seem like overkill, they can make sense depending on your needs. For example, some can pull other lawn-care and gardening devices, like trailers and aerators. Expect to spend anywhere from around a thousand to seven thousand dollars or more, again depending on motor size, options, and accessories. There's no such thing as a small riding mower, although there is some size variation among them, so you'll need to consider where you're going to store it.

Most rotary mowers are gas-powered, and most people opt for them. There are electric rotaries on the market, but they can be hard to find and more expensive than comparable gas-powered models. Battery-operated electrics are easier to use, as you don't have to worry about dragging a power cord as you go, but they're heavier and can be tough to keep charged.

These days, most decent mowers are mulching mowers; it's probably hard to find one that's not. These mowers chew up grass clippings into smaller, less objectionable sizes. Most come with a bagging option that lets you pick up debris and leaves; I say, get it. Worst-case scenario, the bag sits in your garage for the life of your mower, but if you do ever need it for whatever reason, you've got it.

Other considerations and options to think about include:

- Safety features. Rotary mowers have moving parts that, well, move very, very fast. As such, they can be dangerous machines to operate. All rotaries have mechanisms to stop them, fast, if necessary. Most have what's called a zone restart, which is simply a lever or switch that brings both blade and engine to a screeching halt. A blade-break clutch, also known as a dead man's switch, is another safety device that's often available on more expensive rotaries. This device is a safety bar on the handle that stops the blade (but not the engine) when it's released.
- Engine power. It isn't necessary to buy the biggest, the best, or the most expensive mower, but it is important to get one with enough engine power to do the job. Lower-priced self-propelled mowers typically come with 2.5- to 3.0-horsepower engines. They're fine for small jobs and for grasses that aren't too dense or too tall. Run one through a good stand of thick Kentucky bluegrass, on the other hand, and you'll risk bending its crankshaft, as the engine simply won't be able to handle the stress. A mower with 3.5 to 4 horses under the hood would be a far better choice here, and probably in general. There are Web sites where you can plug in your lawn size and terrain and determine a range of engine hp that will make you happy. Check the Resources appendix.
- Deck housing. Deck housings come in various materials— aluminum, steel, or plastic—and various widths. All have their advantages and disadvantages. Steel is the toughest, but also the

heaviest, and it can rust. Aluminum is lighter and rust-resistant, but it costs more. The plastic used in deck housings is extremely tough and light—it's the same material used in football helmets—but it can crack if hit hard enough.

- Deck width. Wider decks are definitely a plus, as they'll get you done faster, but mowers that have them are heavier and harder to maneuver in addition to being more expensive.
- Zero-turning radius. If you're thinking about a riding mower, this option, which allows you to turn on a dime because the rear wheels move independently, can make your mowing time even easier and faster. It's one to think about if your yard is extremely large or mowing time is really at a premium. Plus, it's kind of cool.
- Front or rear drive. This is another riding mower consideration. Some people feel front-wheel-drive machines are more maneuverable. New on the horizon: all-wheel-drive machines.
- Cutting-height adjustment. This is typically a lever-based device that moves the mowing deck up or down. If you have to choose between two mowers and it's easier to adjust the mowing height on the pricier one, I strongly encourage you to go for it. You'll find out why soon.

As with just about everything, you tend to get what you pay for with mowers. As you go up the price scale, you'll get more bells and whistles. The machines will be built a bit tougher, engines will be bigger. But remember, the biggest, the best, or the most expensive isn't necessarily the right choice. If you don't think you'll be working on your current yard forever and you don't want to take your mower with you, it doesn't make a lot of sense to blow the bank on it.

Bottom line, get a mower that suits you and your lawn. If necessary, try a few before you buy them. Either borrow from friends or neighbors or go to a rental shop and see what they have available.

When people ask me what mower to buy, I tell them to get the size that fits their lawn; and in 99 percent of the cases I tell them to buy a rotary. They're easier to take care of and service, they're more available, and they can provide a high-quality cut for the vast majority of lawns.

Mowers have seen the future, and the future is robotics. These puppies scurry over lawns just like their indoor vacuum counterparts do. A barrier of some sort, either electromagnetic or mirror-based, keeps them close to home instead of in your neighbor's yard. They're not widely available yet, and they're expensive, but you'll see more of them as the technology improves and prices drop. The newest versions even have computer programs that set their mowing patterns.

Trimming Things Up

If you're serious about making your lawn look good, another piece of equipment that's worth buying is something to put the finishing touches on your hard work. For most people, this means investing in a string trimmer or an edger. Or both.

String trimmers come in gas or electric models. Like gas mowers, gas trimmers are more powerful and you don't have to worry about running out of cord or battery juice. Like electric mowers, electric trimmers are quieter and less expensive. They do a pretty good job on small lawns; for big jobs, gas trimmers are the bell cows.

Options on trimmers include:

- Straight versus curved shaft. Straight-shaft trimmers are more powerful and versatile. Curved-shaft models are lighter and easier to handle, and less expensive.
- Antivibration engine. Machines with this feature don't tire out their users as quickly.
- Rotating head, which means it can be used as an edger.

People operating string trimmers are notorious for cutting grass too closely. You're going to try to be the exception to this rule, which is valiant and honorable, but you'll do some scalping. Just about everyone does, as it's simply too easy to get lulled into the job and begin to cut too close, which is never good. The more you trim, the better you'll get at it.

If you don't have a lot of trimming to do, manual or electric hand shears are another option. It's harder to get an even trim with these, but they're also low on the scalping scale.

Edgers, which cut cleanly defined lines between lawns and hard surfaces—pavement, asphalt, and so on—also come manual or powered. If you have a large lawn and lots of edges to delineate, or if you're dealing with a tough aggressive grass like bermudagrass, go with a power model.

Finally, if you're really anal and you can't stand the sight of leaf clippings on hard surfaces like sidewalks and driveways, you might want to add a leaf blower to your arsenal. You can also use it for tidying up your yard in fall and spring, and for blowing fertilizer off hard surfaces as well (if it's on your sidewalk or driveway it will soon be in a gutter and then in a sewer line somewhere).

Now let's move on to what mowing correctly is all about, and why it's so important.

ACHIEVING THE PERFECT CUT

Once you have the right equipment and it's in prime operating order, mowing correctly boils down to two things: mowing at the proper height and mowing at the right frequency. That's it. These two factors are the cornerstone of every lawn-care program, as they're also the key influences behind the other two major cultural practices—irrigation and fertilization. Changing mowing height, even slightly, can affect how much and how often you have to feed and water your lawn.

Getting the Right Height

First up is mowing at the right height. The rule of thumb here is to never cut off more than one-third of the leaf blade during any single mowing. Why is this so important? Remember, you damage grass blades every time you cut them. When you cut them too short, you're not only inflicting physical harm, you're also further diminishing their already diminished capabilities. In other words, you're hitting them when they're already down.

Scalping your grass—cutting it too low—is something you never

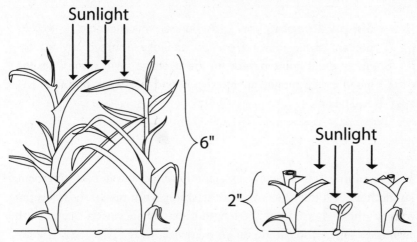

On the left, grass plants mowed to a proper height; on the right, scalped plants that are mowed too short. Note their little buddy in the center; that's a weed seed that can now germinate because it's getting enough sunlight. If you don't pay attention to any other diagram, pay attention to this one, as it will get you further down the road than all the rest. Don't scalp your grass!

want to do, period. If you do it, you run the risk of damaging your grass where it hurts it the most—at the crown, command central for all of the plants' growth. Scalping grass isn't like scalping people, you're not lopping off the tops of their heads, but you are cutting too close, not at ground level but simply too close. Scalped grass can recover, but it does so at a price. You typically have to water it more, and it's more vulnerable to things like crabgrass and diseases, which take time and money to fight. Continual scalping will open the top of the turf—the canopy—and give weeds the one requirement they need to germinate—light—that they don't get when lawns are dense. So, avoid these problems on the front end. Don't scalp your grass!

If you like to keep your grass fairly short, following the one-third rule will mean mowing more often. As an example, if you're keeping your lawn at two inches, you'll have to mow it when it gets to three inches. During peak growing season, this might mean mowing every other day or so. Mowing more often encourages lateral growth, resulting in denser, thicker turf with minimal weeds.

Keeping your grass longer, on the other hand, makes the one-third rule easier to follow by allowing you to go longer between mowings.

Simply keeping your grass longer will eliminate up to 20 percent of the mowing you do annually. That's a savings of about eight hours a year for the average lawn owner, not to mention less money spent on gas and less wear and tear on equipment.

What's more, that longer grass length reduces water requirements, strengthens pest tolerance, and boosts photosynthesis. In short, keeping grass at the higher end of the length range for its variety is one of the healthiest things you can do for your lawn.

Each grass species has its ideal mowing heights. This is another good reason for knowing what's growing in your yard.

Grass Species	Recommended Height
annual rye	1.5–4″
bahiagrass	2–3″
bermudagrass, common	0.75–1.5″
bermudagrass, hybrid	1.5–4″
blue gramagrass	2–3″
buffalograss	1–3″
centipedegrass	2–4″
fine fescues	1.5–4″
Kentucky bluegrass	1.5–4″
perennial ryegrass	1.5–4″
St. Augustinegrass	1–2.5″
Supina bluegrass	1–2.5″
tall fescue	2–6″
zoysiagrass	1–3″

If you want to mow less frequently, plant a slow-growing species and keep it at the high end of the scale. That said, you should plan on mowing your grass about once a week or so during peak growing season no matter what. If thunderstorms are rolling through on a regular basis and dumping lots of moisture, you might have to mow more often,

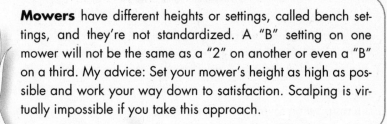

Mowers have different heights or settings, called bench settings, and they're not standardized. A "B" setting on one mower will not be the same as a "2" on another or even a "B" on a third. My advice: Set your mower's height as high as possible and work your way down to satisfaction. Scalping is virtually impossible if you take this approach.

maybe even every couple of days or so. Prolonged drought? Every ten days to two weeks might be all your grass needs.

Is it ever okay to cut more than one-third? Yes, there's an exception to this rule. If you live in the North, and there's usually good snow cover through the winter, you can cut your grass a little shorter on your last mowing of the season. Doing so will leave less of those brown, dormant leaf blades behind, and your lawn will look greener when the snow melts in the spring. Just remember that the one-third rule is most important when the grass is under the most stress—for example, high temperatures for cool-season grasses, cool temperatures for warm-season grasses, and drought, wear and tear, and pest damage.

If you have to cut a little more during the early spring or late fall and/or get a little behind due to rain or vacation, it's not going to end the world. What we're trying to prevent here are continual scalping practices that will lead to poor turf conditions. Everything in moderation.

Why are cutting heights so important? Basically, the height of the grass blades and the length of roots are related. If you cut grass too low for its type, it won't root as deeply as it should. Lawns of shallow-rooted grasses dry out faster, need more frequent watering, and are less able to spring back from drought. They're also compromised when it comes to things like fighting off weeds, as they lack the nice thick canopy that keeps the sun from hitting weed seeds and seedlings down below. As weeds take hold, the grass gets even weaker. Remember how grass grows? If you stop mowing or don't mow frequently enough, it won't spread out; it will thin out and have a harder time competing with weeds.

BEFORE YOU MOW

Cutting grass entails more than just whipping out the mower and going at it. Do some prep work before you start your engine, and both you and your grass will be better for it.

Be smart. Know how the equipment works. Even if you're not much on reading owner's manuals, this is one time you'll want to.

Dress right. Skip the sandals. Wear shoes, preferably sturdy ones, especially if you have to power your mower up and down slopes. Want to know how many emergency room trips are caused by lawn mowers? It's best not to get that knowledge firsthand. Wearing long, close-fitting pants is also a good idea. Not only will they protect your legs from anything that your mower might kick up, but shoes look less dorky with them.

Pick things up. Pick up anything that could turn into an injury-causing projectile should the lawn mower pick it up—rocks, twigs, kid's toys, dog's toys. Pick up pet droppings, too. And paper scraps. You'll find out why if you ever run over a candy wrapper and shred it into a thousand small pieces.

Get out your string trimmer or edger and hit the spots that are too tight for your mower, such as the areas around planting beds or pavement. If you cut them first, you can run your mower over the cuttings to chop them up.

Now you're ready to mow.

PUTTING BLADES TO BLADES

Start by giving yourself an outline to work from. Mow a strip at the ends of the lawn that matches the direction you're going to mow in (north and south or east and west). Mow a similar strip around flower and shrub beds. You're going to work your mower between these strips, and turn the mower on them.

Overlap each cut by one to two inches to avoid giving your lawn a Mohawk haircut with each pass. Don't pull the mower back toward you when you finish a strip, as doing so not only makes another pass over the same grass and inflicts more damage, it can also inflict damage on you. Reverse your direction on the turning strip instead.

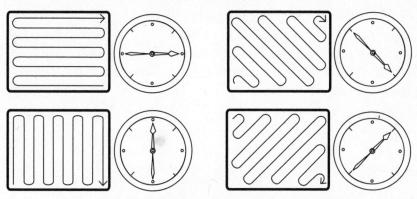

Always change directions from mowing to mowing to prevent boredom for you and your lawn.

Always change up your pattern from mowing to mowing. Mowing in the same direction every time is not only boring, it can cause problems for your lawn—specifically, compacted soil and wear spots, which will serve as embarrassing reminders of the pattern you trod over and over and over again. To avoid them, mow by the clock—in other words, base your mowing pattern on the numerals on a clock face—and change it every time you mow. As an example, mow from twelve to six one day. The next time, mow nine to three. Then do the diagonals—ten to four, and eight to two.

If you really want to get fancy, you can give your lawn a snazzy checkerboard pattern like the ones you see on athletic fields. This looks hard, but it isn't. You will, however, need a piece of equipment called a roller, which attaches behind the mower unit. Newer mowers sometimes come with this feature; you can buy roller kits to attach to older mowers. The roller simply pushes the blades down in the direction you're rolling. Going the opposite direction on the next pass will push the blades in the opposite direction. The opposite orientation of the leaves will reflect the light of the sun. Patterns will be most distinctive on bright days or under the brightest of lights.

Lots of people find mowing boring. Lawn geeks, however, being cut from cloth that's a little different, typically don't. We tend to enjoy the time we spend with our turf much more than nongeeks. This isn't to say that mowing can't get a little, well, tedious, especially if you have to do it more often than you'd really like. A little creativity can help relieve that boredom. Finding a potential lawn geek—maybe one of your kids or a neighborhood kid—and getting him or her started on his initiation might be a very good thing here, both for you and the kid. Supervise your budding geek right and you'll not only have a great-looking lawn, you'll be able to take pride in helping to establish the next generation of lawn-care experts.

CHAPTER 8

Watering It Down

There are two basic ways to water a lawn—the right way and the wrong way. Here's how to know what's right and what's wrong for yours.

Water is a resource that no living organism can go without. In the turf world, the ability to manage water—that is, the ability to precisely provide the right amount of water to specific areas of turf—is what gives the people who tend golf courses and athletic fields the ability to attain perfection. This has come about from vast improvements in irrigation technology, to be sure, but it still boils down to one simple thing: nothing good comes from overwatering turfgrass.

If I had to list ten problems related to watering, nine of them would be about putting down too much instead of not enough. Bottom line, if you have the ability to water, you'll be more likely to put on too much than too little. It's nothing to be ashamed of; thousands of people before you have done it, including thousands of turf managers. So, what I want to do in this chapter is explain how to supply what the plants need.

Of the three primary cultural practices, watering can be and often is the easiest of the lot. It's also the practice that lots of people—probably you, too—tend to be a bit cavalier about. We let automatic sprinkler timers determine when and how much lawns get watered, whether they need it or not. We get out the hose and give things a quick spray-down when our lawns look parched. Or we simply look to the

I have a neighbor who I'd like to drown because he waters too much. Even during the spring and fall, when it's cooler and wetter, he leaves his sprinkler system on autopilot. He puts down so much that it soaks into my yard; the area gets so wet that when it's time to mow the mowers leave ruts. Plus, the excess water causes the grass in that part of the lawn to first grow too much and then grow too little because the nitrogen in the soil has been all leached out. It's the one part of the yard that gets diseases and I know why. Now obviously I'm just kidding about drowning him, but I'm not kidding about the irritation he's causing me and my lawn. The point here: Pay attention to what you're doing and don't just assume that more is better. It's not.

skies and send novenas to Mother Nature, on whom we can typically depend for doing at least part of the job, and relegate our lawns to dealing with what they get.

If any of these methods describe your watering approach, and you're wondering why your lawn doesn't look better, well, you shouldn't. You can't just dump a bunch of H_2O on your yard whenever the spirit moves you and call it good. Nor can you, in most situations, depend on automatic sprinklers to apply the right amount of water when it's needed, or count on the heavens to supply manna to your grass often enough and in sufficient quantities to keep it happy.

Grasses are amazingly resilient plants, and they can go with the flow (or without it) pretty darned well, but they'll look and feel a whole lot better if you take watering seriously. So, let's take a closer look at what watering seriously—or, better put, watering wisely—is all about.

MEETING THEIR NEEDS

Watering your lawn the right way boils down to this: supplying the right amount of water often enough to meet the needs of the grass plants that comprise your turf. That's all there is to it.

What does meeting their needs mean? Bottom line, water is the must-have ingredient for plant health. It's what keeps them standing upright, as it plays a key role in maintaining cellular structure. Withhold it, and plants wilt.

Plants need water for moving nutrients from the soil to their roots and then to their leaves. They need it for moving fertilizers and pesticides both into them and through them. They need it for photosynthesis—the chemical conversion of sunlight into carbohydrates—to occur. They use it to cool themselves off—the environment, too—by releasing water vapor through their leaves (the scientific term for this is "transpiration"). Applied in a specific way called syringing, which you'll read more about later, water is also what keeps plants from frying when it's boiling hot outside.

Of everything you just read, here's what you're going to focus on: supplying the right amount of water often enough. That's it. Let me repeat that:

Supplying the right amount (not too much). Often enough.

Easy, right? Well, it can be once you figure out what the right amount of water is, and what often enough means. When you do, you can successfully meet the needs of your lawn, which, by the way, can be a pretty demanding entity depending on where you live, the kind of grass it contains, and the watering system you have in place. Or not. If water regularly pours from the sky or you have an automatic watering system equipped with things like moisture sensors and timers, you might play a middling role at best in this relationship.

Most people aren't so lucky, but it's still possible to minimize your role in the watering equation once you know how.

AN INCH . . . MORE OR LESS

Let's start with supplying the right amount of water. Interestingly enough, for being almost all water—water can comprise up to 90 percent of a grass plant's weight when it's actively growing (as a comparison, humans are about two-thirds water)—turfgrass doesn't need much water to stay healthy. Unlike humans, who need something like two quarts a day—the medical community keeps rethinking this, but that's about what we lose every day through the various ways in which we exchange fluids with the world around us—grass plants only need about one inch or so of moisture a week. The operative phrase here, however, is ". . . or so."

The one-inch rule only applies in a perfect world and to a perfect lawn, meaning one that's healthily and deeply rooted in ideal soil and that uses its water supply as efficiently as possible because it's been taken care of exactly as it should be—in other words, it's also mowed to a favorable height, it's fertilized properly, thatch is under control . . . the list goes on.

Since ours isn't a perfect world, and that perfect lawn is something you're probably still working toward, chances are that your lawn needs more than that one inch. But, then again, it might not. Lots of factors can affect water needs, including:

- The weather. If it's consistently hot and dry where you live, your lawn will need more water. If it's also windy, it will need even more water to make up for evaporation—heat, low humidity, and wind can eliminate as much as one-third of an inch per day from your turf. Flip these factors around, and your lawn might need considerably less than one inch a week, especially during certain weeks of the growing season—for example, spring and fall, when you're more likely to have rainfall and cooler temperatures, both of which should factor into your equation.
- Stress levels. Lawns suffering from foot traffic, disease, or prolonged drought conditions typically need more water.
- Life span. Newly established lawns need more water than the old fogies do. For watering guidelines for sod and seed, turn to chapter 6.
- Air supply. Lawns that are aerated on a regular basis (see chapter 10 for what this means) and that have an appropriate thatch level soak up moisture better. They also have deeper root systems and can better survive drought conditions.
- Amount of shade. Shady areas require less water.
- Soil composition. Grass on sandy soil must be watered more often and with smaller amounts of water each time than grass growing on clay or loamy soils.

Another factor in the watering equation is knowing how deeply rooted the grass plants are and how deep moisture is traveling in your turf. This step requires measuring the root zone. To test this, dig into

 **Keep in mind** that the roots on some grasses, mainly cool-season grasses like perennial ryegrass, Kentucky bluegrass, and Supina bluegrass, will shrink in response to drought or extreme heat. As roots get shorter, you'll have to water more frequently.

your sod after you've watered. There are special soil probes for this, or you can simply use a shovel. Spread the hole so you can see how far the water has penetrated. Ideally, you'll see a well-spaced mass of roots growing vertically into the soil. They should extend anywhere from three to six inches. You want to water so the soil is moistened to that depth.

Periodically digging into the sod is also a good way to determine watering effectiveness throughout the growing season. You don't have to shovel into it every time. Just take a long screwdriver and plunge it in after watering.

Water requirements also vary with grass type. Some simply need more water than others. From most to least, here's how they rank:

Cool-season grasses
Supina bluegrass
annual bluegrass
perennial ryegrass
Kentucky bluegrass
fescues

Warm-season grasses
St. Augustinegrass
bahiagrass
centipedegrass
zoysiagrass
bermudagrass
buffalograss
blue grama

Do you even have to water your lawn? If you're in an area where average precipitation is high and the potential evapotranspiration (the technical term for the estimated amount of water a lawn would use if water is always plentiful in the soil) is low, you might get by without watering. Keep in mind, though, that you'll also have to deal with dormant grass at times (grass that has turned brown and is growing very slowly or not at all). As long as it's not dormant for too long, and it's in good shape before it goes to sleep, things should be fine. If it's thin when it went dormant, weeds will crop up when your lawn starts growing again.

How can you decide how much to give your lawn? There's no magic formula. You must include your grass, the soil, the surrounds (microclimate), the time of year, and specific weather. There are some constants here (grass, soil, and possibly microclimate, although that can change when trees leaf out); other factors that change gradually (seasons); and finally, weather. Put all of these in the mix and then get ready to adapt to changing circumstances; remember that watering schedules should be flexible, just like our daily schedules should be. Always give yourself some wiggle room for the unforeseen.

DETERMINING WHAT YOUR LAWN NEEDS

Is your lawn getting enough water? If it's currently in good shape, chances are that it is. But it's fairly easy to tell for sure.

Start by looking at it. Color is a good indication of general grass health. Grass that looks lighter than it should could be wilting, as grass blades fold inward to conserve water when they don't get enough of it. As they do, the turf will take on a grayish or purplish blue cast. It's somewhat apparent to the naked eye, and even more so if you don polarized sunglasses and look at your lawn in direct sunlight between two and five p.m.

Footprints that stay in the lawn long after you walk on it are another surefire indication of a parched lawn. Healthy lawns recover from foot traffic fairly quickly. Footprints that stick around for more than an hour or so indicate a condition called dry wilt. The turf needs a drink.

Color varies depending on the species, which is another reason why it's good to know what you're actually growing. If, for example, your grass is naturally lighter in color than others, you might think it needs water when it actually doesn't. This is especially true of older lawns (more than twenty years old) with older varieties that aren't as dark green.

Dry spots on an otherwise dewy lawn can indicate moisture problems. Spots that look drier than the rest of the grass in general are also a pretty good indication of dehydrated turf, but not always. Dry spots can be caused by lots of different things, insects and diseases among them.

How about too much water? This one's pretty easy to determine. If puddles start forming and earthworms come out of the ground gasping for air when you water or when it rains, there's too much water down below or there's a drainage problem. In either case the turf roots will be living close to the surface because roots can't grow into saturated soil. The result's going to be short roots, and short roots are a problem when and if the water does get turned off or the plant gets stressed in any way. The turfgrass will either die or you'll be forced into watering even more frequently to match the short root system.

If you want to get really geeky, you can even determine exactly— well, almost exactly, close enough for this geek anyway—how much water your lawn is truly getting. If you think your lawn is suffering from water problems either way, either too much or too little, doing so can be a good idea.

The amount of water that soil can take up in a given period is called its infiltration rate. When the infiltration rate is exceeded, water collects and runs off.

Measuring Mother Nature

Depending on your local weather people for predictions and mea-surements of how much moisture actually rains down upon your turf is an imprecise approach at best. Precipitation amounts can vary widely, even from block to block. Measuring them yourself is a far better way to tell how much moisture your lawn gets from above.

You'll need a rain gauge for this. These inexpensive plastic devices are available just about everywhere; the weather folks at your local tele-vision station might even give them away. You can make one if you're so inclined. All you need is a container with markings up the side to measure what goes in it. Just about anything will work as long as it's deep enough to hold at least a cup of water. Water will splash out of shallow containers. If it's cold where you live, opt for plastic over glass, for the obvious reason.

Where you place the gauge will affect how accurate your readings are. For best results, find a spot away from trees or buildings, both of which can deflect moisture from the gauge. Wide-open spaces are also bad choices as they'll expose the gauge to wind and evaporation.

The National Weather Service—in my book, a pretty definitive source for such things—recommends positioning gauges at least fifteen to twenty-five feet away from a single-story house if placing on the ground. If possible, put it twice as far away from a two-story house, and at least twelve feet away from a standard privacy fence.

This is tough if acreage is limited, so here's the easy approach. If you have a fence, mount the gauge on a fence post. If you don't, find something else to mount it to. A piece of outdoor furniture can work, as can a porch or deck railing.

Position the gauge so there's nothing overhead that will either block the water or channel more of it than there should be into the container or otherwise interfere with collection. Secure it so it doesn't blow over in the wind. Check water levels and empty the gauge regularly, preferably daily and at the same time each day.

Measuring What You Provide

Now that you're keeping track of how much water your grass is get-ting from Mother Nature, you can easily figure out how much you need to water to meet your lawn's weekly needs—that is, if you know how much moisture your watering systems are putting down. This step can also determine if the coverage is what it should be. Here's how to do it:

1. Eat tuna fish sandwiches for a few days. Save the cans. (Cat food cans also work for this.)
2. Place them in the area you want to test. Do this in a grid pattern, every fifteen feet; you can cover nine hundred square feet with nine cans this way. Put the first one fairly close to the sprinkler or irrigation head, then space the others evenly.
3. Water for twenty minutes or until water begins to run off your turf instead of sinking in.
4. Measure the water depth in each can.

This can get a little complicated when measuring in-ground systems, as you have to measure the whole lawn in sections, but it's a good way to see how your sprinklers are distributing water. It can tell you if your sprinklers are overlapping too much and putting down too much water (this will go a long way to explaining wet and dry spots, let me assure you); it can also tell you about irrigation heads that aren't adjusted correctly and throwing at an inconsistent arc much more accurately than just eyeballing it.

Don't be too concerned if the differences are less than 20 percent. If they're greater, you'll have to work with nozzle sizes and arcs on your sprinkler heads. But the one thing that's constant is having a level head; that is, the arc should look the same all the way around, it shouldn't be six feet high on one side, ten feet high on another side. The heads need to be turning in level circles; if they don't they won't deposit water consistently, and there will be too much in some areas and not enough in others.

One of the telltale signs of heads being out of adjustment are brown or dark green rings on your turf from either too much or not enough water; they'll match the arc or lack thereof. You can do a can test before these things ever rear their ugly heads, but once you see these rings in July the horse is out of the proverbial barn, and the grass is already under stress. Jump on it by doing a can test early in the season, ideally before you have to start watering on a regular basis.

Let's say your sprinkler runs twenty minutes before water starts to run into the street. This tells you that twenty minutes is as long as you should operate your sprinkler at any one time.

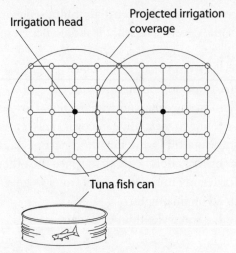

Space the cans evenly near the sprinkler or head you want to test.

Now the question is how often to water. You check and see that the can that collected the least amount of water has a quarter inch in it. If your yard needs one inch of water a week, you'll have to water four times a week, for twenty minutes each time, to give it that inch.

If your sprinklers put down a quarter inch of water in thirty minutes before water starts to run off and go to waste, you'll want to water for thirty minutes four times a week. And so on.

If it rains a quarter inch, you can forgo one day of watering that week. A half inch of rain and you can maybe skip a couple of cycles, depending on the time of year. So a half-inch rain will give you that babysitter you've been looking for and you can go to the movies one afternoon (but not Hawaii). If you quit for a week in mid-July on a lawn

Overwatering is the second-most common mistake that people make when taking care of their lawns (scalping still wins the prize). It's simply bad for grass, not to mention a waste of money and resources. Grass roots struggle with waterlogged turf, as soil pores filled with water have little if any room to spare. Soggy soil and sopped leaves are also ideal breeding grounds for lawn diseases.

that got a one-inch rain on Monday, it will show by the end of the week. That's because all of the rain that hit the lawn didn't stay in the soil— some drained away. Your soil can only hold so much (otherwise it's a lake, remember?).

SPRINKLING IT ON

Your lawn doesn't give a whit about how it gets watered. All it cares about is getting enough fluid to keep it happy. You can accomplish this happiness with whatever suits you, from a sprinkling can to a multi-thousand-dollar in-ground multizone irrigation system.

So, the question is, is there a best approach? No, not really. A good ol' sprinkler-and-hose combo can be as efficient as or even better than automatic systems.

If you have a choice, choose the watering approach that best matches the following:

- Your budget. Manual systems are vastly cheaper than in-ground setups and always will be.
- Your lifestyle. If time is short or you just don't want to spend hours moving hoses around your yard, automatic might be the better choice.
- Lawn size and shape. If you're dealing with a large lawn, manual systems might simply be impractical. Irregularly shaped lawns and lawns with lots of slopes might call for automatic systems as well. On the other hand, automatic systems can be overkill on small lots.

If you don't have a choice, your goal is to use whatever's at hand in the most expeditious way. Regardless of the approach you take, always measure its effectiveness. Do the test detailed above to determine how long it takes to apply a specific amount of water. Check for gaps in coverage.

Hose and Sprinkler

If you water manually, you already know what the basic components are all about. You've got your sprinkler, and you've got your hose.

If you like what you have and it seems to be doing the job, there's no reason to fix something that isn't broken. If you're not entirely pleased with your current setup, get some new stuff. Doing so might be a good idea anyway, especially if your equipment is older, as newer products have improved quite a bit.

The type of sprinkler—fixed, portable, or traveling—is really up to you. So too is the sprinkler configuration—impact, rotary, and so on. Depending on your lawn, you might need more than one type, maybe an oscillating or soaker sprinkler that dispenses water more slowly for sloping areas and a couple of impact sprinklers with adjustable heads for getting into the corners in other areas. If you have kids, they might get a kick out of a traveling sprinkler—the tractorlike ones that move along hose lines.

If you're starting from scratch, here are some recommendations:

- Match the sprinkler to the yard. The packaging should note the sprinkler's maximum coverage. Movable sprinklers are designed for use with five-eighths-inch-diameter hoses, which deliver fifty pounds of water per square inch. Even though they all start with the same amount of water, how widely they distribute it varies. Some are designed to cover small areas; others can spread water as far as the eye can see.

- Buy good stuff. It's frustrating when parts blow out when you power things up. Yes, it costs more on the front end, but solid equipment will save you money in the long run.

- Buy a sprinkler timer if you don't already have one so you don't have to worry about being home to turn them off and on. Some portables have them built in; others mount between faucet and hose.

- Buy good hoses. Cheap ones will just frustrate you. Choose rubber or a rubber-vinyl combination over straight vinyl—they're sturdier and they kink less. Go for as many plies as you can afford—the more plies, the more substantial the hose. Get one long enough to easily reach every part of your lawn. Hoses that are too long, however, can be hard to move, as they get heavy, so you might want to buy two shorter hoses and put quick-release couplers on the ends. If you have two outdoor faucets, make things really easy on yourself and buy two hoses.

No matter what type of sprinkler system you use, make sure water is getting to all areas of the lawn. Many sprinklers miss corners and edges, which typically dry out faster than other lawn parts anyway, so they really need good coverage.

Impact sprinklers are my personal favorite for manual watering. These look like automatic sprinkler heads, and, of the manual sprinklers, they do the best job of distributing water uniformly and efficiently. The best ones let you adjust the pattern from complete circles to variously sized arcs. If you get the kind that are mounted on spikes, you can stick them in the ground wherever you want. Buy enough of them and you can leave them in place and just move the hose around. Or, if there are garden beds nearby, just leave the hoses in the beds between watering. Put quick-release couplers on the hose and the sprinklers, and all you have to do is snap them together. Quick and easy.

Automatic Systems

Automatic or permanent irrigation systems are fast becoming the preferred approach for all but the smallest yards, for a variety of reasons. Chief among them are advances in irrigation technology. Irrigation has become a big business, and lots of research dollars have been and are being spent on technologies that make better use of what's increasingly becoming a very precious resource, especially in drought-prone areas.

Things like rain or moisture sensors, which shut systems off when they detect moisture, are fairly standard issue on new systems. Not only are they good conservation measures, but they also save you from the embarrassment of having your sprinklers come on full blast during a downpour. Some municipalities require them, and there will probably come a day when all of them will. I would even argue that if you have to keep an area green and you're paying substantial bucks for the water, an automatic system equipped with sensors will actually pay for itself over time. It has been proven many times over on golf courses and athletic fields and if necessary can be proven on home lawns.

On the horizon are things like evapotranspiration controllers that take the guesswork out of programming watering times by calculating the correct amount of water to apply and adjusting sprinkler run times accordingly. According to Bell Labs, the day's not far off when sensors in a typical lawn sprinkler could call up the National Weather Service, check the day's forecast, and turn itself on or off depending on whether rain is predicted.

Automatic irrigation won't guarantee a great yard. Plenty of things can go wrong with even the most modern, advanced systems. They can develop underground leaks. Timing devices can malfunction. Sprinkler heads can clog or break. Plus, they can be overkill if you don't have to water all that often. That said, they can also be a real asset if precipitation is scarce where you live, and they can add value to your property.

Bottom line, automatic systems can be wonderful, but you can't just leave them to their own devices. Not only do they require annual maintenance, but it's important to keep an eye on them during the growing season to make sure they're working properly.

The cost of installing automatic sprinklers is a big deterrent for lots of folks, and there's no two ways about this; they are expensive to install. Small, fairly basic systems start at around two thousand dollars; zoned systems with special features like drip irrigation can start at three times this much. Shopping around to compare prices is highly recommended if you're thinking about installing one of these babies. If you're fairly handy and your lawn is fairly simple (that is, it's relatively small, flat, and square), installing the system yourself might not be out of the question, but discussing it in more detail is outside of the scope of this book.

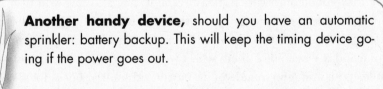

Another handy device, should you have an automatic sprinkler: battery backup. This will keep the timing device going if the power goes out.

Realizing the role that weather plays in watering needs is a great way to get in tune with your grass plants. Evaporation levels are lower when temperatures are lower. They're also lower when it's humid, and when it's cloudy. Turf loses more water when it's windy. The amount of water your turf will need on an 81°F, sticky, cloudy, humid day will be substantially less than what it will need on a 75°F clear, windy, bright sunshiny day.

Interval Training

Most experts will tell you to water "deeply and infrequently." I have problems with this concept as the terms "deep" and "infrequent" are too ambiguous. Infrequent watering might be daily if roots are only a half inch deep due to stress. My preferred approach is to match watering to your grass's needs. Know what kind of grass you're growing—in general, warm-season grasses have deeper roots and can go longer between waterings. They also do better during hot weather. Monitor root depth. Measure what Mother Nature is providing. Keep an eye on the weather. Know what kind of soil you're dealing with. Sandy soil doesn't hold water well, so you'll have to water more often. Soil that's high in clay doesn't absorb water well, so you'll have to be sure that you don't apply more than it can take. Always be sure to put down enough water to moisten as much of the root zone as possible.

If you're starting from scratch, try watering every two to three days. See how your turf responds. If the weather is cooperating, this pattern could work all summer. If the weather turns hot and dry, the turf will start to stress and the grass roots will shrink. Your watering intervals should shrink as well.

Good Timing

Early in the morning, ideally between four a.m. and nine a.m., is prime watering time. If there's any wind at all it's typically minimal, which means more water will hit the ground, assuming your sprinklers are adjusted correctly. Sunlight levels are low so evaporative loss is less.

Watering early in the day also allows plenty of time for it to leave the soil surface before nightfall. Remember, surface water is not something you want hanging around after dark.

Watering at high noon or thereabouts, which you'll read more about shortly, can be good in some situations, but it's not as efficient since some of the water will evaporate before it hits the ground.

Nighttime watering is rarely a good idea in hot and humid conditions, and especially not if conditions are such that the ground might remain wet for longer than it should. You can water at night, if necessary, however, when evening temperatures fall below 55°F. If you live in the Southwest or in another area where it's extremely hot during the day and the humidity is low, watering at night will minimize evaporation.

Dealing with Special Situations

What we've discussed so far will meet basic needs. But sometimes needs go beyond basic. Things like drought conditions, high temperatures coupled with wind, and hilly turf call for some special watering approaches and techniques.

Cooling Them Off   Temperatures approaching 100°F or more, especially when coupled with high winds for more than half of the day, can stress out turfgrass faster than fast. Golf course superintendents restore peace and tranquillity to putting greens in these conditions by lightly sprinkling things down just enough to wet the grass leaves but not enough to get water into the soil. You can, too.

This technique, called syringing, reduces surface temperatures and gives the turf a temporary breather. It doesn't replace longer, deeper watering, but it can tide plants over until their next big drink.

Syringing is also a good approach for the following:

- Turf suffering from a patch disease (see chapter 13 for more on these).
- Newly seeded lawns. Syringing will help keep seedlings cool and moist while they're establishing themselves.

Dealing with Drought   Remember what I said earlier about grass being able to go with the flow, or without it? Depending on the

> **Stick** to your guns if you decide to let your grass go dormant during a drought. Don't water it from time to time because you feel bad for it or think that doing so will help it recover faster when conditions are more favorable. It won't. In fact, doing so will stress the plants more than if you just left them alone.

type of grass you're growing, it's okay to not water it during dry spells. Many Kentucky bluegrass varieties will survive just fine. They'll turn brown and go dormant, but they'll green up and start growing again when rain returns. Fescues don't go dormant from a color standpoint, as tall fescue won't turn deep brown and fine fescues aren't that green to begin with, but they grow very slowly when it's dry. In fact, even perennial ryegrass that is in decent health before the water is shut off will survive a short drought, and warm-season grasses can go an extended period and still recover. The grass will lose color as the production of chlorophyll decreases without water in the plant, but this is a natural defense. It's not something to be concerned about, but you may object if a neighbor or two decides to water and their lawns start looking greener again.

If your grass is already stressed from wear, disease, or insects, or if it's overrun with weeds, don't let it go dormant. Grass under stress needs water to help it recover. Denying it can and probably will make matters worse.

The key to letting grass go dormant naturally with the best chance of recovery lies in how you've taken care of it. If you've followed a good mowing and fertilizing schedule, grass density will be high. This is extremely important when water returns after a drought, as the water will benefit any weed seeds in the soil as much as the grass. If the grass is dense, fewer weeds will germinate. If it's not, you might have lots of weeds, in which case you'll have to take action (turn to chapter 11 for help).

Sticking It to Slopes   Sloped areas can be really tricky to irrigate well, as gravity pulls the water to the bottom of the area before the top can absorb it. So you end up with a puddle down below and dry spots above. Water very slowly or apply it in short intervals. Turn off the water after a few minutes, give the turf time to soak up what's there, then turn it on again. Repeat as necessary.

Wind and Heat   Short periods of heat and windy conditions, or short-term droughts, might require adding one or two more sessions to your weekly watering schedule, and possibly even watering daily. Keep an eye on moisture levels by probing the soil.

Soggy Sod   Lots of things can cause soggy soil, and it's not something to ignore, as it can lead to serious turf problems. Zoom in on any soggy spots right away, and try to determine what's going on before bigger problems erupt. Things to look for here include:

- Malfunctioning sprinkler heads. Fix or replace as necessary.
- Poor coverage. You may need to change nozzle sizing, spray pattern, or actually move the sprinkler head.
- Soil compaction or layering. Turn to chapter 10 for help with this.
- Drainage problems, either at the surface or below. Turn to chapter 16 for help with both.

Stay in the Game

It's important to keep an eye on things regardless of how you put water down. Every so often, turn your system on and watch the sprinklers at work. Remember my favorite lawn geek adage: Grass does not lie. If your grass is sporting circles in various shades of green, it's definitely a good time to check how those sprinklers are spraying and make any necessary adjustments. On automatic systems, periodically check the valve box. It shouldn't be full of water; if it is, one of the valves is probably leaking and you'll need to replace a worn washer or gasket. With sprinkler-and-hose combinations, check connections to make sure they're tight. Hoses can spring leaks; look them over periodically as well.

Remember, you're an important part of the watering equation. Do your part, follow the rules, and your turf will thank you. Finally, and most important, nothing good ever comes from overwatering. You end up with weakened plants with short roots, waterlogged soils that promote diseases, weeds, and soil compaction, and you end up paying for the water that caused the misery. It pays to learn your lawn's needs.

CHAPTER 9

Feeding the Beast

Just like people, there's no one-size-fits-all when it comes to how lawns should be fed. Knowing the basics will help you make the right nutritional choices for yours.

One of the questions I get asked the most when I'm teaching turf management classes or when I talk to garden clubs is "Can you give me a fertilizer program for my yard?" The answer is "I wish I could." As with the question "Can you give me the formula for raising my child?" the answer is that we can only give you guidelines that you can use to fit your specific needs, but no specific formula.

So we're going to talk about guidelines here. What I need you to understand is how fertilizer works, how it interacts with the plants, and how over- or underfertilizing an area can be detrimental and at the end of the day actually cause you problems like weeds, diseases, and insects.

Unlike humans, plants manufacture their own food. So when we apply fertilizer to turf, we're not really feeding grass plants as much as we're providing some important nutrients to help their internal production centers do a better job. We're stocking the pantry with ingredients, but they're cooking up the meal.

All fertilizers are building blocks. They have to interact with the other nutrients plants need—hydrogen, carbon, and oxygen—to form the starches and sugars that the plants use to grow and develop.

The basic practice of fertilization is pretty simple. You buy fertilizer. You apply fertilizer. Knowing what kind of fertilizer to buy, how much to apply, and when to apply it so it will do your grass the most good is also pretty easy to figure out, once you know how. Of all the cultural practices, this is the one you'll spend the least amount of time and the least amount of money on.

Figuring things out means taking things up a notch when it comes to technical language and terms, which can make for some sloggy reading. Part of the reason for this is because there are chemicals and equations involved, which can make things look more complicated than they are. Once again, this isn't complicated stuff, so hang in there if this is new to you.

Like mowing, you have some choices when it comes to fertilizing. You can do it yourself or pay someone else. If you're a true lawn geek, applying it yourself is highly recommended. Doing so truly makes you master and commander when it comes to your lawn's health. Plus, you'll save a lot of money. If you decide you don't have the time or inclination to do it yourself, knowing more about what fertilizing is all about will keep you from making bad choices when it comes to hiring help.

Most scholarly discussions of fertilizing start with a fairly lengthy discourse on plant nutrition. Unless you're going into turfgrass management as a career, you really don't need to know everything there is to know about this. So I'm just going to cover the basics.

BASIC NUTRITION—PLANT STYLE

Just like humans need vitamins and minerals for things like bone and tissue growth, energy metabolism and whatnot, grass needs nutrients to grow and survive. Humans need some thirteen vitamins and about twenty-two minerals to keep their bodies operating the way they should. Grass plants need seventeen nutrients.

The three most important nutrients for all plants—hydrogen, carbon, and oxygen—are nonmineral nutrients derived from two sources: air, which yields carbon and oxygen; and water, which yields hydrogen and oxygen. Via photosynthesis, plants use the sun's energy to change these substances into amino acids and carbohydrates, which is what

> **While** the fertilizer business has definitely boomed in recent years, supplying additional nutrients to plants is hardly a new practice. Until somewhat recently, however, it was a fairly nasty practice. Until synthetic fertilizers were developed, lots of people spread manure on their lawns, which was not only smelly and ugly but also introduced weed seeds to the soil.

nourishes them. You can't have one without the other, by the way. If all it took was fertilizer you should be able to grow grass in the shade. But you have to have sunshine to produce photosynthesis. If all it took was fertilizer and not sunlight, every domed stadium in the world would have grass.

The other fourteen nutrients are minerals that come from the soil. They dissolve in water and plants take them up through their roots. But plants require more of certain nutrients than what's naturally available in soil, and sometimes the nutrients that are in the soil aren't in forms that plants can use all that well. This is why we fertilize.

Lawns need big doses of certain nutrients, in particular nitrogen, phosphorous, and potassium. When you buy fertilizer, these are the nutrients that you'll pay the most attention to.

Nutritious Nitrogen

Nitrogen is the most abundant mineral in plants and the most important for healthy, vigorous growth. It's also the one most responsible for grass color, which means that the color of your grass is a good indication of nitrogen level. If it's low, your turf will look pale. Deny it nitrogen long enough and it will turn yellow. The plants within will grow more slowly and spread less vigorously. Weeds will increase in number as your turf continues its downhill slide. Not a pretty sight. And so easily avoidable.

Nitrogen comes in two forms. One is soluble in water, the other isn't. Water-soluble, or quick-release, nitrogen delivers a fast nutrient hit to grass plants. Insoluble, or slow-release, nitrogen delivers a slow and steady supply. A good-quality fertilizer for routine maintenance will have some of both, for reasons I'll go into shortly. There are specific times when you want to use one over the other, which I'll also go into shortly.

Because it's the most abundant plant element and it's the most important for healthy growth (and because it also easily washes through the soil, or is lost to the atmosphere, or is used by other microorganisms), nitrogen is also the nutrient we supplement in the largest amounts. But it's definitely possible to have too much of a good thing here. The chemicals that contain nitrogen are salts, which means they're caustic. Apply too much of them and you'll burn your lawn. Apply a little less than too much, but more than your lawn needs, and you might not get lawn burns, but you probably will have to deal with too much grass. You'll have to mow it more often, and you'll have created a haven for insects and diseases.

Excessive growth can also lead to scalping by overzealous caretakers in panic mode. Faced with runaway turf, they forget the most important commandment—*never remove more than one-third of blade length when you mow*—and they simply whack the turf down to size. This opens the door to weeds (again), stresses the plants, and makes them more susceptible to insect and disease attack.

Plentiful Phosphorous

Phosphorous is the second most abundant element found in plants. It's a key player in protein synthesis, which is particularly important to young grass plants, as it helps them develop healthy roots.

Grass plants are very good at conserving and reusing phosphorous. It also doesn't move around much in the soil, which means that specifically focusing on this nutrient in a fertilizing program is almost never necessary. Low phosphorous levels can be a serious problem, but you'll almost never encounter them.

Purposeful Potassium

Potassium is the second most necessary macronutrient after nitrogen, but it's listed third on fertilizer labels so it gets discussed last. It plays a key role in many of grass's physiological processes and, as such,

You might hear people say that adding potassium will make grass stronger. Great if you're selling potassium, not so if you're depending on it to make your grass strong. The myth got started back around 1980 or so when a turf professor made the statement that if you added potassium you could make your turfgrass stronger. Well, that's what people thought he said, anyway. What he really said was that if your grass is deficient in potassium you'll lose wear tolerance and strength, but you could add potassium and increase it. He didn't say, "Put on twice as much potassium and the plant will be twice as strong," but that's how folklore gets started and it's difficult to change.

is essential for overall lawn health and hardiness. Without it, grass doesn't handle stress well, doesn't grow as well, recovers more slowly from damage, and is more disease-prone. Problems occur when turf doesn't have enough potassium, but you don't build up "plant muscle" by putting on excessive amounts of potassium. That's the issue with all fertilizer; more does not mean better.

Potassium is typically applied as soluble potash, or potassium chloride, which comes from potassium salt deposits. It moves through soil fairly quickly, but not as quickly as nitrogen does. Sandy soil is often low in potassium for this reason, while clay holds it tighter than a drum.

Other nutrients, like iron and calcium, are also important for grass health, but they're usually available in the soil in sufficient amounts for healthy growth. Don't let anyone try to talk you into specially packaged containers of micronutrients—things like calcium, zinc, iron, and so on—for your lawn. Most good fertilizers contain small amounts of these nutrients, just to be on the safe side. Feeding more than this is almost never necessary, and usually only with very sandy soils.

HOW MUCH FOOD?

Lots of factors affect how much food your grass needs. Soil type and health and its ability to provide nutrients to grass plants are biggies. Soil rich in organic matter does the best job of holding and releasing nutrients, which is why soil preparation is such an important step in establishing lawns. So are things like:

- how much your lawn gets used, as stressed-out turf needs more nutrients to support its recovery.
- grass type, as different grasses have different nutrient needs.
- moisture; precipitation and your watering habits affect absorption and leaching levels.
- mowing height, which affects root growth and the plant's ability to get to nutrients in the soil.
- temperatures, a biggie when it comes to growth rate, and again, nutritional requirements.
- sun and shade, as grass grown in shade needs less nitrogen.
- the age of your yard; older lawns that have nutrient residuals built up in organic matter will need less fertilizer.

Another big factor, and a real good one, is whether you leave grass clippings behind when mowing. Doing so can eliminate one to two pounds of nitrogen supplementation per year.

You can spend a lot of time testing and measuring these factors to determine your grass's fertilizer needs, or you can rely on years of plant research to tell you what you need to know. If you're like me, and you like things easy, the latter approach is the way to go.

Remember, nitrogen is what makes the world go around in the wide world of fertilizing. Knowing how much your grass needs pretty much determines your fertilizing program.

There is one basic thing to keep in mind here, AND I'M GOING TO SHOUT IT OUT IN BIG CAPITAL LETTERS SO YOU GET THE POINT AND I DON'T HAVE TO KEEP REPEATING MYSELF:

NEVER APPLY MORE THAN ONE POUND OF QUICK-RELEASE NITROGEN PER THOUSAND SQUARE FEET

Soil testing might seem like a good idea when determining how much fertilizer to apply, but it's typically not. When it comes to the three main nutrients, tests don't tell us all that much, as no one's ever been able to determine the optimal levels of any of them for best turfgrass growth. Soil tests are good, of course, for determining things like soil pH and composition, both of which can also affect fertilizing needs. And if you suspect a serious nutritional problem—rare, but they can happen—a test can help you get to the root of the problem faster. One great example is low phosphorous levels, particularly in newly established lawns based on topsoils that were once subsoils from digging out the basement.

OF TURF AT ANY ONE TIME. EVEN BETTER, APPLY ONE-HALF POUND PER APPLICATION, AND DO IT MORE OFTEN.

Why? Remember, nitrogen is a salt. Applying too much of it can burn your lawn, as the grass can't metabolize it quickly enough. So it just sits there and eats away at things. And it can promote excessive growth, which is another thing you don't want.

Now, if you're only using a *slow-release* product less frequently, you can apply more than this, which is one reason for opting for them. Still,

If you're at all concerned about fertilizer polluting streams or waterways, keep in mind that grass does a great job of absorbing and storing nutrients. When applied correctly, the chances of fertilizer leaching into water supplies are minimal. Always sweep up (or use the leaf blower; it's usually not an amount that will hurt your grass) any fertilizer that lands on hard surfaces. If you don't, it could go down the gutter and into a sewer and a waterway. This isn't your lawn's fault, it's your fault, but lawns typically take the blame. In most states laws dictate that lawn services must sweep up any spilled fertilizer, but the law does not apply to home owners.

you'll never want to apply more than three pounds of nitrogen per thousand square feet, *ever*. You won't burn the grass but you will likely never do it again. It's kinda like the boy who touched the hot stove, lesson learned. You will also mow your brains out as the fertilizer will release in heavy amounts all year long.

You have this down, right? You're not going to apply more than one pound of nitrogen per thousand square feet of grass at any one time. And you'll consider applying even less more often. Like people, plants do better when they get the nutrients they need in a steady manner, not when they gorge at a buffet table every so often and starve themselves between feedings. But hold that thought for now.

Next up is knowing how much nitrogen your grass needs. Based on research, we know that different grasses have different nitrogen requirements. How much they need is expressed as pounds per year per thousand square feet. Here's how they rank:

Grass	Pounds
St. Augustinegrass	3–6
Kentucky bluegrass	3–6
bermudagrass	2–6
bahiagrass	2–4
tall fescue	2–4
zoysiagrass	2–4
perennial ryegrass	2–3
fine fescue	1–3
centipedegrass	1–3
blue grama	1–2
buffalograss	0–2

Say you're growing Kentucky bluegrass and your yard is four thousand square feet. You'd want to apply between twelve and twenty-four pounds of nitrogen to your lawn annually.

Why is there a range for each grass? The length of the growing season where you live, as well as all the other factors previously listed, has a lot to do with it. The key really is that grass does best when it gets small doses of nutrients throughout its growing season. Grasses expected to grow most of the year, if not all, need more fertilizer in general, and therefore more nitrogen, than those that go dormant when the weather gets cold.

Now that you have a general idea of your grass's annual nitrogen needs, it's time to figure out which product to buy. The labels on fertilizer products will tell you what you need to know once you know how to decipher them. So let's walk you through a sample fertilizer label, using our example of a four-thousand-square-foot lawn of Kentucky bluegrass, which needs three to six pounds of fertilizer per thousand square feet per year.

READING THE LABEL

All fertilizers must bear content labels similar to the one on page 157.

There's lots of information here. The most important is the "guaranteed analysis," which tells you how much you're getting of the big three nutrients—nitrogen, phosphorous, and potassium. This is always stated as a ratio representing the amount of each ingredient, by weight, in the product. Fairly common ratios are 20-10-5, 15-5-10, 10-10-10, and 16-16-16. In our diagram we have a ratio of 20-5-10, meaning there are four parts of nitrogen to one part of phosphorous to two parts of potassium.

Note that this is the guaranteed *minimal* analysis by law; there would be nothing wrong with the fertilizer having *more* than this amount. Of course, manufacturers aren't looking to give away their product, so this is tightly controlled in the manufacturing process. The issue can be a little more complicated with organic fertilizers because, simply put, constantly controlling Mother Nature isn't possible. The amounts in natural products are often higher than listed. This in turn can affect the growth of the grass, and potentially cause inconsistent results. It might not be noticeable in your lawn or in a golf course rough, but it's not a choice when you need tight control and predictability, like on a putting green.

With these numbers you can determine the weight of each nutrient in a given package. The formula for this is: weight of package times percentage of nutrient. So, in our 50-pound bag of 20-5-10 fertilizer, we would find 10 pounds of nitrogen (50 pounds × 20%) , 2.5 pounds of phosphorous (phosphate) (50 pounds × 5%), and 5 pounds of potassium (soluble potash) (50 pounds × 10%). Concentrate on the nitrogen; remember, it makes the turfgrass world go around. It is the product that you're paying for when you're buying fertilizer.

Basic Lawn Fertilizer
20-5-10

Guaranteed Analysis

Total Nitrogen (N).. 20%

      Ammoniacal Nitrogen.......................... 5%

      Urea...15%

Available Phosphate (P_2O_5)........................... 5%

Soluble Potash (K_2O)....................................... 10%

Derived from: Urea Nitrogen, Ammonium
Phosphate, Muriate of Potash.
Equivalent to: 700 lbs $CaCO_3$

Net Wt. 50lbs

Rogers Fertilizer Company
5555 North Street
East Lansing, MI 48823

A typical fertilizer label.

Let's say you've decided you're going to put down three pounds of nitrogen per thousand square feet per year and you have a four-thousand-square-foot lawn; you're going to need twelve pounds of nitrogen. Going back to our fifty-pound bag, that bag will only have ten pounds of nitrogen, so you'll need to buy a second bag.

Of course you're not going to put down more than one pound of nitrogen per thousand square feet at a time, so you'll have to split those twelve pounds into three applications during the season. Most fertilizers

Fertilizer labels also list other active ingredients, like micronutrients, and their percentages so you know how much you're applying of them, too. Inactive ingredients—the carrier or filler product that nutrients ride on their journey to their intended target—comprise the majority of what's in a fertilizer bag, and account for most of the weight.

will probably tell you how to set your fertilizer spreader to apply this one pound of nitrogen. If not, you can figure it out yourself. What you need to determine is the percent of nitrogen that's in the fertilizer. In our example there's 20 percent, which means that to get one pound of nitrogen you're going to use five pounds of fertilizer per thousand square feet. Since you have four thousand square feet, you're going to put down twenty pounds of fertilizer each time (logic would tell you that if you want to put down a half pound of nitrogen, you'd need ten pounds of fertilizer). You should be able to work from there if you use the same fertilizer every time.

CHOOSING YOUR PRODUCT

Nitrogen is nitrogen is nitrogen, which means that any fertilizer containing it will technically work. Is there one best fertilizer product? If there were, it would be one that you only had to apply once per growing season and that released nitrogen in such a way that it would give the lawn a steady supply of nutrients throughout the growing season. (That perfect product doesn't exist yet, although there is a way you can apply a small amount of nitrogen per day and make your grass very, very happy, which I'll go into later on.)

That said, you'll see lots of different products on the shelves. Technically, they'll all work as long as they have nitrogen in them. Here's how to choose among them.

Release Me

Remember, nitrogen comes in two forms—soluble, or fast-release, which greens things up fast; and insoluble, or slow-release, which sticks around longer and provides more food over a longer period of time.

These days, most fertilizers contain both soluble and insoluble nitrogen, and they're typically the best choice. For the most part, you want a good balance of both, but not always. Let's say you just interseeded your lawn to spruce up its density or to change its characteristics. Or you had a big party and your grass is looking a little puny and pale. Putting down a fertilizer that's heavier on soluble, fast-release ni-

Here is one of the best pro tips I know when it comes to fertilizing: Always have some urea fertilizer around. Urea fertilizer is a very common, quick-release synthetic fertilizer that is a component in almost all commercial fertilizers. By itself it will be in a bag listed 46-0-0 and is very inexpensive, but it can be a lifesaver. It's the best thing for greening up or perking up a lawn fast. Apply it at a rate of one-half pound of nitrogen (or roughly one pound of product) per thousand square feet. Don't go any higher than this or you risk burning your grass. Be sure it gets at least a tenth of an inch of water after you apply it, either from you or Mother Nature. It will respond to the fertilizer in two to four days if you water it in. The intense color will only last from two to three weeks but it's a great way to get a lawn ready for showing off.

trogen will give your seeds a good start and make your poor, beat-up grass look a lot better faster than a slow-release product will.

Too much soluble fertilizer can also cause excessive growth, and, in large amounts, it can burn your grass. On the flip side, too much slow-release nitrogen might not provide enough nutrition when your turf needs it the most.

Other things to keep in mind when you're weighing soluble versus insoluble: The more insoluble nitrogen in the product, the more you can apply without risking fertilizer burn. As percentages of insoluble nitrogen go up, however, so do prices.

High-quality fertilizers containing both types of nitrogen will meet your grass's needs immediately and for some weeks—typically six to twelve—into the future. This is what you want to buy; it will be commonly available in all major brands.

Although they're not required to do so, many products will list the percentages of soluble and insoluble nitrogen. If you don't see them, you can still get an idea of how much of each is in the bag by checking the content label. Here's what to look for:

Quick-release
ammonium nitrate
ammonium sulfate

ammonium phosphate

urea

Slow-release

ureaform

isobutylidine diurea (IBDU)

polyon (resin-coated urea)

sulfur-coated urea

milorganite (or sewage sludge, an organic material)

animal manure

Complete Me

Because most soil lacks the big three nutrients—nitrogen, phosphorous, and potassium—most fertilizers contain all three of them in various amounts. But you can purchase fertilizer without phosphorous or potassium if your lawn doesn't need it. You can also buy products that contain just phosphorous or just potassium. For the most part, however, you'll want to stick with fertilizers that contain all three, with phosphorous levels the lowest.

Is there one best place to buy fertilizer? Not necessarily, although you might find it easier to shop at places that professionals frequent. They have better products in general—they have to, or their target market wouldn't buy from them—and less consumerism, meaning fewer and easier choices. That said, you can buy fertilizer anywhere you want. Comparison shop if you want, as prices do vary, but don't make your decision based on price alone. What's actually in the bag is most important, and that's what your decision needs to be based on more than anything else. If you are comparison shopping, the easy way is to compare how much each pound of fertilizer is costing you, as this is the driving force. Remember to try to compare apples to apples, in this case soluble nitrogen to soluble nitrogen, to get a true comparison.

Phosphorous, while important, is typically present and accounted for in established turf, which is why the fertilizer you buy for general fertilizing doesn't need to contain much if any of it. Look for fertilizer with a low second number on the bag, such as 20-3-15 or 25-0-25. Establishing new lawns is another matter, though. For them, starter fertilizers, which contain more phosphorous, are the way to go.

Stink or No Stink

You can also choose an organic product if that suits you. These contain animal or plant waste. They feed both the grass and the soil, as they also encourage microorganism growth.

The nitrogen in organic sources is nonsoluble, which can be a plus, as it releases slowly and delivers a steady food supply throughout the growing season. The downside to these fertilizers is that their nitrogen levels can vary quite a bit—since these products are derived from natural sources, levels can't be calculated as precisely and controlled like they can be with synthetic products. Also, organic fertilizers can be kind of stinky, and they're more expensive in general. Plus, the nitrogen in organic fertilizer is temperature sensitive, which means that the soil temperature must be over 50°F for it to work well. Lower than this, and the fertilizer will just sit until the weather warms up. Not exactly what you want to help seeds along or speed up turf recovery, especially in the spring, when temperatures are low.

The best time and place to use natural fertilizers is in the summer on mature lawns. The nitrogen in these products needs microbial activity to release it, and this activity is highest when temperatures are the warmest, so if you want to see a good response put it on during late spring and early summer, when temperatures are warming up. You don't want to use them on young lawns because these lawns need fertilizer immediately, and slow-release fertilizers (which organic fertilizers definitely are) don't release enough nitrogen quickly enough to push things along.

Weed-and-feed products will kill certain weeds and feed grasses at the same time. If you have lots of broadleaf weeds in your yard, they might be a good choice. If you're battling grass weeds you won't be happy, because most weed-and-feed products on the market right now are only effective on broadleaf weeds. I'm not a big fan of these products overall because they rarely do a good job on weeds—the herbicide must leave the fertilizer particle and come into contact with the weed through watering or rainfall, so if there's no moisture around they're not very effective. You can usually get 85 percent control, but I am a 95–100 percent guy. If you're an 85 percent person it might be okay for you, but I prefer a separate weed-control application with a liquid because I know the herbicide will come into contact with the weed. I prefer to have the control of these two applications. Lawn geeks like control.

TIMING IS EVERYTHING

You want to do the majority of fertilizer applications when it's going to do the most good—namely, when grass is actively growing. *At a minimum*, your grass should receive an annual nutritional boost. This isn't the best approach, but if you use a slow- or timed-release product, your turf will receive a fair amount of nutritional support for a good part of the growing season.

The better approach is to feed lightly and relatively often throughout the growing season. Remember, cool-season grasses are most active when temperatures are between 60°F and 75°F—in other words, in spring and fall. I typically recommend the "holiday calendar" guideline for fertilizing these grasses, which simply means timing applications around Memorial Day, Fourth of July, Labor Day, and Thanksgiving. This schedule will give your lawn a good start in the spring and support it into the fall and winter. The key to this is putting down the right amount, which can be as simple as reading the directions on the back of the bag. Always remember, twice as much is never twice as good.

You don't take twice the recommended dosage for medicine, so don't do it to your grass. Warm-season grasses, again, grow best when temperatures are above 80°F, which makes hot summer weather prime time for fertilizing them. Fertilizing then will build strong roots and strengthen the plants so they can better survive low-growth periods with their greater potential for stress. For these grasses, time fertilizer applications around the first three holidays, and be prepared to fertilize the first of August if you are watering (watering makes the grass grow and uses up the nitrogen faster). Omit the Thanksgiving feast.

PUTTING IT DOWN

Fertilizer does its best work when it's applied in the right amount and in the right place. Too much fertilizer causes dark green streaks that might turn an ugly brown. Too little fertilizer, and you'll get the opposite—light green streaks that might turn an ugly brown. They both mean you misapplied the fertilizer. Fertilizer doesn't lie. Maybe better put, it can't.

You have some choices when it comes to fertilizing equipment. For large yards, and if you need to get things done fast, opt for a rotary or broadcast spreader. They're efficient, accurate, and quick. Most cover a five-to-ten-foot-wide path, depending on the fertilizer you're using and how fast you walk. Divide the fertilizer rate in half and apply in opposite directions, and you'll never have to worry about skips or overlaps again.

For smaller lawns or lawns with lots of tight areas, a drop spreader might be the better choice. These drop fertilizer straight down from a hopper, which makes application more precise in tight areas. Drop spreaders typically cover a two-foot-wide strip, but, since their wheels ride several inches wider than the hopper, overlapping each pass by at least the width of the wheels is a must for getting complete coverage.

There are also hybrid spreaders that combine drop spreader accuracy with rotary spreader efficiency. Set to rotary for covering big areas; set to drop for working along driveways, flower beds, sidewalks, the space between your garage and your house, you name it.

Unless you have a really small patch of green, buy a rotary spreader. What's more, buy a good one; professional grade here isn't overkill. Even good ones aren't that expensive, and if you treat them right—specifically, wash them down after you use them, because fertilizer salts will corrode them—a good one will last you a lifetime.

If your yard is very small, and I mean tiny, a handheld crank sprayer might work for you. They're the cheapest option, but not a good one unless you really don't have much ground to cover. They can't hold more than a couple of pounds of fertilizer at a time, and it's tough to get an even application with them if you don't have strong arms, as you have to both hold the hopper level and turn the crank steadily as you walk along. It looks easier than it is, believe me. They'll cover a five-to-six-foot-wide path.

There are also liquid sprayers, which for home use are usually handheld devices that attach to garden hoses. They're easy to use, and relatively inexpensive. I don't recommend them for fertilizing, though. It can be difficult to get an even application if you don't do a good job of directing the spray. If your water pressure isn't steady, the product will go on unevenly. And, if you have a large lawn, you'll have to refill the device pretty often, which can be both a pain in the rear and messy. They're pretty good for applying herbicides, however, primarily because even coverage isn't the major concern for herbicides. Overapplications won't show up like they would with fertilizer; twice as much fertilizer is going to show up as twice as green, but twice as much herbicide and you won't have twice as much dead. Dead is dead.

Based on the above, I'm going to assume you're going to use a spreader, and, hopefully, a rotary spreader. Here's how to do it right.

- Cut, then feed. Freshly mowed grass is easier to move through, and you'll see the wheel tracks better—you'll find out why this is good in a moment.

Fertigation, which applies minute amounts of fertilizer to turf via in-ground irrigation systems, is another fertilizing option. It's a great way to give your grass ongoing nutritional support, as it receives a little sip of fertilizer every time you water, and it's inexpensive, too.

- Watch the wind sock. Working with dry particles always goes best when the air is calm or as close to it as possible. Early mornings are often good, as wind is typically lower then. (Early-morning dew, by the way, is great on fertilizing days, as wheel tracks show up really well in it.)
- Watch your tracks. If your spreader covers a six-foot-wide area, you want to keep the wheel tracks at least this far apart on every pass. This is why you want to see those wheel tracks. If you're using a drop spreader, they're even more important. Remember, you have to overlap your passes slightly to avoid application gaps with these machines. If you're in a situation where you can't see your wheel tracks, you might want to put flags at each end of the yard spaced the width of your spreader, and just walk to the flags.
- Walk, then drop. Don't turn your spreader on before you start walking. Instead, start walking first, then turn it on. And don't stop walking before you shut it off. Turn it off first, then stop. This might take some practice, but master it and you won't have to worry about burns or streaks marking every starting and stopping spot.

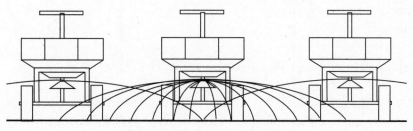

Match wheel tracks to spreader coverage.

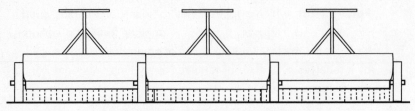

Overlap your passes slightly to avoid application gaps.

- Make a pass. Start the job by making one circuit around the perimeter of your yard to give yourself room to turn on.
- Go this way and that. Worried about patchy application? Cut the amount of fertilizer you need to put down in half. Then apply it in two directions.
- Give the green some juice. Water your lawn after you're done. Doing so will boost the fertilizer's efficiency. Or, even better, fertilize just before it rains.

What I'll always tell you about fertilizing is that not only is it the least time-consuming of the three main cultural practices, it's probably also the cheapest in terms of actual cash outlay. The necessary equipment is pretty inexpensive and the chemicals aren't that pricey either. What's more, fertilizing saves you lots of money over the long run, just like preventive medicine does for humans, as it can prevent lots of nasty things from happening on your turf.

Start the job by going around your yard first, then back and forth.

Doing the job right takes a little more time and effort on the front end, no doubt about it, but you'll be a fertilizing pro in no time flat. Which is a good thing, when you realize that someday pesticides will be all but unavailable, and fertilizers will be all that's around to nurture your lawn's good health.

CHAPTER 10

Lawn CPR

You've watered it, you've fed it. Now what? Like all living organisms, your lawn needs to breathe, too.

For argument's sake, let's start this chapter off with a look at the future. It may or may not be your exact future, but humor me here. There's a method to my madness.

Let's say you've done a great job at establishing and working on your lawn. It's an honest-to-God work of art, lush and green, weed- and spot-free, worthy of a full-color photo spread in the best lawn and garden magazines. People ooh and aah over it. Your kids love to play on it. Your dog sits by the door and begs to be let outside so he can run circuits on it, especially along the fence line in back. The neighborhood association taps you as the host for the annual new-neighbor barbecues and the Fourth of July ice cream socials, and you say yes because, well, you're proud of your accomplishments and secretly, deep inside, you like the attention.

These are all good things, as they mean that your hard work has paid off in a lawn that people and pets enjoy using. All that turfside activity can also put your grass plants into a death grip, however, struggling for the oxygen, water, and other nutrients they need to stay healthy. Kids cavorting, people partying, dogs hauling butt along fence lines—it smashes down the grass and compacts the soil surrounding its roots.

Even occasional foot traffic causes a certain amount of compression, and it will build up over time. It can also encourage excessive plant detritus—a.k.a thatch—which can also choke the nutrient supply to grass roots.

What can you do to keep your lawn from flatlining? You can—and you should—give it a breath of fresh air. Doing so will restore healthy oxygen flow to your grass and increase its ability to suck up other good things—like fertilizer and other nutrients—as well.

There are two ways to improve oxygen and nutrient flow to your grass. You can poke holes into the soil through the thatch, or you can remove excess thatch. Both approaches are beneficial; either will improve the overall health of your lawn by restoring the channels that let air, water, and nutrients through to the soil.

Which line of attack should you choose? It depends on what's going on underfoot. A healthy lawn should feel a little springy when you walk over it. What if yours feels hard as cement? That rock-hard feeling can have lots of causes, such as construction traffic if your home is new construction, or if your kids and pets trample the lawn on a regular basis. Regardless of the reason, what you're dealing with here is soil compaction, and poking holes into the turf is the best way to treat it.

Or, let's say your lawn feels like a soft feather bed underfoot. This indicates a thick thatch layer. Remember, thatch is not only unavoidable, it's part and parcel of a healthy lawn. You want a bit of it, as it protects grass plants from drought and heat stress by holding moisture at the root level. But remember, too, that thatch can get out of hand for various reasons. When it does, it holds back too much moisture and cuts off nutrients to grass roots. Aerating will help the thatch break down faster, as it will restore the oxygen and nutrient flow to the tiny organisms that play a key role in the process, but if the layer is especially thick and ugly, dethatching is the call here.

Or maybe you water the heck out of your lawn but it's still dry no matter how much H_2O you lay on. Thatch or compaction, or both, could be the culprits. You'll have to do a little digging—literally—to figure out the best approach here. Take your shovel or spade, pick a spot in your lawn where the problem seems most severe, and carve out a soil sample. Or, better put, try to. If the soil is severely compacted, the blade might just deflect off the surface of the turf instead of digging in. If you have to jump on that blade to muscle it in, you can stop right there, as you have your answer. Aeration is definitely the call.

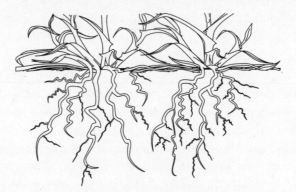

This is what turf should look like.

If you were able to remove a chunk of turf, examine it. Remember that healthy turf will contain grass roots extending three to six inches below the surface. There will be spaces in the soil between the particles and it should crumble fairly easily. The thatch layer should measure between one-half and three-quarters of an inch.

Your turf, however, won't look like this. If it's compacted, you'll see short, stumpy grass roots struggling to grow in densely packed soil. If thatch is the culprit, the roots may or may not look okay, but they'll definitely be topped off with a thick layer of dead plant matter. If thatch and compaction are really severe, the roots might actually be growing in the thatch layer instead of the soil.

Either way, you want to get things flowing again. It's time to break out the heavy artillery.

This is what turf shouldn't look like.

ADDING AIR

Soil gets compacted, particularly if it gets a lot of traffic. In the turf-grass management world, we've got to alleviate the compaction without taking the field out of play. This means reducing the density. The original concept called for pulling plugs of soil out of the ground by hand, but along the line someone thought there should be a machine to do it and invented one. (His name, by the way, is Tommy Mascaro. He was an inventor and I met him early in my career; he owned a turfgrass equipment company and invented the aerator in the early 1950s.)

Aeration, which basically calls for punching lots of small holes in the soil, is the technical term for improving turf 's ability to absorb good things like air, water, and nutrients. It makes these good things more available to grass roots, which will eagerly suck them up like a duck on a June bug and be very grateful to you for helping them out.

Aeration is best for breaking up soil compaction, which is a fancy term for heavy soil. Heavy soil contains too many solid particles (read silts and clays) for the space it takes up, and this is what prevents the good stuff—air, water, and nutrients—from circulating in the soil and nourishing grass roots the way they should. When there's not enough space for air and nutrients in the soil, grass roots are shallow and weak

If you're living in a newly built house, your yard was sodded, and it isn't looking too good, suspect soil layering. This happens when different-textured soils are stacked on top of each other, and it's fairly common on construction sites, especially when subsoils are excavated, brought to the surface, and covered with a layer of topsoil. It also happens when sod is placed directly on soil that's significantly finer- or coarser-textured than what's in the sod. The layers prevent good water movement, which results in poor root development and compaction. Aerating will break up the layering, help the layers merge together, give the roots more room to grow, and improve water and oxygen flow. For best results, plan on poking holes through the layers every year for at least a couple of years.

for two reasons. First, because they can't get enough nutrients to be anything other than puny. Second, the lack of space gives them little room to grow in.

Aeration also works well on thatch, as improved airflow will help break it down faster. In fact, if you don't find the looks of your lawn's thatch layer truly objectionable, don't bother removing it. Punch holes through it instead. Not only is it easier, it's kinder to your lawn.

HERE A POKE, THERE A POKE

You can poke those holes by simply taking a tine or fork and going at it. There are also devices you can buy or rent that look like rollers with spikes that will do the same thing. This approach is known as solid-tine cultivation. It's been done for years, but we've taken a good look at its effectiveness, and guess what? It isn't all that great for lawns. The holes made by tines, forks, or spikes are pretty thin, so they don't accomplish much. In fact, research has shown that solid-tine cultivation can actually make compaction worse. It doesn't remove any of the soil, it just pushes it to the sides of the holes, which compresses the soil around the holes even more than it was. The space in the newly created holes doesn't compensate for the compression, so the problem is pretty much what it was before you started, if not worse.

The other, and better, approach is known as core cultivation, which means pulling cores or plugs out of the soil. This leaves larger voids, and since some of the turf is actually removed, it doesn't compress the soil around the holes.

If you don't have access to a core aerator and you do have a solid-tine device lying around, using it is better than nothing, especially if soil compaction is limited to a small area. But it's only a little better. Core cultivation is the superior approach and the one you should take if you can.

You have two choices when it comes to core aeration: hiring a lawn service to do it for you or doing it yourself. If you go the DIY approach, rent a core aerator. This is not a piece of equipment to buy, as a good turf aerator, meaning one that's big enough and heavy enough to really do the job right, costs around fifteen hundred dollars new. Even if you aerate every second or third season, which you might have to do if your

Every so often, I'll come across some well-meaning soul who heard or read somewhere that wearing old-fashioned spiked golf shoes while he's working on his lawn is an easy way to aerate it. Well, it isn't, and the reason why should be fairly obvious. The spikes on golf shoes are only about three-eighths of an inch in length, which isn't anywhere near long enough to penetrate even a fairly thin thatch layer and definitely not long enough to do the roots any good.

Wearing golf shoes will definitely improve your traction should you need to do something with your lawn when it's wet, but that's about all they're good for when it comes to lawn care. Devices called aerator sandals, which sport long, thin tines, are a variation on this theme. In theory, their longer tines will do a better job, but those long, thin tines are scary buggers, no two ways about it. They look like they'd do a better job of landing you flat on your face (or your rear) should you somehow catch them in the grass as you're walking. I don't know about you, but I'm just klutzy enough to make this a real possibility. Another reason not to go this direction: these devices deliver solid-tine aeration, which you now know is about one step up from doing nothing.

lawn gets lots of use or there's lots of heavy clay in your soil or you're dealing with a soil layering problem, it's not enough to support the cost.

Not convinced? Spread the use out over twenty years. You're still only going to use that aerator maybe eight to ten times, tops. At best the cost per use would be a hundred and fifty dollars. The typical rental on a good aerator is about eighteen to twenty dollars an hour. Unless your yard is really huge—and if it is, you'll probably want to hire a company to do the aerating for you, as it's really, really hard work on big lots—it will probably take you a couple of hours to aerate your yard. That's still a lot less than a hundred and fifty dollars per use.

Smaller core aerators for residential use are available for a lot less money, but they're also questionable purchases. Some of them attach to garden tillers or lawn tractors, so you'd have to have one of these as well. They're also smaller and lighter than commercial models, and, as such, aren't as efficient. Typical commercial and rental aerators, for example, have twenty-four tines. Smaller ones for home use are typically half this size, meaning you'll have to make twice as many passes to get the same hole density, and it will take you twice as long.

Bottom line, even if you're a gadget geek and you really want to add a turf aerator to your arsenal, resist the temptation. Spend your money on something you'll use more often, like a heavy-duty rotary spreader. You'll be happy you did. Trust me on this.

You can find rental aerators at most lawn and garden stores or home improvement centers. Hardware stores and general machine rental shops also typically have them. Most rental shops carry manual and power aerators. Manual aerators are going to give you a better workout, if you're after that, and they're a good choice if you don't have a huge yard. If you do, a power aerator is probably a better choice. They're heavy, though, and you'll need at least a small station wagon to transport one.

As mentioned, these machines typically aren't all that expensive to rent, but this might be the perfect time to get to know your neighbor better by telling him what you're up to and seeing if he's interested in using the machine and sharing the rental cost.

You'll want to rent an aerating machine that removes soil plugs approximately two to three inches deep and one-half to three-quarters of an inch in diameter. That's about the size of your little finger. When you get it home, your goal will be to punch around thirty to thirty-five holes in every square foot of turf, which might seem like a lot but isn't. It does, however, require making more than one pass over the grass. Spacing your passes evenly will result in evenly punched holes, which is

A good rental shop should offer directions on how to use their equipment, and you, being a good renter, should listen and follow those directions. Even if you think you know how to use whatever it is you're renting, let the person doing the explaining do what he's paid to do. It covers his behind, and it might save you from some embarrassing or harmful operator errors.

also what you want. Holes two to three inches apart are ideal; four to six inches apart is adequate.

You'll want to aerate during the growing season, for the obvious reason—doing so gives the grass ample time to heal and fill in open areas. This means aerating cool-season grasses in late spring or late summer to early fall and warm-season grasses in spring.

Make sure the soil is moist before you get started. Working on bone-dry, hard-as-a-rock soil is not just frustrating, it's physically exhausting. Early mornings, when the turf is cool and dewy-moist, are typically good times. Aerating the day after a rain shower or the day after watering your lawn also works.

Focus your efforts on compacted areas. Most aerators cover a fairly small area on each pass. You'll have to make two to three passes over your lawn's hard spots to punch enough holes in them. Save your resources and your energy by skipping the areas that don't need attention.

The excavated soil plugs look a lot like goose droppings. If you hate looking at them, or you think your neighbors will and that bothers you, you can break them up by running them over with a lawn mower (use an old mower blade) or pounding them apart with the back of a rake. Doing so will give your lawn a cleaner, more uniform appearance. There's also a device that looks like a horizontal chain-link fence that you can drag over the cores, which does a fine job of breaking them down, but it's a grueling process. If you have a lawn tractor, pull it out of the shed for this one. Or find a strong kid.

If you don't mind your lawn looking like a gaggle of geese just visited it, and your neighbors are okay about it, too, just leave the cores alone. They'll dissolve over the next few weeks, maybe a little faster if you get some rain. You can help them along, of course, by sprinkling them down, especially if you're not expecting rain. Mowing will break them down as well.

After you aerate, your lawn's going to look a bit chewed up. (Not as bad as it's going to look after dethatching, but bad enough.) There's not much you can do about this beyond letting nature take its course. Before too long, grass roots will start to grow into the spaces where the plugs were, and your lawn will look much healthier than it did before.

The downside to aerating is that it can also bring up weed seeds from down below as you pull the plugs out. If you're doing it late in the season, this shouldn't be too much of a problem, as winter will probably

Since aeration's such a good thing for lawns, it's almost better to plan on doing it regularly instead of waiting until your lawn needs it. For lawns that get low use, meaning they're not trampled by kids and pets on a regular basis, every three to five years should be often enough. Lawns with average use, every couple of years or so. Plan on doing it more often, even annually, if your lawn is where the neighborhood kids hang out and play and the soil has lots of clay.

set in before they get the chance to germinate. Apply a preemergence herbicide the following spring to catch any seeds that might be lurking. If you aerate in the spring, use a preemergence herbicide before you do.

After aeration is a great time for a quick fertilizer application. A light touch of urea will help your lawn look better faster. Turn to chapter 9 for more information on how to do it.

DETHATCHING

A healthy thatch layer is a good thing. It helps provide nutrients, conserves moisture, and shades and protects the crowns of grass plants. Normal thatch production can vary quite a bit depending on the type of grass you're growing. Grasses that spread by rhizomes or stolons will produce more thatch than bunchgrasses do. You won't see much thatch, if any, in perennial ryegrass or tall fescue lawns. Of the spreaders, grasses that do so via stolons are usually the worst.

If the thatch layer on your lawn is healthy, there's no reason to remove it. How to determine if your lawn needs dethatching? The turf sample approach, as previously discussed, is a surefire way to tell. Dig up a small piece of your turf with a sharp tool. Make sure you get a cross section that goes through the thatch into the soil beneath it. If the dead grass layer is more than a half inch, you need to dethatch or aerate. It's as simple as that.

One of the biggest misconceptions I've run across in lawn care is that leaving grass clippings behind after mowing results in excessive thatch buildup. Clippings are 85–90 percent water, and they break down very quickly. Thatch is dead plant stems and roots. Too much thatch indicates that they're not breaking down as quickly as they should, but grass clippings have nothing to do with this process.

If your lawn is producing excessive thatch, question your maintenance practices, in particular fertilizing and watering. Excesses of either will contribute to excessive thatch accumulation. Get them in balance, and thatch can be reduced naturally.

In addition to excessive fertilizing and overwatering, thatch can get out of hand because of low microorganism levels (remember, they help digest thatch). When it does, it literally becomes a catch basin for nutrients and water. Instead of sinking into the ground where grass roots can get at them, they stay in the thatch, above the roots. Your grass plants will continue to seek out water and nutrients and will use them wherever they're found, which means that they'll root in the thatch, if that's where they find sustenance, instead of in the ground. Instead of being at the interface between thatch and soil, their crowns will ride above the thatch, which means they won't get the light and drought protection they need to be healthy.

If your grass is never stressed, it can survive all of this, in theory anyway, but you'll have to support it by almost continually laying on water and fertilizer. If you ease up on either at any time, the grass will stress out almost immediately because the water and nutrients in the thatch won't be enough to support it in its time of need.

The type of grass you're growing will determine the best time for dethatching. Late summer or early fall is good for cool-season grasses. It gives them enough time to recover before cold weather sets in but cuts down on their having to compete with weeds. Spring is also okay for dethatching cool-season lawns, but then you run the risk of greater weed

Some will say you have a thatch problem; the wise owl will say you have a cultural problem. Check the cultural practices that led to the thatch problem so that once it's fixed it doesn't happen again.

Some grasses, notably St. Augustinegrass and zoysiagrass, are prolific thatch producers. Unfortunately, their growth habits also make them poor candidates for dethatching. If you have to dethatch them, proceed carefully and give them as much recovery time as you can by doing it as soon as you can in the spring.

development, as the weeds will be germinating at the same time. So put down a preemergence herbicide.

For warm-season grasses, late spring—right after the plants green up but before it gets too hot—is good timing. Follow the dethatching with a preemergence weed control to minimize unwanted plant invasion, and, again, a nice light urea meal.

Lots of people will tell you to remove thatch by dethatching and then raking it up. I'd rather punch holes and drag the soil back into the thatch layer. It makes more sense and in my mind is less work; it's a lot less mess and you don't have to rake the stuff up. The microorganisms from the soil will speed the breakdown of the thatch. That said, I'd be remiss if I didn't tell you how to rake your lawn, so here goes.

Depending on how bad the thatch layer is and how much you like manual labor, you can go self-propelled or not. If you have a small yard and the thatch is relatively shallow, you can use an implement called a thatch or cavex rake. These tools have bladelike tines that cut through the thatch. A stiff lawn rake can also work if the thatch layer is one-half to one inch thick. Anything more than this, get a thatch rake. Or rent a power rake or vertical mower. These machines are about the size of a lawn mower and about half again as heavy as one, but they make quick work out of thatch. If you have a large yard, you should be able to power rake it in about three or four hours. Working it over with a thatch rake could take days.

Mowing is the first step in dethatching. This is one of the few times you don't want to follow the one-third rule. Instead, you want to go pretty low. Doing so will make the job ahead easier. And this is definitely one of the times you'll want to remove the clippings.

If you use a thatching rake, angle the rake so that the tines slightly

 **If "even terrain"** is a term you'd never utter in conjunction with "my lawn," don't even think about using a power rake. It will scalp the grass when it hits high spots and won't do anything at all when it skims over low spots.

cut into the ground. Use a push-pull stroke, and work in small areas. Make a couple of passes instead of trying to remove all of the thatch on one pass. Remove the debris with a regular lawn rake, or with the other side of your thatch rake, if it's designed for this. Be prepared for a lot of debris—even a smallish yard can produce numerous leaf bags full of the stuff.

If you use a power rake, and it's your first time, practice a little first on a faraway corner of your yard before tackling the whole thing. As mentioned, these machines are heavy, and they can run away from you if you're not careful. The same thing goes for aerators, by the way. Get to know them a little before you start tearing up your yard, literally.

A little thought needs to go into timing if you're planning to use a preemergence herbicide in the spring. It's difficult to put down a preemergent and then dethatch and put down new seed and expect good things to happen. So, if you're going to dethatch, seed and go with siduron that particular year (see chapter 5 for more on this). Fertilizing and watering are musts.

Finally, here's one fact you're just not going to get around: Excessive thatch has to be removed manually, not biologically or with chemical "snake oils." People have tried to come up with hocus-pocus solutions for decades. You'll see advertisements for miracle products that claim to dissolve thatch and alleviate compaction. Run from these products (and get ready to work).

Once your turf is happy and breathing nicely again, keep it that way. Mow it right, water it right, fertilize it right . . . yeah, I know, it's a broken record, but this stuff works. And your back and your wallet will be happier for it, too.

PART FOUR

Crisis Control

CHAPTER 11

Weeding Things Out

Does your lawn have more weeds than grass? Here's how to identify, control, and understand how they got there in the first place.

When people call and ask me to come out and look at their lawns because they have "weed problems," I place a little bet with myself as I'm on my way out there. I already know they don't have a weed problem. What they have is a cultural practice problem—they have a mowing problem or a watering problem or a cultivating problem, all of which lead to weeds in their yard. So I place a bet on what I think I'll see.

Weeds are the result of poor-quality turf, not the cause. When you correct the cultural practice, you'll stop the proliferation of the weeds. Keep it going, and it doesn't matter how many times you kill the weeds, they'll keep coming back.

That's weed control in a nutshell. Optimize your cultural practices, minimize your weeds, and vice versa.

Ralph Waldo Emerson wrote, "What is a weed? A plant whose virtues have never been discovered." Well, to me, and to most people who deal with turfgrass for a living, a weed is any plant that's growing where you don't want it to.

That said, there's a basic truth about weeds that's important to get your head around: You'll always have some in your lawn. Always. No getting around it. Here's why: Weed seeds can remain viable in soil for thirty years and even longer. There can be up to forty million weed seeds in the top six-inch layer of a thousand-square-foot area of soil. That's more than five thousand seeds in a square foot. No way will you ever be able to get rid of all of them.

Nor, for that matter, should a weed-free lawn be your goal. Surprised? Don't be. A weed-free lawn is virtually impossible.

LIFE WITH WEEDS

Yup, it's true. A weed-free lawn is akin to a Utopia. It's not literally impossible, but the time and money you'd have to spend creating it doesn't justify the end result. Plus, it's simply not necessary. The best groundskeepers will tell you that their goal is not weed-free turf. It's turf that looks good—that's consistent in color and texture—and that performs the way it should with as few weeds as possible. To us geeks, however, while perfection is just temporary and always fleeting, it is kinda fun to chase.

Still, one of the best lawn geek secrets is that great-looking lawns can have some weeds. Don't believe me? Try a simple test. Take a stroll around your neighborhood. When you find a good-looking yard, stop right where you are and take a look. Can't see any weeds? Get down on your hands and knees, and you'll see them, all right.

Interestingly, weed control is a fairly contemporary concern. According to the Weed Science Society of America (you had to know there would be such a thing, right?), state laws aimed at controlling plant diseases were enacted between 1721 and 1766, but laws specific to weeds didn't come along until one hundred to two hundred years later. The word "weed" didn't even appear in college texts or extension bulletins until roughly the early 1950s, some ten years after the discovery of one of the most powerful herbicides, 2,4-dichlorophenoxyacetic acid, a.k.a. 2,4-D.

> **Turfgrasses**—for example, tall fescue or zoysiagrass—can also be weeds when growing in areas where they aren't wanted, like in the middle of your prized stand of Kentucky bluegrass, as they interrupt the consistency and the conformity of your lawn's appearance.

Weeds will definitely annoy you when you're right on top of them and they're staring you in the face. But how many crazy people are going to drop down and inspect your grass up close and personal? You have to put things into perspective, which here means taking a curbside view. This is the distance from which most people will see your yard, and, from an appearance perspective at least, it's what really matters.

And, don't forget, there are weeds and there are *weeds*. I have seen lawns absolutely full of low-growing weeds that pass the curb test. This isn't to say you wouldn't want to get rid of them, but you can probably live with more of them than you can with disruptive weeds like dandelions. There's no way to disguise their yellow flowers when they start cropping up.

Controlling weeds, however, isn't just a matter of vanity. Sure, they detract from the overall appearance of the turf, but looks aren't everything. They also make it more difficult for grass to grow in general, and, in turn, make life more difficult for you, too. And more expensive! Weeds compete with turfgrasses for water, sunlight, and nutrients. Weed-choked lawns require more watering and feeding than those where weeds are under control. You'll not only spend more time on these cultural practices and get poorer results, your costs for them will be higher, too.

Laying on more water and fertilizer also upsets the balance among the big three cultural practices. When you feed more, grass grows faster. Faster-growing grass means you'll have to mow more often. Mowing more often can result in overgrowth or scalping, which opens the door for even more weed invaders, not to mention other problems.

It just makes sense to tackle weed problems before they get out of hand, knowing that you can have a nice-looking lawn with some weeds, or unwanted plants, within reason. You just have to accept the fact that your yard will never be entirely weed-free for very long, as there are always more weeds lurking around the corner. Knowing how to take care of them and when to take care of them in the most efficient manner is the key to having a relatively weed-free lawn.

Another factor to consider when determining your weed tolerance is how your yard fits in with others on your block. Lawns that are too perfect stick out as much as ones where you can't see the grass for the weeds. Plus, you have to live with your neighbors. Making your lawn a showplace if the others aren't might not be the best idea. On the other hand, doing so might motivate your neighbors to improve their green spaces as well.

CONTROLLING THE ENEMY

While good cultural practices have always been the best way to create healthy, weed-free turf, herbicides are also very much part of modern turfgrass management. Over the years, some people used them appropriately and judiciously, others didn't. Some preferred to create gorgeous green spaces by spraying the heck out of weeds instead of using herbicides as part of a well-planned cultural program. They were a bandage, or a crutch.

Back in the day, some of the chemicals used on grass were, to put it mildly, fairly noxious stuff, and their application rates were ten times that of today. Over time, most of them were taken off the market. The ones that remain are applied at far lower rates than they once were. They have come a long way.

You'll still hear a lot about the evils of lawn chemicals, and that's not necessarily a bad thing. Many of them are toxic if they're used incorrectly. When used appropriately, however, herbicides can and do play an important role in lawn care, and they're a part of every lawn geek's lawn-care lineup.

THE IPM MODEL

The evolved, modern approach for battling weeds and other turf invaders employs a philosophy called Integrated Pest Management, or IPM. Begun back in the 1960s, IPM takes a "least-risk approach" to preventing pest problems or responding to them when they arise. It includes correct, judicious, and educated herbicide use, when necessary, but also emphasizes lowering herbicide use through employing other methods, including sound cultural practices, biological controls, and so on.

No matter the pest, IPM puts chemical use at the bottom of the totem pole. Following IPM rather than going gangbusters on the chemicals means spending more time working on your lawn, but you'll get healthier turf as a result. You still might have to use herbicides, especially if you're battling some of the more tenacious weeds or you inherited a lawn with problems and you're putting it back into order, but they'll be a partner, not the first line of defense. Then, once the problem is controlled, you can rely on gentler IPM measures to keep things that way.

The following is a good IPM model for managing weeds as well as other turf pests—insects, animals, and diseases.

IPM for Lawns
1. Preventing
   - Managing and monitoring soil and site health
   - Following a solid lawn-care program—mowing, watering, fertilizing, aerating, managing thatch—based on your turf's specific needs
   - Planting improved grass varieties resistant to insect and disease attacks
2. Monitoring
   - Regularly inspecting turf for problems
   - Keeping an eye on the weather
   - Using past knowledge to predict when problems might erupt
3. Diagnosing
   - Identifying the cause of the problem
   - Using established thresholds to determine when action is warranted

4. Correcting
   - Correcting cultural practices that led to the problem
   - Implementing an appropriate cultural program if not already in place
   - Specific cultural controls based on type of pest
   - Physical or mechanical removal
   - Biological controls—bacteria, fungi, nematodes, predatory and/or parasitic insects, insect growth regulators (IGRs)
   - Biological (natural) pesticides—neem oil, insecticidal soap, pyrethrins
   - Synthetic pesticides

The Enemy, Up Close

Identifying the intruder is a key IPM step, as knowing the enemy is the only way to effectively battle it. Let's begin with the basic weed categories. There are two:

- Broadleaf. These are dandelions, plantain, oxalis, and so on. They're called broadleaf because they have wide leaves with large veins. Two other features characterize these weeds—their leaves radiate outward from their centers, and they often have flashy flowers.
- Narrowleaf, or grassy. These include crabgrass, bermudagrass, quackgrass, and basically any grass that's growing where it's not welcome. This group also includes a group of plants called sedges, which resemble grasses but have hollow, triangular stems.

Organisms like moss and algae don't fall into either of these categories, but if they're appearing in your lawn and you don't want them there, they're weeds too.

Weeds are also categorized as annuals or perennials. Annuals go through an entire life cycle in one year. Perennial weeds keep going, year after year after year. Some go dormant or stop growing for part of the year, but their root systems stay alive. Dandelion is an example of perennial weeds.

Both broadleaf and grassy weeds can be annuals. Crabgrass,

> **While crabgrass plants** have life cycles similar to annual flowers, the big difference is that when they die they put out a tremendous amount of seed to ensure their species' survival. You potentially have to battle that seed output, and subsequently weeds, every spring, as it keeps coming after you like a river. Don't think you've taken care of it one year and you won't have to do it the next year. Whatever the month is that crabgrass comes up in your area, it's going to come up. Now combine this weed's efforts with your practices that encourage it (poor mowing practices and so on) and you can clearly see that battle lines are drawn.

knotweed, and annual bluegrass are the most common annual weeds. Annual weeds are also divided into two groups—winter and summer—based on their growing seasons. Summer annual weeds germinate from seed in the spring and die in the fall, just like annual flowers do. Crabgrass and spurge are good examples of summer annual weeds. Winter annuals germinate in the fall, live through the winter, form seeds in the spring, and then die. Common chickweed is a winter annual.

Some weeds are biennials. These noxious critters grow and store food reserves in their first year to support their flowering and seeding activities to come in their second year. After that, they typically die, but not always. And here's something that proves the amazing adaptability of plants, and, seemingly, especially weeds. Annual weeds can, in certain places and in certain conditions, behave like perennials if they want to badly enough. Crabgrass in Hawaii is a great example—if the weather is consistent and favors the weed, it will continue to grow year-round.

Good Cultural Practices

The big three cultural practices—mowing, watering, and fertilizing—play a big role in IPM, as, again, they can and do minimize the need for herbicides. Here's what you can do culturally to whack out weeds.

- Mow your grass at the right height and frequency. This ranks high on the control list, as mowing too low can make lawns friendly habitats for weeds that have adapted to low mowing heights—crabgrass, in particular, but there are others, too. Mowing at the right frequency—meaning never cutting more than a third of the leaf blade at a time—will prevent scalping and keep density up, which will block the light weed seeds need for germination.
- Water correctly. Turf that's watered properly is less hospitable to germinating seeds, as the soil surface dries out between waterings instead of staying wet.
- Fertilize correctly. Apply fertilizer when it will do your grass— not weeds—the most good.
- Aerate when it's called for. Time it for when it's best for your grass, not for the weeds.
- Control weeds mechanically. If there aren't many, pulling or digging them out can work, but only on ones that don't resprout from rhizomes, taproots, bulbs, and whatnot. Mechanical control can work on the seedlings of these plants, however, if you catch them early enough.

If you make a conscious, concerted effort to implement these practices, I guarantee you'll see a decrease in weeds. You might not get rid of all of them or the process might not be fast enough, so you can help this along by applying an herbicide at the right time, at the time when that particular herbicide will kill that plant (more about this later). A great example is a preemergence herbicide scheduled to go down in April. If it goes down at the right time, it will keep crabgrass from germinating. If you apply it after the crabgrass germinates, it will do absolutely nothing. At that point you might as well light a match and burn the money you'd spend on that herbicide because that's all it's worth—nothing.

One approach to weed control that I often suggest (it comes from my weed scientist friend and colleague Ron Calhoun) is to "reset the clock"—in other words, start over. Apply an herbicide in correct form (product, rate, and timing) to control weeds and then start using cultural practices correctly, as the misuse of these practices were the causal agents of the weeds in the first place. This gives a fresh start and you can have a nice lawn in four to six weeks with minimal use of herbicides. The key is the consistent, correct use of the cultural practices, almost like a diet or workout regimen.

Biological Control

Biological control, which uses naturally occurring organisms to issue cease-and-desist orders, is still a bit out there when it comes to battling weeds. So far, the biggest problem in this area is finding organisms that will kill weeds while leaving grasses and other plants alone. There aren't any biological weed controls on the market yet, as researchers haven't found organisms that will respond consistently in various climates and environments, but they're working on it.

Going Natural

Other natural controls are also part of IPM. For example, herbicidal soaps and corn gluten meal have proven effective on some weeds and in some situations.

Herbicidal soaps kill weeds by burning their leaves. These products aren't selective, so they're best used for spot treatment. Since they only kill what they contact, they don't work quickly on perennial weeds, which are best controlled systemically. With repeated application, however, they will suppress their growth.

Corn gluten meal is a naturally occurring plant protein that both inhibits seed germination and fertilizes turfgrass. Since it only works on seeds before they germinate, it's a preemergent control only. It can also take a while—and I mean years here—to get full control with this product if your lawn is under heavy crabgrass attack. It does a better job on relatively healthy lawns that aren't battling significant crabgrass problems.

On the horizon is a product that you might even have in your backyard that will provide good control of dandelions, provided you're mowing and fertilizing on a regular basis. We've been researching this in some form since about 1990; it began with a study of mulching fallen leaves into turf to see if it decreased turfgrass quality (it did not).

But after five years we noted that turf treated with maple leaves had very little to no dandelion activity in the spring. Alec Kowalewski, one of my graduate students, started a project in 2004 to identify a particular maple species; his work showed two things; that sugar maples provided better control than other species, and just like all the rest of the natural products they're not as effective as herbicides and must be coupled with at least low to medium cultural practices—fertilizing and mowing.

So if you have a maple tree (in particular a sugar maple tree), go ahead and mulch those leaves back into your turf. If not, stay tuned as our research continues.

Calling In the Chemicals

If you're dealing with a particularly weedy lawn, this IPM step, which calls for selective and mindful use of herbicides, can get it into shape faster than all the other approaches combined. Couple it with mowing, watering, and fertilizing correctly, and all you'll have to do is spot treat some broadleaf weeds from time to time.

There are preemergence and postemergence herbicides, and selective and nonselective herbicides. You'll find all you need to know about selecting the right ones and using them correctly in chapter 12.

WAGING THE WEED WAR

Ready to go on the warpath? The weeds that cause you problems will vary somewhat depending on where you live, but some can be pains in the you-know-what just about anywhere. The ones here fall into the latter category. At some time during your tenure as a lawn geek, you'll probably have to deal with them. To (hopefully) make it easy to find your particular pest, I've grouped them as grassy or broadleaf. IPM controls, beginning with the least harmful, accompany each description.

Annual Grassy Weeds

As mentioned, these are grasses and sedges. They resemble turf-grasses or are turfgrasses growing where they aren't wanted.

Crabgrass, Smooth and Hairy Both are summer annuals that germinate in late spring and early summer. Their leaves are bluish or apple green, and show up really well through polarized sunglasses.
Control methods:

- Hand-pull if not widely spread.
- Apply a preemergence herbicide in spring before soil temperatures reach 60°F.
- Apply postemergence herbicide like dithiopyr (Dimension), quinclorac (Drive), or MSMA when plants are small, first thirty to fifty days after germination. After fifty days, Drive is your best bet. You can apply Drive at any point during the growing cycle. Multiple applications might be necessary for best control later in the season.

smooth crabgrass

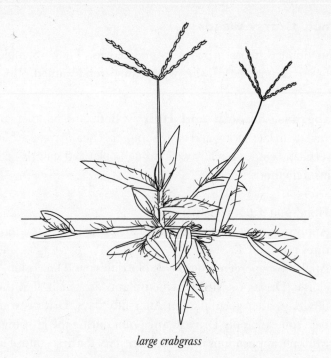

large crabgrass

One thing to remember about controlling crabgrass or any annual plant right before the end (last two to three weeks) of their life
cycle (for summer annuals, the end of summer, for winter annuals,
the end of spring) is that no action will often be as effective as
action. The plant is going to die anyway, so wait it out with a
plan to prevent it from happening next season, save the money
you would spend on the chemical, and make sure you fertilize
and overseed the bare areas that will be formed when the
weeds die.

Annual Bluegrass   You first met annual bluegrass in chapter 2,
where I warned you about it cropping up in your lawn. It definitely has
some value for providing ground cover in extremely moist and shady
areas, but there are parts of this world that will consider this plant a
weed.

annual bluegrass

If there's annual bluegrass in your cool-season lawn in the North . . .
I wish you good luck, as it will be virtually impossible to control it. But
you know what? It's not really necessary. It's not all that obtrusive. Live
and let live, in this case.

Control:

- If already established, keeping your grass a little longer will
  lower the amount of sun reaching the bluegrass seedlings.
- Don't overwater. Annual bluegrass responds well to it. Don't
  overfertilize either, for the same reason.
- Apply preemergence herbicide in late summer to early fall.
- In warm-season lawns in the South and the transition zone,
  where annual bluegrass acts like an annual but disrupts turf
  uniformity in the winter on an otherwise dormant lawn (primarily bermudagrass and zoysiagrass), apply glyphosate in late
  winter when the grass is still dormant but the weeds are growing. This won't hurt your lawn, as the grass must be actively
  growing to take up the chemical. Only the weeds will get it.

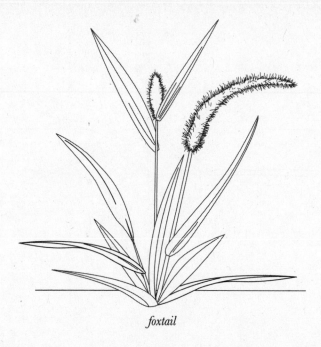

foxtail

Foxtail   Also known as yellow or green foxtail; the seed head on this summer annual looks like the tail of a fox, hence its name. It's found throughout the United States, but primarily in the Midwest and East.

Foxtail germinates later than some weeds in this category, and it can be a real pain in the rear in newly seeded lawns. If seeds are present they'll sprout when soil temperatures reach 65°F.

Control:

- Don't seed or aerate when conditions are ripe for foxtail seeds to germinate.
- Apply preemergence herbicide containing siduron if establishing turfgrass from seed. Otherwise any preemergence herbicide will do.
- Spot treat with nonselective herbicide. Painting it on leaves with a brush is most effective and least disruptive to the other grasses.
- Apply a postemergence grass herbicide like quinclorac (Drive) if none of these got it.

Goosegrass   Goosegrass is a summer annual that looks like crabgrass but with a silvery center. It's sometimes called silver crabgrass

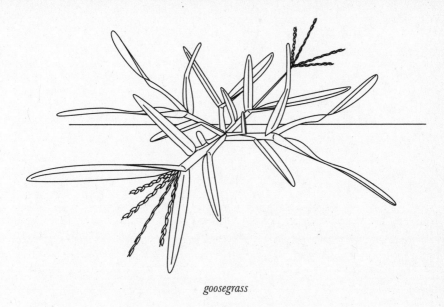

goosegrass

for this reason. It can crop up almost anywhere, but it prefers hard, compacted, poorly drained soil. It also likes warm temperatures, so it tends to hang out more south of the transition zone.

Goosegrass's seed heads contain three to seven spikes and look a little like zippers. It is a particular headache, as it germinates later than some annual grasses.

Control:

- Aerate compacted areas.
- Apply preemergence herbicide oxadiazon in late spring or early summer.
- Spot treat with fenoxaprop if in cool-season grasses.
- Spot treat with nonselective herbicide.

Perennial Grassy Weeds

Like annual grassy weeds, these weeds look like grass. They come back year after year.

Dallisgrass Also known as watergrass, this coarse-textured, highly invasive plant loves the hot, humid conditions found in the South. It spreads via seeds from seed heads that resemble rattlesnake

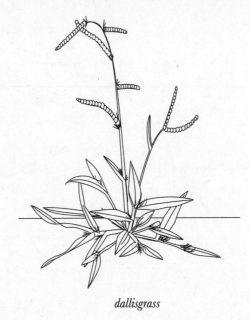

dallisgrass

tails, and it can also form short, thick rhizomes that turn into thick clumps.
Control:

- Hand-pull when plants are young.
- Don't aerate during prime germination season, which is when soil temperatures reach 60°F to 65°F.
- Apply preemergence herbicide when germinating. This is recommended even if some plants have germinated, as seeds will still be in the soil and application will prevent them from cropping up later.
- Use postemergence herbicide containing MSMA or DSMA.

Nimblewill   This perennial grass has fibrous roots and spreads via stolons. It forms dense mats that look like bermudagrass, typically in moist, shady, underfertilized areas.
Control:

- Water and fertilize appropriately. This weed can be crowded out by preferred grasses. It's kind of a weak plant; I rarely see it in what I consider to be well-maintained lawns.

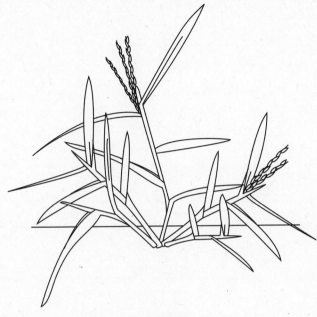

nimblewill

- There are no selective herbicides to control, so you'll have to use glyphosate or fluazifop if you need to get it out now.

Quackgrass This coarse, tall grass has lots of aliases—quake grass, dog grass, twitch grass, devil's grass—which speaks to its ubiquitous nature. It appears across the United States but isn't much of a problem in the South. It spreads aggressively via rhizomes, which makes manual control virtually impossible. It sometimes comes along with straw used to mulch new lawns.

Control:

- Take good care of your lawn. A solid program of mowing, watering, and fertilizing will encourage the turfgrass and discourage the quackgrass.
- Apply glyphosate or fluazifop in May or September when actively growing.

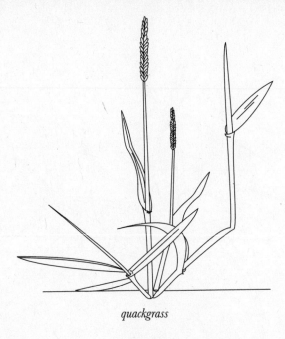

quackgrass

Tall Fescue   If you're growing a stand of tall fescue as turf, it's not a weed. If you're not, it is. As you might remember, tall fescue is a cool-season grass, and, of course, it's a perennial because it comes back year after year.

Control:

- Kill it by covering the affected area with clear plastic for three days. Remove the plastic, cut out the affected area. Reseed.
- Spot treat with glyphosate when clumps appear.
- Treat with the herbicide chlorsulfuron, or sulfosulfuron (if you have a Kentucky bluegrass lawn).

Yellow Nutsedge   Also known as nutgrass or swampgrass, yellow nutsedge has triangular stems with waxy, grasslike, yellowish-green leaves. It reproduces via seed, rhizomes, and small, hard tubers called nutlets, which makes it a tough little plant to control. Given the right conditions—poor drainage and warm weather—one yellow nutsedge tuber can produce almost two thousand plants and upwards of seven thousand new tubers in a single growing season. It's found throughout the United States.

tall fescue

Control:

- If only a few plants, pull by hand. Let a couple of weeks go by, then check the area for any regrowth from nutlets, and repeat.
- Check irrigation frequency and coverage—overwatering favors this weed.
- Improve drainage via aeration or other means.
- Mow at the low end of the range for your grass in spring and early summer, when sedges are most actively growing.
- Fertilize cool-season grasses in the fall after frost.
- Apply postemergence herbicide containing methanearsonate in late spring to early summer, when sedge is actively growing. For best control, time applications to three-leaf to flower growth stage. If you don't catch sedge at this stage, herbicide application won't do much, if anything, to control it. You'll be better off waiting until the following spring.
- If available, halosulfuron, sulfentrazon, or imazaquin-based herbicides also provide control.

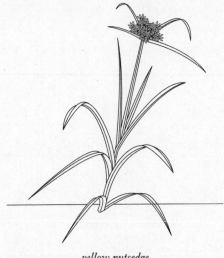

yellow nutsedge

Creeping Bentgrass   You met bentgrasses briefly in chapter 2 when I told you not to grow them. If they appear in your yard because some other danged fool decided to do so, treat them as weeds.

• Kill it by covering the affected area with clear plastic for three days. Remove the plastic, cut out the affected area. Reseed.

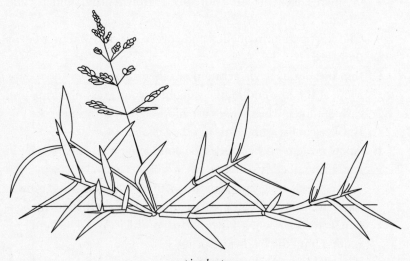

creeping bentgrass

- Spot treat with glyphosate when clumps appear. For best results, paint it on with a brush.
- Spot treat with the nonselective herbicide fluazifop. Be ready to overseed in cool-season lawns.

Broadleaf Weeds

These plants are tenacious, stubborn, and, like all weeds, born with a strong will to survive. What's more, they're tougher to live with, as they disrupt turf uniformity much more than grassy weeds do.

Broadleaf Summer Annuals

Knotweed   Found across the United States, knotweed often pops up in crevices between sidewalks and turf but can appear in stressed-out turf almost anywhere, and especially in areas where soil is dry and compacted. Its tough stems and leaves form dense, wiry mats that can reach as wide as three feet across. It's also a prolific seed producer. It can resemble spurge, especially when it's young. It is the first summer annual to appear every year.

Control:

- Knotweed can be pulled, but not easily. The hard-as-a-rock areas this weed favors make it tough to get all the roots.

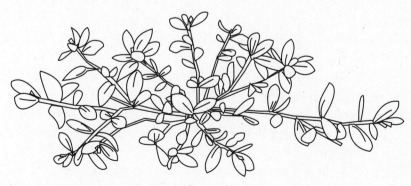

knotweed

Wondering if you have knotweed or spurge? Break one of the stems. If it's spurge, you'll see a milky sap.

- Aerate affected areas. If compaction is due to established paths, consider removing the grass in these areas and installing gravel, pavers, or stepping-stones instead.
- Preemergence herbicides can be effective if applied in late fall or winter.
- Apply 2,4-D or a three-way herbicide combination (2,4-D + MCPP + dicamba) to young plants. If in sidewalk cracks, dab on a little glyphosate. As plants get larger, postemergence herbicides are less effective and you may use a three-way containing carfentrazone.

Oxalis   Another weed found throughout the United States, oxalis (also called yellow wood sorrel) can be a perennial depending on where it grows. It can look a lot like clover when not in flower, but look closer and you'll see the distinctive, heart-shaped leaves that distinguish it from clover. When in bloom, there's no mistaking it, as it has yellow flowers.

Oxalis spreads via seeds that literally burst from their pods when they're ready to fly the coop. They can fly so vigorously, in fact, that they can land several feet away from their mother plant.

Control:

- If not many, hand-pull, as single plants can be easily removed.
- Apply a preemergence herbicide, properly timed.
- Apply a three-way herbicide product when plants are young yet actively growing. Best timing is two weeks after dandelions quit flowering.
- If oxalis appears later in the summer, apply a three-way herbicide containing carfentrazone or triclopyr.

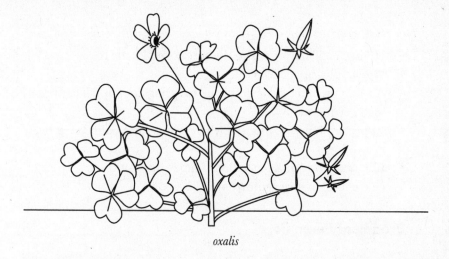

oxalis

Spurge   Two spurges—spotted and prostrate—infest lawns. Both have hairy or purplish-red spotted leaves and red stems, and form low-growing, circular mats. They thrive during the summer and they like dry areas on thin lawns.

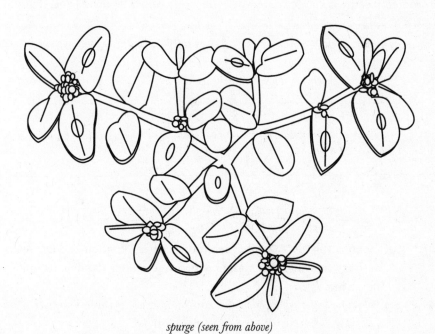

spurge (seen from above)

Control:

- Hand-pull if not extensive. Be sure to get all the roots.
- Water your lawn correctly.
- Apply a preemergence herbicide in spring and/or fall to prevent seed germination.
- Apply a three-way product when plants are young yet actively growing.
- If spurge appears later in the summer, apply a three-way herbicide containing carfentrazone.

Broadleaf Perennials

These plants germinate in the fall, and you can zap them with preemergence herbicides at that time. If you don't get them then, you can treat them with a postemergence herbicide later. Fall, however, is the best time for control.

Broadleaf Plantain   Broadleaf plantain is a shallow, fibrous-rooted weed with large, veiny, oval-shaped leaves. The leaves and stems

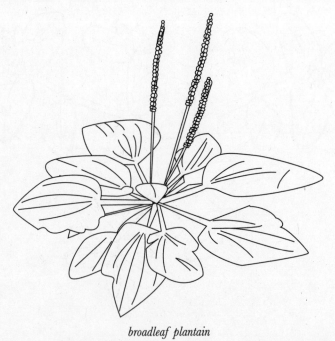

broadleaf plantain

can range from dark green to purplish in color, and can be smooth or covered with short hairs. It grows in a rosette pattern and has seed heads that look like rattails.

June through September is the main growth period for this weed. It spreads by seeds and underground shoots.

Control:

- Broadleaf plantain has shallow roots, which makes it fairly easy to pull by hand. Be sure to get all the roots when you do.
- Apply a three-way herbicide product to established plants in the fall.

Dandelion   You might not recognize some kinds of weeds, but you'd have to be from the planet Neptune not to know this one, as widespread and ubiquitous as it is.

Dandelions are a particular problem, as they spread so easily, both by seeds flying off their puffball seed heads and underground through their thick, fleshy tap roots.

Control:

- Can dig out, but the entire taproot must be removed, as new plants can root from root sections. Don't try to pull by hand; use the appropriate digging tool, which is designed to penetrate deep with minimum damage to surrounding grass plants.
- Keep turfgrass as healthy as possible in general to avoid open spaces where dandelions can take root.

dandelion

- Apply postemergence herbicide in the early fall (just before tree leaves begin to fall) when dandelions are germinating.
- Apply a three-way product in spring two weeks after they flower.

Field Bindweed Also known as creeping jenny, perennial morning-glory, bell-bine, and sheep-bine, this particularly noxious and pervasive perennial weed looks like a flowering vine. It's actually not a bad-looking plant and was probably cultivated as such at one time. Now it's just a bad, bad weed.

Field bindweed is a particular problem in pastures, and it regularly crops up in lawns that are carved from them. If it's in your lawn, you'll know it. Not only will it do a great job of twining around and through just about every grass plant in your yard, it will also wrap itself around things like shrubs, other vines, plants in flower beds, small trees, fence posts—basically almost anything it can find.

This weed has an extensive vertical and lateral root system. Vertical roots can grow as deep as fourteen feet and more. Lateral roots

field bindweed

can turn into secondary vertical roots at various points along their growth. When they do, they start growing both roots and shoots at those points. It also spreads by seeds and rhizomes, with an average plant setting close to six hundred seeds annually. When seeds are a month old, they form a tough, waterproof covering that makes them virtually impossible to kill. All of this makes bindweed extremely difficult to get rid of.

Control:

- Young plants can be controlled by hand-pulling or hoeing, but only if they're very young, about three to four weeks past germination. Older stands will also respond to cultivation or hoeing if you keep at it. Attack them every two to three weeks, as soon as bindweed reaches six inches long, and repeat as frequently as necessary. Water as little and as infrequently as possible.
- If the problem is extremely severe, and you've given up on the grass in the area, cover it all up with black polyethylene mulch. Overlap the edges of the plastic to ensure that no sunlight reaches the soil or the plants. If it does, you'll get bindweed peeping up through the cracks as sure as the sun rises in the desert. Put something over the plastic—mulch, rocks, and so on—both for aesthetic purposes and to hold it in place, as it's going to be there for a while. It can take three years or more of light-exclusion therapy to work, but it will if you give it enough time. That said, bindweed seeds are almost impossible to kill. Be prepared for new bindweed babies to emerge when you take the plastic off, and deal with them as necessary.
- Apply a three-way postemergence herbicide when flowering in spring and in early fall, when active growth starts up again. Combine with quinclorac (Drive) for best control.

Ground Ivy   Also known as creeping charlie, run-away-robin, or gill-over-the-ground, ground ivy is a low-growing broadleaf perennial with round, dark green, scalloped leaves and small purplish flowers in the spring. It spreads through its creeping stems and by seeds.

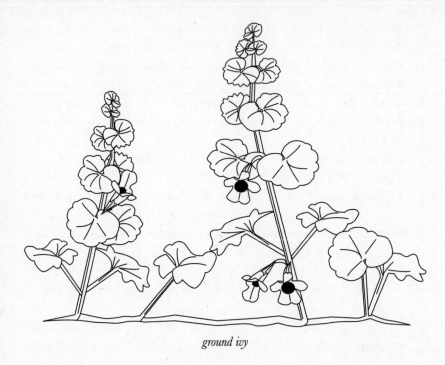

ground ivy

Ground ivy likes moist, shady areas where grass can be a bit thin regardless of what you do, which makes it difficult to get rid of. If grass is sparse in sunny areas, it will invade them, too.

Control:

- Pull young plants by hand in late summer to early fall—mid-August through mid-September.
- Cull thicker, more extensive growth with a dethatching rake. If you take this approach, you'll pull out some grass, too, so have some shade-tolerant grass seed on hand to work into the bare areas.
- Treat extensive stands with a three-way postemergence herbicide in spring (products containing triclopyr are the best here), just prior to and during flowering, and again in early fall when active growth resumes. Combine with quinclorac for best control.

White Clover   You might remember that white clover was part and parcel of the earliest lawns. Since it was ubiquitous and accepted, it

white clover

was also part and parcel of modern-day lawn seed mixes for many years. These days, it's just a plain ol' weed.

White clover is a low-growing plant with three-part leaves and distinctive, white to pinkish white blossoms. It's not the world's worst-looking weed, and some people even find it attractive. What's more, it adds nitrogen to the soil. It can make big brown patches in your lawn in drought conditions, however, and in early fall when it goes dormant. Since it's an aggressive grower on both above- and belowground stems, it's a good idea to get rid of it.

Control:

- Make sure grass is adequately fertilized. Clover is a sign of low fertility; it thrives because it can fix its own nitrogen from the air.
- Spray with three-way postemergence herbicide in the fall.
- In late spring or early summer apply a three-way herbicide with quinclorac, fluroxpyr, or carfentrazone.

NOT WEEDS, BUT NOT WELCOME

Turf algae and mosses are two more turf invaders to know about. Turf algae are single-cell organisms that can take up residence almost anywhere if conditions are right for them. They're not pathogens, and they don't directly infect turf or turfgrasses, but they can grow into turf-damaging mats that interfere with oxygen exchange in the soil. When the mats dry out, they turn into stiff, hard crusts, which makes things worse.

Give them the right soil pH—different algae species have different pH requirements—and the right weather conditions—extended periods of warm, overcast, rainy weather—and an algae bloom can develop very quickly. What's more, it will hang around and compete with your turfgrass as long as conditions remain favorable for its growth.

Control:

- Improve air movement and sunshine in the area by trimming branches on trees and shrubs if possible.
- Avoid frequent shallow watering, especially in warm, humid, overcast conditions.
- If soil is compacted, aerate to improve oxygen flow and surface water drainage.
- One homemade remedy that I've seen work is to use Dawn Ultra dishwashing liquid, mixed at three ounces per gallon of water, and then spray it on, sprinkle it, paint it, whatever. It's believed that the Dawn has an algicide in it, thus contributing to the effectiveness. But know this, the algae will come right back if you don't change the environment; it has no choice, like any other weed.
- Apply algae-control products before crust forms. Iron or other pH-altering materials can create an unfavorable environment for algae growth.

Mosses are primitive plants that form soft, velvety mats over soil surfaces. These mats can get very thick when and where conditions are favorable—typically, in cooler, more humid climates and on lawns with damp, poorly drained, shady areas. If they do, they can choke out grass plants.

There are two main moss groups. One contains chlorophyll and grows on the surface of the soil. The other doesn't and spreads underground. They both reproduce by wind- and moisture-borne spores.

Moss can indicate a variety of issues—drainage problems, compacted soil, too much water, unbalanced soil chemistry, too much shade, or improper fertilization among them. Identify and correct the problem, and getting rid of the moss can be easy.

Control:

- Alter growing conditions so they favor turf over moss. Follow good watering practices. Be sure to let the soil surface dry between applications.
- If possible, trim back branches on trees and shrubs to improve airflow and allow more sun to reach the turf.
- Apply moss-control products containing lime, iron, or copper to alter soil pH when moss is actively growing during spring and summer.

Weeds are always present and help to remind us that a perfect turf is rarely attainable. Mostly, though, weeds are opportunists. They grow where we allow them to because of improper environment or improper practice on our part. Getting rid of weeds is usually simple; staying rid of them often takes a change in practices.

CHAPTER 12

Building Your Herbicide Arsenal

The inside scoop on the best herbicides to have on hand for battling weeds.

Go to any lawn and garden store and you'll see tons of different products on the shelves—enough to send you into a state of brain freeze. There are branded products—some of them so well established and promoted that you'll recognize the names; others not—generics, store brands, you name it. So, how do you choose among them? It's actually pretty easy, once you know a little more about the herbicide business.

The basic things to know about herbicide selection are:

- All annual grassy weeds are best controlled before they germinate in the spring.
- All other weeds are best controlled as small plants, the younger the better.

Pretty easy, right?

The herbicides you need to control them fall into two general categories: preemergence and postemergence.

HITTING WEEDS BEFORE THEY HAVE A CHANCE

Preemergence herbicides are designed to knock out weeds before they even think about poking their heads up from the ground. (Actually, these weeds do germinate but they are killed so early they are never noticed.) In most cases, these herbicides are used on annual grassy weeds, primarily in the spring to battle crabgrass, but they're also applied in the fall to prevent annual bluegrass.

These herbicides stick around for a while—anywhere from ninety to a hundred and twenty days. This residual effect is a good thing, as it will keep controlling weed seedlings through the growing season if you time your application right. If you have a long growing season and heavy weed pressure (bare soil, sparse plants, lots of traffic), however, a second preemergence application at forty-two to sixty days into the growing season will be very beneficial

Most of these products are nonselective, which means they'll kill any seeds they come into contact with. This means you can't use them anywhere you want to start a yard from scratch. If you're establishing a yard vegetatively via sprigs, sod, or plugs, however, you can use these herbicides. Siduron is the sole exception. This herbicide will let grass seeds germinate but will stop summer annual grasses dead in their tracks.

Benefin, bensulide, DCPA, dithiopyr, oxadiazon, pendamethalin, prodiamine, and simazine are examples of preemergence herbicides.

HITTING THEM WHEN THEY'RE UP

Postemergence herbicides control weeds after they germinate. They're the preferred approach for most broadleaf weeds, the second-best approach for controlling crabgrass, and the only hope for controlling most perennial grasses.

For broadleaf weeds, you want a selective postemergence—a product formulated to kill these weeds while leaving desirable plants alone—that contains three chemicals: mecoprop, or MCPP; 2,4-D; and dicamba. This combination is sometimes called Trimec, which is the brand name it was sold under when it was patent-protected. Now it has various names—Three-Way, Weed-B-Gon, lawn weed killer, you name it.

Quinclorac is also relatively safe to use on new grass seedlings, which is key when you're establishing grass in the spring. That said, if you have St. Augustinegrass, centipedegrass, or bahiagrass, tread a little lightly; it will definitely kill the weeds, but it might ding the grass a little. It's fine on zoysiagrass and bermudagrass and all cool-season grasses discussed in this book.

Every store is going to have at least one Trimec-type formulation. Find it and buy it; choose a branded product or go with a generic, it doesn't matter. They'll all kill the vast majority of weeds in your lawn. This is a must-have for your arsenal.

You'll need at least one more selective herbicide to use with Trimec to get broadleaf weeds like creeping charlie and oxalis. Triclopyr and quinclorac are two good choices here. Triclopyr has been around the longest and gives good control when application is timed correctly. Quinclorac is a relatively new herbicide that, when mixed with the three-way combination, is very effective on tough broadleafs and can control crabgrass throughout the season.

Quinclorac is still under patent. It's currently sold only as Drive. It's more expensive than other herbicides and it can be hard to find. It's scheduled to come off patent in 2007, however, so its availability will go up and its price will go down. If there's a LESCO where you are, you can find it there. It's available in 1.5-ounce and sixteen-ounce packages, which will be enough to last you at least a couple of years.

If you live in Alaska, California, New York, Massachusetts, South Carolina, or Vermont, Drive is a no-no for you; these states prohibit its use.

You can go to some larger stores and find a three-way combination herbicide mixed with another herbicide called carfentrazone. This combination is sold under the Spectracide label for summer annual broadleaf weed control. This product can be very good in the summer if you missed the late-spring application window, as it will control weeds like oxalis, spurge, and knotweed.

Perennial weeds can be controlled throughout their life cycles, but earlier is always better. Annual weeds have a sliding scale in terms of control. The later the season, the worse the control.

Broadleaf weeds are controlled with herbicides like Trimec, sometimes in combination with quinclorac (Drive) or carfentrazone. Annual grasses can be controlled with products like MSMA, DSMA, fenoxaprop (Acclaim), and quinclorac. Drive has shown to be the most effective and to have the most activity on mature plants.

GET 'EM ALL

A nonselective herbicide is the final must-have product. This will kill anything and everything green. You can use it on things like sidewalk cracks and other areas where you don't have to worry about killing other plants, and it's also useful if you're renovating your lawn, as it will kill everything in its path. Glyphosate is an excellent choice here. You'll find it as Roundup, its original brand name, but since it's off-patent it's also available under other names.

Other nonselective herbicides include:

- Reward. This herbicide delivers control similar to Roundup but isn't quite as good systemically.
- QuikPro Dry with Roundup. This product contains a quick-kill combo of glyphosate and diquat. Both ingredients are nonselective; only glyphosate is systemic. Neither sticks around too long after application, which means you can plant pretty soon after using them.
- Scythe, which is used for fast burn-down of plant material.
- Brush Killer BK-32, for controlling perennial weeds, good on bamboo.

When All Else Fails   There are other herbicides for battling weeds, but they can be difficult to find, as they're not typically available at your average lawn and garden store or big-box retailer. Turf specialty stores are better bets, but since these stores are aimed at professionals who buy in large quantities, you'll have to follow suit and buy by the gallon (at least). Products like quinclorac might be available in smaller amounts. If not, you'll have to buy the pro sizes or call in a professional to handle the problem.

These herbicides include:

- metsulfuron (sold as Manor), for controlling bahiagrass and other tough broadleafs in warm-season turfgrass
- chlorsulfuron (sold as Corsair), for controlling tall fescue in warm- and cool-season turfgrasses
- halosulfuron (sold as SedgeHammer), for controlling nutsedge
- imazaquin (sold as Image), which controls broadleafs, sedges, and grassy weeds in warm-season grasses
- Fusilade, for nonselective control of grassy weeds in cool-season grasses, particularly good for zoysiagrass
- MSMA and DSMA. These are postemergence herbicides for grassy weeds, crabgrass, dallisgrass, and so on. They'll work on both cool- and warm-season grasses; most require multiple applications to complete the job.

CHOOSING YOUR BREW

Preemergence herbicides for home use are usually applied in granular form, although liquid formulations are available. Broadleaf herbicides are liquid or granular, with the granular formulation coming layered (the herbicides are coated on the granules) or combined with a fertilizer (this is a common form of application for preemergents as well). Liquid products dominate the market for postemergence grassy weed control.

The application method doesn't necessarily match the product's formulation. As an example, an herbicide might be meant to be sprayed on as a liquid, but it must be mixed in a tank of water first. The form can be powder or granules.

Buy separate equipment for applying herbicides. Removing all traces of the chemicals in herbicides from sprayers and spreaders is difficult, and you don't want to run the risk of putting down herbicide, even in minute amounts, when you're using equipment for something other than weed control.

Here's my suggestion for best results: Use a granular product for preemergence control and apply it with a spreader. For broadleaf weeds, go with a liquid application, which will ensure good contact with leaf surfaces. A granular weed-and-feed product is a second-best choice here, as it will miss some weeds. If you do use a granular weed-and-feed, use it in the fall, not the spring. Apply in the morning to wet turf.

Use liquid herbicides applied with a sprayer to control all other weeds.

Applying Them Right

Since herbicides are either spread or sprayed, you'll need a spreader and/or a sprayer to put them on with. In theory, you can get away with one or the other, but in the long run it's best to have both pieces of equipment at your side. Sprayers can be handheld, backpack, or pull behind, depending on the size of your lawn. Rotary spreaders are best for most granular applications. If lawn boundaries are a major concern, then add a drop spreader to your lineup. There are also guard attachments for rotary spreaders, but they can be tricky. Or opt for a new-generation spreader that you can switch from drop to rotary on demand.

In addition to your application equipment, have a measuring cup that you use for measuring herbicides and nothing else (rinse it out into your sprayer), and a good set of rubber gloves. A mask is a great idea when mixing, especially when working with powders.

Timing

Timing is everything in life; has been and always will be. It's no different when applying herbicides for weed control.

Killing weeds is easiest when they're young. Older plants, especially when they're getting ready to flower or set seed heads, are very resistant to herbicides. The problem is, this is also when they're the ugliest, and typically when you most want to kill them.

Take dandelions as an example. They're fairly innocuous before they start flowering; pretty darned ugly when they're in flower, but this is when you'll want to send them to their graves because their bright yellow flowers are disrupting the looks of the turf you've worked so long on. But hold your horses, bucko, this is the worst time to do it. You'll be better off waiting a couple of weeks, after they're done flowering or seeding, as their defenses will be lower then. Do so and you'll probably hit some summer annual weeds as they start germinating too.

The best time for controlling winter annuals and all perennial weeds is in the early fall, right about when the first frost hits or when nighttime temperatures dip below 40°F. This is when they germinate, and they're all at their most vulnerable. A well-timed blanket application over your entire yard will do a nice job of controlling them, leaving you with a much cleaner yard the following spring. What's more, you can use about half as much herbicide in the fall as you would in the spring, as the plants are so small and young.

Summer annual grassy weeds like crabgrass and foxtail are also best controlled when they're young. Here, the best approach is to apply a preemergence herbicide in the early spring before soil temperatures get above 60°F. If you miss this window, postemergence herbicides in the early summer are your best bet, with dithiopyr and MSMA your options. Controlling mature crabgrass is extremely difficult unless you can get your hands on quinclorac (Drive). Usually the best approach, if you

Two to three weeks after dandelions are through seeding is the best bang for your buck for spring weed control. The exact dates will vary, depending on where you live.

miss the window of opportunity with them, is to simply ride things out and let the grass die with the first frost. Overseed and fertilize the affected area, and get ready to control it with a preemergence herbicide the following spring.

To recap:

- Control annual grasses by applying a preemergence herbicide in early spring.
- Control broadleaf weeds by applying a postemergence broadleaf herbicide a couple of weeks after dandelion seed heads are gone. This will also hit some summer annuals before they germinate.
- Control winter annuals and all perennials in the fall with a postemergence herbicide. Circle your calendar for the early fall, as this is your best time to really be successful for the following year. It is two to three times more effective than any other time.

Stay with this program for a couple of years, keep up with your fertilizing and mowing, and you'll be down to occasional spot spraying in the spring for broadleaf weeds, and maybe putting down a preemergence herbicide as an insurance policy. You might even be down to just a little hand-weeding at this point. Your lawn will be the envy of the neighborhood.

Applying Them Right

There's a right way and a wrong way to put herbicides down. Here's the right way:

- Read label directions and precautions carefully, and heed them. This is a must. Herbicide labels contain a lot of information and none of it is to be taken lightly.
- Determine how much herbicide you need, and mix only that amount so you don't have to dispose of what you don't use.
- Mix products carefully to avoid spilling.
- Be sure your equipment is correctly calibrated. Poorly calibrated equipment can lead to poor results if you don't apply

enough of the product, or grass damage if you apply too much. Plus, you run the risk of environmental contamination.

- Store all products and equipment securely, far out of the reach of children and pets.
- Dispose of empty containers and excess product properly.

Most of the time, in most situations, you'll be able to get the vast majority of weeds in your lawn with two or three products. If you learn how to use these products correctly, you'll be the envy of everyone in your neighborhood.

CHAPTER 13

Spots, Blights, and Other Really Ugly Stuff

A five-thousand-square-foot lawn contains some four million turf-grass plants. If the environment surrounding them gets out of balance in some way, lawn diseases can happen. The good news? Most diseases can be avoided if you know how.

We live in a germy world. Stuff like bacteria, funguses, and viruses are always present. What's more, you want them to be. Without them, you don't build up your natural disease defenses. One little germ could spell the death of you.

The same is true for turfgrasses. The organisms that can make them sick are always present in the soil. And, again, you want them to be. Many of these organisms are beneficial. They do good things, like helping break down thatch. Some of them supply essential nutrients to grass roots. Some prey on other organisms that can also cause turf problems.

Like us, grasses have developed both chemical and physical defenses to protect them against disease-causing organisms. Taking care of your lawn properly supports the plants' natural defenses. Most of the time, this is all you have to do to keep things shipshape. But things can happen to weaken those defenses, even on the best-maintained turf. When grass plants let their guard down, for whatever reason, lawn diseases can happen.

Like humans, grass plants are very capable of protecting themselves from things that can make them sick, but are vulnerable when things happen that throw their natural protections out of whack. Unlike humans, who are imbued with things like free choice and will and what-not, and who can maybe avoid behaviors or at least make informed choices about ones that might put us in harm's way, the grass plants in our care aren't so lucky.

When grass plants get sick, they're not to blame. When things go out of kilter in their world, they can't turn their forefingers around and point at themselves or kick themselves in the rear for staying out too late or enjoying that one last tequila shot that their better sense told them not to have.

Sadly, if your lawn comes down with a disease, you probably con-tributed to the problem. But this is an area of lawn geekiness that you might never have to visit if you take care of your lawn right. If you aren't a good caretaker, you can definitely put your grass at risk, and es-pecially so if the conditions are favorable for disease development.

The good news is, things that you might do to make your lawn sick are pretty easy to avoid, and avoid them you should, as this is an area of lawn care that's easiest to deal with by never having to deal with it at all.

HOW DISEASES HAPPEN

Grass at Risk

If every plant is a potential disease host and things that can poten-tially harm them are part and parcel of their surroundings, how does grass get sick?

Every disease, plant-based or human, without exception, has three basic components:

Cool-season grasses are more disease-prone than their warmer-blooded kin. Heat, humidity, and lack of sunshine are the biggest contributors to disease for these grasses. Couple these factors with bad cultural practices and diseases can re-ally get out of hand.

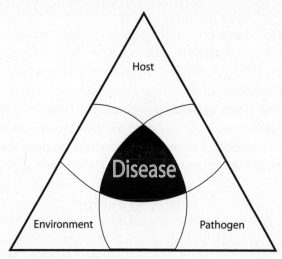

The Disease Triangle. All three components must exist for a disease to develop.

- a host
- a pathogen, or disease-causing agent
- a reason, or the right conditions

The third factor—the right conditions—is the big variable in the turfgrass disease equation. This means that conditions—the environment—play a key role in plant diseases.

When only one or two elements of the equation are present—say, a susceptible plant and a pathogen—disease can't develop. Even plants in less-than-optimum health usually have resistance levels high enough to keep them safe. But it's a delicate balance. Change the equation by adding conditions favorable to disease development, and that delicate balance can quickly become anything but.

There are two big contributors to "favorable conditions": you, and Mother Nature. Between the two of you, there's lots you can do to create disease-favorable conditions.

Moisture is the biggest factor regulating turf diseases, as fungi, the organisms that cause most of them, are moisture-dependent. Too much moisture is typically the culprit, but not always. This one, obviously, you can control to a certain extent with your own watering practices, or if rainfall is the issue, drainage plans.

Even when you plant the right grass in the right climate, some are more likely to get certain diseases than others. All grasses have their Achilles' heels when it comes to diseases, and none of them are disease-free. This means that dealing with diseases is part and parcel of dealing with turf. Plant Kentucky bluegrass and you'll need to be on guard for things like leaf spot and powdery mildew. Switch to perennial ryegrass and you'll have to watch for things like pythium blight and brown patch.

Good ol' Mom, on the other hand, has her hand firmly on the controls of the other big factor: temperature. There isn't much you can do about this variable beyond choosing the right grass for your area and taking care of it right. If you push the envelope and plant a species that's maybe a little borderline for where you live, you increase the probability for disease, as the plant isn't as well adapted to the area. Get a little loose about taking care of it, and the probability of disease-favorable conditions developing also goes up.

Of all the disease-causing organisms that can wreak havoc with your lawn, you really only have to worry about fungi, as they're behind practically all lawn diseases. Viruses can cause lots of different plant-based diseases, but they typically focus their attack on things other than grasses. St. Augustinegrass decline, or SAD, is the only major virus-linked lawn disease. Bacteria can contribute to some plant diseases, but they rarely cause lawn diseases.

So, fungi are the focus here. Knowing more about them, and why and how they can become a problem, can go a long way toward your never having to deal with their ugly side.

Fungi, Friend

Simply put, we couldn't live without fungi. They're some of the world's most important organisms. Without them, we wouldn't have lifesaving drugs like penicillin and other antibiotics. Things like mushroom burgers or grilled portobello sandwiches? Not on the menu, as mushrooms are fungi. And forget about quaffing a cold beer when you're hot and sweaty and itchy after mowing on a hot day. Fungi are what power the fermentation process in things like beer, champagne, and bread.

Fungi don't do photosynthesis, which means they have to feed on other things, like dead organic matter—thatch—and other stuff that falls to the ground. If you've ever shuffled through a pile of wet leaves during the fall and come across some yucky-looking stuff that maybe looked like mold, it was probably fungi going about their job. As they munch, they convert the materials in these tissues into other compounds—carbon, nitrogen, and other essential mineral nutrients—that they and other organisms can use.

The vast majority of fungi aren't problem children. They go about their jobs pretty quietly. But not all fungi are friendly. And sometimes even friendly fungi can go bad.

Fungi, Foe

Fungi can also cause a number of plant and animal diseases: in humans, fungi are the organisms behind ringworm, athlete's foot, and several more serious diseases. Plant diseases caused by fungi include rusts, smuts, and leaf, root, and stem rots.

Unfriendly fungi, or pathogens, fall into two main categories. Some are parasitic, meaning they feed off living hosts instead of dead tissue. These fungi are especially skilled at invading plants, as they really, really need what's inside of them. In fact, most fungi in this group can't live outside of plants.

Other unfriendly fungi are facultative saprophytes, which is the technical term for good fungi gone bad. Even these fungi are beneficial most of the time, but if plants are weakened in some way, they'll push their way in. Reason enough to keep plants healthy by following good cultural practices.

When fungi invade plants, they develop thin, transparent fibers called hyphae. These fibers eventually twist or mat together to form fungal bodies called mycelia. At this point, plants are considered infected. After an incubation period lasting anywhere from several days to several weeks, disease symptoms will begin appearing. On individual plants, symptoms include leaf spots and blights, wilting, yellowing,

The spots that indicate many plant diseases represent the entry points for the fungi. Cells at the entry sites quickly die from a high concentration of toxic compounds that accumulate in them. Small circles of dead cells, called necrotic lesions, then form at the sites. These spots can be great diagnostic clues, as they're typically unique to the disease that causes them.

stunted growth, and root rot. Symptoms can also appear as spots, patches, circles, or rings on affected areas.

More often than not, more than one fungus is to blame for plant diseases, which is one thing that makes diseases so tough to identify. Oftentimes, a pathogenic fungus first wreaks its harm, only to be joined by one or more friendly fungi gone bad. When this happens, they can do serious damage very quickly.

Most of the time, beneficial fungi and other microorganisms living in the turf keep pathogenic fungi in check. Given the right conditions, however, pathogenic fungi can increase in number, overwhelm their natural enemies, and seek out vulnerable grass plants. The result: lawn disease.

Fungi reproduce by dust-sized particles called spores. Just about anything can spread them—wind, water, people, animals, tools—you name it and spores will ride it. They'll even travel from place to place in soil and plant material. The good news about spores is that they're short-lived. If they don't land on a suitable host within a few hours of developing, they typically die. The bad news about them is that they can quickly cause diseases if they find good hosts and the conditions are right.

Mycelia can take on various hues, depending on the fungi, and are often used for identification purposes.

Fungi can overwinter in soil, dead plant material, or in the grass plants themselves. Many fungi form tough mycelia masses called sclerotia. These can stay viable in soil or on dead plant tissue for months, sometimes years. Again, when conditions are ripe for invasion, they'll attack.

IPM FOR TURFGRASS DISEASES

Integrated Pest Management (IPM) is pretty easy when it comes to turfgrass diseases, for a couple of reasons. First, remember the disease triangle. All three parts must exist for disease to develop. Take away any one, and, voilà, no disease.

You can positively affect two of these factors—vulnerable plants and favorable environment—with good cultural practices. As such, good lawn care should always be the first line of defense. Anything you do to diminish or remove the conditions favoring disease development will prevent these diseases from happening or send them packing as quickly as possible when they do occur.

Second, pesticides—in this case, fungicides—are the only other available control. We've tried to develop others, but nothing much has come of it so far.

Battling turf diseases with fungicides on home lawns is almost never necessary, though. You should use them only if the outbreak is widespread or weather conditions are such that problems are going to continue for a while.

Taking Care of Business

I'll say it again. Proper lawn maintenance will minimize or eliminate two components—vulnerable plants and favorable conditions—that lawn diseases need to erupt. What's more, it can cure lots of fungi-based diseases even after they rear their ugly heads.

Let's review the specific elements of proper lawn care that can prevent and/or cure grass diseases.

Watering Remember, fungi love moisture. You can't control what falls from the skies, but you are master of the universe when it comes to your watering techniques. If they include things like

Always keep a close eye on moisture levels in shady spots. They never need as much water as sun-kissed areas do. If you have an automatic irrigation system and some of the heads are in the shade, you might have to shorten watering times or change the nozzles to ones that put down less water.

flooding your lawn and leaving it wet for long periods or watering after dark, you can almost bet on lawn diseases knocking at your grass's door.

Watering in the morning is always a good idea, as it gives your lawn time to dry off before sundown, but it's an especially good practice if other conditions are ripe for diseases. To ward off almost all lawn diseases, follow the other good watering practices, which you should know by heart by now. Water to match root depth, minimize watering after dark, especially when it's hot and humid, and let the lawn dry out between applications.

Fertilizing   Applying too little or too much fertilizer—in particular, quick-release or soluble nitrogen—can open the door to many fungal diseases. You always want to establish and follow a fertilizing program that matches your grass and soil types. If a turfgrass disease breaks out, see if there's a fertility component and adjust your program accordingly.

Never overfertilize. Doing so always causes problems, but it can bring on diseases faster than fast when it's hot and humid out. I know I've harped on this a lot throughout this book, but always remember, when it comes to fertilizer, twice as much is never twice as good. And remember, you can always add more fertilizer to your lawn, but you can't take it off. It's not like blankets on a bed.

If you have any questions about your soil's fertility levels, get them tested.

Mowing   Cutting your grass lower than its minimum recommended height and continually scalping your grass are, simply put, bad practices, whether or not diseases are a concern. It weakens the grass

Turf diseases associated with low fertility include rust, red thread, and dollar spot. The good news is that a simple light, soluble nitrogen application can clear up symptoms in a hurry.

and makes it less able to cope with any stressors, including fungal attacks. Not keeping your lawn mower's blade sharpened is another bad practice. Mowing with a dull blade inflicts jagged cuts on leaf ends. Grass that's working overtime at healing its wounds is easy prey for disease invaders during stressful conditions.

Aeration/Thatch Removal   Simply put, fungi love thatch. Not only do they find grass detritus a cozy hiding spot, they even help break it down. Nice of them, isn't it? Excessive thatch, however, can create overly moist conditions where fungi can run amok. Punching holes in it or raking it up periodically will help keep everything in balance.

Chemical Control for Fungi

Fungicides are the pesticides that kill fungi or stop spores from germinating. Like other pesticides, most fungicides fall into two basic categories: contact and systemic. Contact fungicides coat plant surfaces with a protective barrier that keeps fungi at bay. They can't help plants already under attack, but they will stop diseases from spreading to other plants. They'll work on most lawn diseases.

Mowing can spread turfgrass diseases, as the fungi can ride the blades from yard to yard. If you use a lawn service, ask what they do to keep diseases from spreading. Simply hosing down the underside of mowing equipment is all that's necessary if there's an outbreak.

Fungal diseases can become resistant to chemicals after repeated applications, which is another reason why fungicides should be the approach of last resort.

Systemic fungicides enter plants through roots and/or leaves and kill fungi lurking within. They're also effective on most lawn diseases, and they're the only products that can tackle systemic diseases.

If you have to use fungicides, know that one application isn't enough to control most diseases. Rain and irrigation will wash away contact products. Systemic products last longer but will lose their effectiveness over time.

I don't make specific fungicide recommendations here for one simple reason: I don't want you to use them! Focusing on cultural practices is the far better approach, and is typically all that's necessary. Pay attention to your lawn and let it tell you what it needs. Make your first reaction to spots and blights proactive instead of reactive. Think about what these things are trying to communicate. Maybe it's time to fertilize or aerate. Maybe you're watering too much. Maybe you were too lazy to rake up the leaves last fall, and now there's ugly moldy stuff cropping up as the snow melts. So, go out and rake them up now.

Simply doing right by your lawn will take care of most diseases. Trust me.

THE DIRTY DOZEN (PLUS ONE)

I'd like to think that you'd never have to read this section. You might like to think it, too. But here's the deal: You could do everything right with your lawn, and the weather could knock things out of whack anyway. The result: blotches, spots, and other indications that a disease is present. They might be isolated—remember, conditions must be favorable for diseases to appear and those conditions might not be uniform across your lawn. Powdery mildew can form on shaded turf but not in sunny spots. Mushrooms might crop up where an old stump was two years after you ground it out. Dollar spot or red thread might appear on hilly areas that dry out before the rest of your lawn does.

Unless you're a plant pathologist—an expert who diagnoses and manages plant diseases—figuring out the specific problem-causer can be tough. Not only can diseases be extremely difficult to diagnose, they often look like things that aren't disease, like insect damage, fertilizer burn, drought damage, even dog pee. Always suspect things like these before diseases.

Just as you now know that turfgrass cannot lie, also know that it will never die naturally in straight lines. Always look for patterns when you see a problem. If you see them, you can then pinpoint the problem a lot easier. If you can see a straight line, there's probably something other than a disease going on. For example, if you walk outside and you see a bunch of brown grass, then you look at it closer and see that it's a square patch of brown grass, you might then realize that it's the exact same shape as your septic tank, and that maybe the problem's related to the fact that the soil there is very shallow and it dries out fast, and so does the grass. So, instead of suspecting a disease, you know the problem's because the grass is dried out.

I'm not saying that turf won't get diseases, it does, but when you see a disorder in your turf, look for a pattern first. Always look for a pattern.

That said, there are some basic clues, some characteristic signs, and a few symptoms you can count on. One is timing. Some diseases prefer spring and/or fall, when conditions are cool and wet. Others like hot and humid weather during the summer. Remember the disease triangle. Other key clues relate to where you live and to the type of grass you're growing, as some diseases prefer certain species over others.

As you go through the profiles, you'll see some common themes: over- or underfertilizing, too much moisture, compaction, and so on. Once again, this speaks to the basic cause of these diseases—bad lawn care—and to the cure—good lawn care. I can't repeat this often enough. Proper cultural controls are key to controlling all diseases. Always start with them first. Stick with the program, give things a little time, and diseases usually clear up.

One May, a woman in Colorado called me to report an odd problem she thought I could help with. A month earlier a dead spot about the size of a card table appeared in her lawn. Four weeks later, the dead spot had spread to encompass her entire lawn. She'd been putting down insecticidal soap but hadn't seen any improvement. My first thought was: insects in Colorado, not very likely, and in April even less. So I told her to describe her lawn to me. She said it was an enclosed lawn with brick walls on three sides and the house on the fourth. I then asked her if any of the grass was alive, and she said just a little bit of it along the fence lines. Next question—where the gas line came into her house. She said, "Right under the front door, I think." I told her to call the gas company. She called back to report that sure enough, there was an underground gas leak. She had actually smelled gas in the area recently, but had dismissed it.

If she had told me that there were spots on the grass that were still alive, I might have suspected some sort of a disease, but with the whole yard involved, it was extremely unlikely that something from nature was the cause.

If cultural controls don't work and the problem continues, or the outbreak is really severe, you might have to resort to a fungicide. Before you do, dig a sample from the problem area and take it to your local county extension office for a firm diagnosis so you know which fungicide to get. Remember that wonky weather patterns can cause lots of fungal diseases. Chances are pretty good that if you're having problems with your lawn, other people are too. The county folks should have a pretty good idea of what's going on, and should be able to advise you based on what they're observing in other lawns.

The diseases here are by no means the only ones that can crop up in turfgrass, but they're the ones you're most likely to encounter. Since this book doesn't concentrate on lawn diseases I didn't include pictures, but don't be afraid to search the Internet and look at some nice color pictures of them.

Brown Patch

This fungal disease causes—you guessed it—circular brown patches, which can range from a few inches to several feet in size. It first appears as rough circles of grass that look a little off—sickly and/or thin. In humid conditions, you might see a dark, smoky ring around the patches in early morning, and especially if the grass is short. This will disappear as the day goes on, leaving a light brown or straw-colored patch in its wake. The grass plants might look like they're drenched with water, but the moisture here is actually the contents of dead grass cells.

Brown patch is caused by a common soil-borne fungus that attacks all turfgrasses and many other plants. This disease can erupt in any high-humidity area and is a particular problem in the Southeast with its hot, humid summers. It likes lawns with thick thatch layers that are overly wet and overly fertilized. It can affect any grass but is most problematic with Kentucky bluegrass, centipedegrass, St. Augustinegrass, tall fescue, and ryegrass.

How it happens.

Too much water and not enough oxygen are key contributors to brown patch. Excessive nitrogen fertilization will also contribute.

How to avoid it.

Always let grass dry out between watering and water early in the morning so leaves aren't wet when night falls. Avoid watering at night if temperatures aren't below 60°F. Keep an eye on the thatch layer, and aerate regularly if there are soil layering issues. When fertilizing, go with light and frequent applications of soluble fertilizers in problem areas. Avoid overfertilizing, especially in the summer when it's hot and humid, as it will contribute to excessive thatch buildup.

How to fix it.

Check watering and fertilizing schedules and decrease or stop. Definitely turn off an automatic sprinkler and begin watering only sparingly, just enough to keep the turfgrass plants alive. I can almost categorically tell you that the grass will improve immediately. Increase light and air circulation by thinning out tree branches in shady areas.

Correct drainage problems if present. Test the soil for nutrient imbalances and correct if necessary.

Dollar Spot

Dollar spot appears as small, round dead spots that typically measure about two to three inches wide. They also sport cottony mycelium that, should you come across it on an early-morning walk, looks like a spiderweb. Grass in dead spots looks like it got a bad bleach job. Over time, the spots can grow together and create one big area of dead grass.

Dollar spot is very common in weather conditions that result in morning dew—warm days and cool nights. It's most problematic in late summer in the more humid areas of the Midwest, South, and Pacific Northwest. It likes Kentucky bluegrass a lot, but can also infect bermudagrass, zoysiagrass, bahiagrass, ryegrass, and fescues.

How it happens.
Consistently high moisture levels in turf will bring it on. Spotty or infrequent fertilizing will make it worse.

How to avoid it.
Make sure grass dries out before the sun sets by watering in early morning. Aeration can also help moisture levels. Follow a regular fertilizing program, making sure nitrogen levels are where they should be.

How to fix it.
Grass can grow out of this disease. You can help it by implementing and following a regular fertilization program, and especially by keeping

Dollar spot can look a lot like brown spot. The difference between the two (besides the fact that they're caused by different fungi): dollar spots sink into the ground.

an eye on nitrogen levels. In the North, on cool-season grasses, a light dose of urea (a half pound of nitrogen per thousand square feet) watered in works wonders. Always consider this remedy first. Core cultivate problem areas, and watch your watering practices. If the problem persists, consider planting a more resistant grass or a grass mixture that includes less susceptible varieties.

Fairy Ring

Fairy rings are dark green or brown in color and can range from a few inches to more than fifty feet wide. Their shape reflects their growth habit—they start at a central point and expand outward from there, and can spread as wide as several feet in just one year. In the spring and fall, especially after heavy rainfall or excessive watering, mushrooms will frequently crop up around them. These indicate the spot where a new fairy ring will grow, fed by fungal strands—mycelia—spreading through the soil. Look closely, and you might be able to see the strands in the thatch and soil.

This disease is caused by fungi that feed on wood debris or other organic matter in the soil. As such, fairy rings often mark the spots where trees used to be. At first, the grass in the rings is darker and fairly lush. As they grow, they often develop inner rings of brown or dead grass. These rings are caused by a lack of moisture from dense fungal growth.

Fairy rings can show up in any turf at any time during spring and summer.

Why it happens.
Wood left behind by tree stump removal or buried in some other way; other buried organic debris.

Fairy ring gets its name from a centuries-old belief that the rings appeared where fairies had danced the night before.

How to avoid it.

Since it's difficult, if not impossible, to remove all of the wood when chipping out tree stumps, good cultural practices are your best defense against fairy rings.

How to treat it.

Reduce thatch and improve water flow by aerating to keep moisture stress to a minimum. Good cultural practices can help prevent brown or dead grass rings from forming and mask the appearance of darker green rings to a certain extent. Remove wood and/or organic debris from soil if possible. Don't just dig out what you find; take out everything in the area down to about one foot and about one foot beyond the ring. Toss the bad stuff, add fresh, clean soil to the hole, and reseed the area. Mowing or raking will take care of the mushrooms.

Gray Snow Mold

Gray snow mold is common in areas where the snow flies early and stays on the ground for a long time. As snow cover melts, it will show up as patches of brown or straw-colored grasses up to two feet wide. Grayish white mycelia, which give this disease its name, will mat grass down.

Cool-season grasses are targets for gray snow mold.

Why it happens.

Compromised oxygen flow in the soil caused by compaction and/or excessive thatch, lush growth from nitrogen overfertilizing, leaving leaves on the ground during the winter.

How to avoid it.

Aerate soil to improve oxygen and water flow. Don't overfertilize. Keep mowing your grass as long as it's growing. Keep thatch level under control. Rake up leaves in the fall.

How to treat it.

Light infections usually recover on their own when temperatures heat up. Rake matted spots when they appear to improve air circulation.

Melting Out and Leaf Spot

These two diseases were classified as one until fairly recently. Thanks to ongoing research, we now know they're caused by two separate pathogens. Since the damage they cause looks similar and they've been a couple for so long, however, I'll discuss them together here.

These diseases form lesions on grass blades. The size, shape, and color of the lesions vary depending on the grass, but they all result in the same thing—leaf and tiller death. As the disease progresses, lots of leaves and tillers die, resulting in thin, or "melted out," turf.

Both pathogens typically target cool-season grasses. Older, more common Kentucky bluegrass varieties are particular favorites.

Why it happens.

Poor cultural practices, in particular scalping or mowing too short; overfertilizing, especially in the spring; and over- or underwatering. Excessive thatch also provides safe harbor for both pathogens.

How to avoid it.

Don't scalp your lawn; cut back on nitrogen fertilizing, especially in mid-spring. Follow good watering practices. Water early in the day; make sure grass is dry at night. If establishing a new lawn with Kentucky bluegrass, choose a newer variety bred to resist these diseases.

How to treat it.

Cloudy, wet weather favors both pathogens. If you can wait things out, the sun often takes care of a big part of the problem.

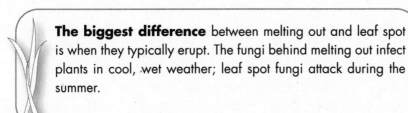

The biggest difference between melting out and leaf spot is when they typically erupt. The fungi behind melting out infect plants in cool, wet weather; leaf spot fungi attack during the summer.

Necrotic Ring Spot

Once known as fusarium blight, this is another fungal disease that causes patchy grass. Like other patch diseases, it creates a frog-eye pattern—rings of dead grass surrounding live grass. As the disease progresses, the spots can grow together to form one huge blighted area.

Necrotic ring spot, or NRS, likes cool, wet weather in spring and fall. Its preferred targets are Kentucky bluegrass, perennial ryegrass, and fescues, but it's not picky and will attack other cool-season and warm-season grasses as well.

Why it happens.

Lack of oxygen from soil compaction, particularly on steep slopes and unprotected areas. High turf temperatures from excessive thatch development and poor air circulation. Overfertilizing—in particular, too much nitrogen. Soil layering can also cause it, which means that NRS is often a problem in newly sodded lawns, where the soil in the sod is finer textured than the soil on the site. The common theme here is that all sodded grasses can be poorly rooted due to soil layering, susceptible to NRS, and difficult to manage after infection because they were the wrong plants for the site. Bottom line, this disease is caused by soil layering, and you have to change conditions by core cultivating. One simple way to tell if you have a soil layering problem is if you can still pull up your sod after six months or a year.

How to avoid it.

Control thatch by aerating and dethatching. Core cultivate to break up soil layering if lawn has been sodded and sod soil is incompatible

Necrotic ring spot resembles summer patch. The difference between them: summer patch is a warm-weather disease; necrotic ring spot is more prevalent in spring and fall.

with site. Finally, you can plant resistant grass varieties or species—Midnight, America, and Majestic Kentucky bluegrass varieties have shown moderate resistance.

How to treat it.

If temperatures are high, a light watering at midday might slow down grass death in stressed turf. If you can't core cultivate right away, the grass will have to grow in the top layer, which means you'll have to go to daily watering and monthly nitrogen applications to get the grass through the summer stress. You might have to core cultivate annually for several years to totally work through this problem and eliminate the soil layering.

Pink Snow Mold

Also called Microdochium patch, pink snow mold is a bit of a misnomer, as it doesn't require snow to grow, just cool, wet weather. It's most likely to appear from late fall to the middle of the spring, and is common in temperate coastal areas.

Pink snow mold appears as small circles ranging from tan to blackish brown in color. As the grass dies, the spots turn tan or white. In cool, wet weather, slimy, whitish-pink mycelia will cover the spots, hence the name.

Pink snow mold likes cool-season grasses, especially Kentucky bluegrass and fescues, but will also attack bermudagrass and zoysiagrass.

Why it happens.

Lack of oxygen flow from compaction and/or excessive thatch, lush growth from too much nitrogen fertilization, and leaving leaves on the ground during the winter.

You'll often see pink and gray snow mold grouped together, but they're caused by different fungi.

How to avoid it.

Aerate soil to improve oxygen and water flow. Don't overfertilize. Keep mowing your grass as long as it's growing. Keep thatch level under control. Rake up leaves in the fall. Areas where snowbanks form are prime snow mold targets, as are any areas where leaves collect and stay on the ground over the winter. Rake these areas as soon as the snow melts.

How to treat it.

Light infections typically recover on their own as soon as the sun starts to shine on the grass, whether the clouds go away or the snow does. You can help things along by raking matted spots as they appear, which will give plant crowns a much-needed breath of fresh air. A small dose of urea (a third to a half pound of nitrogen per thousand square feet) will give affected areas a shot in the arm and help them recover faster. Apply to the entire area; don't just throw fertilizer at the affected spots.

Powdery Mildew

Powdery mildew gets its name from the light-colored powder—it looks a little like dried milk—that forms on leaf blades. The powder is a combination of mycelia and spores. It's mostly unsightly and it typically doesn't kill plants, but it can weaken and thin the grass and make it more susceptible to other diseases.

Powdery mildew likes cool, damp conditions and often crops up during extended stormy periods when skies are overcast more than not. Shady areas with poor air circulation are ideal spots for this fungus. Excessive fertilization also favors it. Kentucky bluegrass, especially when grown in the shade, is a powdery mildew favorite.

Why it happens.

Impaired air circulation; excessive fertilization.

How to avoid it.

Reduce shade; improve air circulation by pruning surrounding trees and shrubs. Monitor fertilizing and watering in shaded areas; avoid excesses of both.

How to treat it.

If it's cloudy for a long time, the symptoms will disappear with the first sign of sun. If the grass is badly thinned by powdery mildew in shaded areas, reseed the area with grasses better adapted to shaded conditions.

Pythium Blight, a.k.a. Grease Spot

Pythium blight first shows up as small, irregular-shaped greasy-looking spots. As the disease progresses, the grass leaves die and the patches fade from green to light brown. Cottony mycelium, best seen in early morning, usually accompanies the spots.

This fungal disease can happen anywhere in the United States but is especially common in the Southeast and after summer rains in the West. Warm, humid weather anywhere favors it. Water and equipment spread it easily; you might see mycelium strands growing along drainage lines or in a pattern matching the one you used the last time you mowed. As such, this disease can spread rapidly and kill large areas in a matter of hours.

Pythium blight will attack all cool-season grasses, with ryegrass being most susceptible. It will also attack bermudagrass if conditions are right. It can attack newly seeded cool-season grasses, especially if (1) you seed in the summer when it's hot and humid and you're out of the establishment window; (2) you have drainage issues and water is sitting around after it rains or you water; and (3) you have seeded too heavily and you have lots of small, weak, diminutive plants—in other words, bunches of small plants trapped in humidity, thus making them more prone to disease.

Why it happens.

Heavy use and/or compacted soil creates ideal conditions, especially during warm, humid weather and especially along drainage lines or where excess water sits for any length of time. High soil pH makes problems worse.

How to avoid it.

Take good care of your lawn in general. Aerate to decrease thatch and improve water penetration. Don't overfertilize or overwater, especially during hot and humid conditions.

How to treat it.

Have soil tested for pH levels; treat if overly alkaline. Prune back tree and shrub branches to improve air circulation. Stay off infected areas to slow disease spread. Cut watering back as far as possible. This is one disease that can merit fungicide application if it's really active, especially during the new yard establishment process (particularly if you're establishing in late spring or summer).

Red Thread

Red thread is what the pink, gooey hyphae of the fungus that causes this disease looks like. It shows up first as water-soaked patches of grass in the spring. Infected blades soon die and turn light tan when they dry out. In humid weather, the hyphae grow on the infected grass blades and sheaths. They also grow beyond the leaves themselves, at which point they'll form small thread masses that are easily seen.

Red thread can appear almost anywhere but it's rarely serious enough to kill a lawn. It prefers cool, moist weather and lawns planted with fine fescue, perennial ryegrass, and Kentucky bluegrass. Bermudagrass is also susceptible.

Why it happens.

Underfertilizing and overwatering; poor soil drainage.

How to avoid it.

Take better care of your lawn in general. Check fertilizer requirements for your grass and establish an appropriate program. Follow good cultural practices when watering. Aerate to reduce thatch and improve airflow.

How to treat it.

Fertilize first. Use a light area application if in between regular applications. Test soil for pH level, and amend as necessary.

Rust

Rust crops up as small red spores on leaf blades. A good infestation can turn your entire lawn yellowish orange, which can be alarming.

Walk through it, and the spores will turn your shoes a lovely yellowish orange, too.

This fungal disease can happen almost anywhere and typically appears during moderately warm weather on dewy lawns. It will develop during the summer and keep going into fall.

Heat-stressed Kentucky bluegrass and ryegrass lawns are particularly rust-prone. It can also appear on tall fescue and zoysiagrass.

Why it happens.

Spotty fertilizing resulting in low nitrogen levels, excessive moisture, soil compaction.

How to avoid it.

Establish and follow a solid fertilization program, and take better care of your lawn in general. Aerate regularly.

How to treat it.

Apply the "miracle dose" of a half pound of urea fertilizer per thousand square feet of turf. Trim tree branches in shady areas to improve airflow and increase sunlight.

Slime Mold

Slime molds are white, gray, or yellow masses that feed on decaying organic matter in the soil. They reproduce by forming tiny, powdery spore balls on grass blades that can range in color from white to bluish gray to black. Like powdery mildew, slime mold spores coat grass blades. If the coating builds up enough, grass blades can turn yellow from lack of sunlight.

Slime molds are not fungi, but they were long thought to be and their life cycles somewhat resemble those of fungi, so they're often lumped together with fungi when the subject of turf diseases comes up. When they grow on things like bark mulch, they can resemble dog vomit, prompting panicky calls to the vet by concerned dog owners who think their pets are sick.

Slime molds can pop up anywhere, especially in cool areas, and will appear after heavy rains or too much watering in spring, summer, or fall. Slimed areas can range from a few inches to several feet in size. All turfgrasses and some lucky weeds are slime mold targets.

Why it happens.
Too much moisture.

How to avoid it.
Reduce supplemental watering. Prevent standing water.

How to treat it.
Slime molds often disappear on their own when climate conditions (or your watering habits) no longer favor them. If they don't, watering them down, brushing them off, or raking them out will make short work of them.

Summer Patch

Formerly grouped with necrotic ring spot and called *fusarium* blight, this disease is caused by a soil-borne fungus that attacks grass roots. It crops up during hot, dry weather, often after a wet period, as crescent-shaped areas of dead turfgrass or circular patches with green centers that look a little like frog eyes. Underground, infected plants are rotted and are brown to black in color. Aboveground, plants die from drought stress.

Summer patch is one of the most destructive diseases of Kentucky bluegrass, but it can affect many grasses, including fescues. It's particularly difficult to diagnose, as the symptoms are so similar to necrotic ring spot. Lab tests are typically required for firm diagnosis.

Why it happens.
Heat stress; soil compaction; excessive thatch buildup, often worse on exposed sites and steep slopes.

How to avoid it.
Follow a balanced cultural program. Aerate regularly to relieve compaction and excess thatch. Don't overfertilize, especially during the summer. Plant resistant grasses.

How to treat it.
Take better care of your lawn in general.

Remember, the best way to control turfgrass diseases is to be your lawn's best buddy. Take good care of it, and evil lawn diseases may never darken your door, or your lawn's roots.

CHAPTER 14

What's Eating Your Grass?

With something like forty million insects in a typical acre of grass, there's no way to get rid of all of them. Nor would you want to, as some types of insects are actually good for your lawn. Here's how to tell the good from the bad, and how to keep the undesirable from getting out of hand.

For whatever reason, insects scare turf managers. Weeds don't seem to bother them, diseases they can prevent with good cultural practices, but with insects they have this fear that they can appear overnight and wipe out turf. It's not very likely, it doesn't happen all that much, but they just don't seem to get over this screaming fear.

Bottom line is, whenever we have educational courses regarding insects, we can get turfgrass managers' attention very quickly. I think one of the reasons is you can't see insects. You've got to go digging to physically see them. At least the weeds aren't hiding out.

Insects are always present whether you like it or not. And your knee-jerk reaction will probably be to get rid of them, especially if your grass is turning yellow or brown and looking a little patchy. But the truth of the matter is, you have to live with them, you'll never be able to control all of them, and the vast majority of them are beneficial.

Of the more than 800,000 insect species on planet Earth, less than 1 percent are considered pests. Of these, less than 100 are considered turf pests. These you do want to control. I didn't say get rid of. Control.

In most cases, insect damage is in short verse because it's only during a certain portion of its life cycle that the insect chews or feeds on turfgrass plants. As the insect moves from one stage of its life cycle to another, it moves out of that feeding frenzy. For the most part, insects live symbiotically with your nice, healthily rooted lawn and no one knows the difference. Oftentimes the insects have natural predators that also keep them in control. Our worst insect pests in the United States are beetles inadvertently introduced here that have no natural local predators. The best example is the Japanese beetle, which you'll read more about later on.

Turf that's properly taken care of can harbor fairly large insect populations without turning as much as a blade. If certain insects rear their ugly heads and do some serious damage, it's usually because you, the caretaker of the turf that they're frolicking in, gave them entrée in some way.

Here's what to do if that's what you've done.

PROBLEM, WHAT PROBLEM?

Since severe infestations can mean using chemicals that can disrupt other aspects of turf health, first up is making sure that something else isn't going on. As an example, most folks think drought damage or sprinkler malfunction when turf turns brown. But turf can also dry up if hungry grubs are doing damage to its root system.

The list of "something else" is actually fairly lengthy. Before you suspect insects, be sure to rule out things like:

- stealth dog peeing
- fertilizer accidents or misuse
- excessive herbicide use
- drought stress and/or damage
- disease

Scalped grass and excessive thatch can also give insect false positives.

Insect damage also tends to be more severe in lawns that are mowed short, watered frequently, and overfertilized—in short, lawns that are getting way too much attention, and not in a good way. This doesn't mean, however, that leaving lawns alone will make them less

Insect damage can be direct, meaning that the bugs themselves cause it, or indirect, meaning that the damage comes from animals tearing up your turf in search of tasty insect meals. The latter can be more destructive than the former, and can happen when the insects themselves aren't causing any significant problems.

insect-prone. A well-maintained lawn, one that's mowed properly, fed correctly, and watered right, is *always* the best defense against an unwanted insect population. What's more, it will be able to withstand the attack and recover with minimal issues.

WHAT, ME WORRY?

For the most part you really don't have to worry about insects. Life at the turfgrass level will stay in balance most of the time. Insect predators keep resident populations in check. New blade and root growth far outpaces the damage insects cause to leaves and roots. You see a healthy lawn, not the insects living there.

Even if your lawn does become infested—meaning it's hosting more bugs than it should or, better said, more than you can tolerate—letting the critters run through their life cycles is typically all that's necessary. Your grass might not look all that great in the meantime, but if your lawn is healthy in general, it will bounce back relatively quickly. If not, recovery can take longer but will happen, especially if you help it along by taking better care of your lawn.

One of the best ways to troubleshoot potential insect problems is to keep an eye on what's going on under your feet. Conduct your insect inspections as part of your mowing program, and you'll kill two birds (bugs?) with one stone. As you go along, note any areas that look a little off. Pay particular attention to any prior trouble spots, especially if they're problem areas year after year. Analyze your cultural practices, and alter them if necessary.

If your lawn repeatedly comes under attack by a specific insect, it might be time to reconsider the kind of grass you're growing. This might seem like a drastic measure, but if there's a better variety or cultivar, maybe one that's less prone to the kind of insects you're battling, or one that's been bred to include endophytes (microscopic beneficial fungi), it might be worth switching. While reestablishment costs might be a little high, you'll probably save money and use fewer chemicals on your grass in the long run.

BUG OFF!

All this said, you'd be the rare lawn geek if you didn't have to battle a bug problem or two at some time during your tenure. As with weeds and diseases, Integrated Pest Management (IPM) is the preferred approach when it comes to ridding your lawn of unwanted insects. Following it doesn't mean you'll never have to use insecticides, but it does reduce the need for them and make them more effective when you have to use them.

Unlike IPM for weeds and diseases, there are a number of control options for battling insect pests. The basics are always the same, however. You start with least harm and work your way up from there.

Identify the Enemy

Determining the evildoers in your yard calls for getting a little personal with them. The damage they cause is one way to know what you're dealing with, but you can't always determine the bug by the damage, as it can be fairly similar across insect families.

One of the easiest ways to ID them is simply getting down to turf level and looking. You might need a magnifying glass for this, as some insect pests are really, really small. Other approaches include:

- Flushing them out. Remove the top and bottom from a large, empty can. A coffee can works well for this, but anything similarly sized is fine. Push the can into the soil where you suspect insect problems. Get it in a couple of inches if possible. Then fill it with water to about two to three inches above the ground. Keep the level up by adding more water for about five minutes. Any bugs in the area will float to the surface. This is a good test for chinch bugs, which feed at the soil's surface.

- Dunking them in. This variation of the drench test calls for removing a square of turf from your lawn and dunking it into a bucket of water. Make the square about four to six inches all around. Again, bugs will float to the surface. This is another good chinch bug test.

- Irritating the heck out of them. Mix one to two tablespoons of liquid dish detergent (scent of your choice or unscented, it really doesn't matter) in one gallon of water. Pour the mixture over a two-foot-square section of the suspect area. This test is good for flushing out armyworms, cutworms, chinch bugs, mole crickets, and sod webworms.

- Digging them up. Remove a turf sample from suspect areas. The sample doesn't have to be huge—about six inches all around is enough. Put it on a flat surface; a thick pile of newspapers or a plywood or cardboard sheet works fine. Then break up the clumps of dirt clinging to the roots with a hand tool—a trowel or a dandelion digger, something like that. Be sure to dig into the thatch line, as that's where grubs hang out. You can collect the bugs or not; doing so can make it easier to count how many there are.

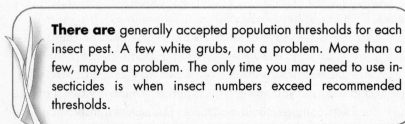

There are generally accepted population thresholds for each insect pest. A few white grubs, not a problem. More than a few, maybe a problem. The only time you may need to use insecticides is when insect numbers exceed recommended thresholds.

Calling In Controls

For the most part, just taking good care of your lawn is all the control you'll need to do. You don't have to grab a can of insecticide the minute you see something crawling in your grass. Nor is spraying your lawn typically necessary or even recommended. Do so, and you also run the risk of killing the beneficial things that lurk beneath along with the pests you're after.

For most insects, successful control via chemicals means hitting them when their defenses are at their lowest. This is when they're young, as soon as possible after they hatch. Most insects hatch out as larvae and they're pretty inactive at this stage. They also lack the hard outer shell that develops later on as part of their metamorphosis into adults, so they're soft and gooey and absorbent.

There is an exception to the rule of not using insecticides as a preventive measure. For insects with no natural predators, like the Japanese beetle and the European chafer, which left their home countries and their predators behind when they came to the United States, preventive applications prior to egg hatch or before grubs hatch out can effectively reduce populations and damage.

As mentioned, the insects that need the most attention are the ones without natural predators. In the United States, there are three: the Oriental beetle (we don't see that one very much), the European chafer, and the Japanese beetle. When an infestation is likely, consider using preventive-type control with halofenozide or imidacloprid prior to egg hatch (middle to end of summer). You'll know if a hatch is threatening because you'll hear about it; this is the kind of stuff that insect experts and university extension offices issue press releases to warn the public about. Sometimes this can be an expensive insurance policy; it can cost about a hundred dollars to treat your lawn, but the peace of mind is worth it and the lawn damage could be worse. This specific insecticide is real easy to put down and buys you assurance you won't have an issue all year; it's too simple not to do.

Beetle larvae are called grubs; moth larvae are caterpillars. Larvae eat almost continually, except when they're overwintering, which is why they can be such a big problem.

Some insects skip the larval stage and hatch right into small, wingless insects called nymphs. It's usually a good idea to attack them when they're young as well.

Most insects are effectively controlled as larvae because they lack adult exoskeletons (unlike all other animals, insect skeletons are on the outside of their bodies). But in some cases, the best control is on the adults before they lay the eggs that turn into larvae.

Biological Controls   This approach pits natural pathogens and predators that already exist in lawns, such as nematodes and bacteria, against unwanted insects. Employ them, and you set up a battle between two naturally occurring organisms. If you do it right, the insects lose.

Sounds great, right? Well, it can be, but there's a catch. Doing it right isn't easy. Biological controls are not only highly selective—in other words, they typically only attack one stage of one species of insect—but keeping them alive long enough to do their stuff can be a challenge. Predatory nematodes, for example, tend to dry out during shipping. They're also not effective if you can't time their application for when insects are most vulnerable.

Biological controls are harmless to humans and pets. They include:

• Predatory nematodes. Nematodes, which are tiny worms, are the most numerous multicellular animals on (and in) Earth. A handful of soil contains thousands of the microscopic worms, many of them parasites of insects, plants, or animals. They'll eat the larvae of various insect pests, including mole crickets, sod webworms, cutworms, and Japanese beetles. Using them is pretty easy; you just mix them with water, apply them to a moist lawn, and let them have their fun. They work best if applied when larvae are young and active, and they need to be kept moist once they're applied. These animals are insect-specific, so it's important to match nematode to insect pest.

- *Bacillus thuringiensis,* or Bt. This is a bacterium that attacks sod webworms and similar pests by producing toxins that paralyze insect guts. It's applied to foliage where and when larvae are feeding and is most effective when mixed with soft water. Like nematodes, it works best on very young larvae. Infected insects stop feeding soon after they ingest Bt, but death might not come for a couple of days. Sunlight deactivates Bt, so it must be applied at night. Repeat applications are usually needed for good control. There are various Bt strains for controlling a variety of insect pests; again, most are specific to the pests they control.

- Endophytes. As mentioned in chapter 2, these are microscopic fungi that grow inside blades and leaf stalks of certain grasses. They're toxic to many lawn pests, including sod webworms, chinch bugs, and billbugs. Some tall fescue and perennial ryegrass cultivars have been developed with endophytes to protect them from these insects.

- Insect Growth Regulators (IGRs). This is kind of a misnomer, as they don't really regulate insect growth. Instead, they mess with it by sending the wrong signals. IGRs contain chemicals that insects naturally produce to govern their molting process. Most IGRs prevent molting, which stops metamorphosis in its tracks. No metamorphosis, no adult insect, end of reproductive cycle. Others, called molt accelerators, cause premature molts with the same results.

In addition to being less than perfectly effective, these controls are also expensive, way more expensive than traditional pesticides, especially when it comes to using enough of them to really be effective. That said, there's been a lot of research and development going on in this arena. While these controls might not be highly practical now, stay tuned for future developments.

When nematodes enter their victims, they release bacteria that break down the insects' internal tissues. Massive infection is the result, and the insects die. The nematodes then reproduce in the dead insects, pick up some of the deadly bacteria, and go on to their next victim. Kinda cool.

Botanical Insecticides   Botanical insecticides, as the name reflects, are derived from plants. The two botanicals in widest use are azadirachtin, or neem, an oil extracted from the tree of the same name; and pyrethrin, a substance derived from chrysanthemum plants.

Neem's mode of action is similar to IGRs'. It's effective on young aphids, cutworms, armyworms, and grubs. It will repel (but not kill) Japanese beetles, which can keep them from visiting your lawn and leaving their spawn—white grubs—behind. It must be applied as soon as pests make their presence known and reapplied as long as they remain active, which makes it an expensive control.

Pyrethrin is stronger than neem and more effective than any biological control. It's also effective on many types of insects, which is good and bad. Good, as it's effective. Bad because it will kill beneficial insects along with the pests. For this reason, it's better as a spot treatment on infestation areas than broadcast over an entire yard.

Both neem and pyrethrin break down quickly after they're applied, which is also good and bad. It makes them even less toxic, but because you have to keep on applying them for effective control, they

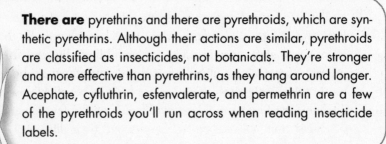

There are pyrethrins and there are pyrethroids, which are synthetic pyrethrins. Although their actions are similar, pyrethroids are classified as insecticides, not botanicals. They're stronger and more effective than pyrethrins, as they hang around longer. Acephate, cyfluthrin, esfenvalerate, and permethrin are a few of the pyrethroids you'll run across when reading insecticide labels.

can get costly. (Many newer pyrethrin-based products hang around a bit longer.)

Insecticidal Soaps These products are derived from the potassium salts of fatty acids. They work by washing away the protective coating on insects' outsides and damaging their inner cell membranes, and are only effective if bugs come into direct contact with them.

Insecticidal soaps work quickly but also lose their effectiveness quickly. When they dry out, they're done. They're most effective on soft-bodied pests like aphids, sod webworms, and grubs. For best results, they must be mixed with soft water, as hard water limits their effectiveness.

Traditional Insecticides If you're in a particularly dire situation, like you're under siege and you're in serious danger of losing your turf, don't even think about messing around with other controls. Used appropriately, traditional insecticides are safe, and in some situations they might be your only hope. But, again, weigh the consequences. These chemicals can wipe out the problem, but they can also wipe out insects that aren't problems. Remember Newton's third law, "For every action there's an equal and opposite reaction"? Take away too many beneficial insects, and insects that weren't problems before can become problems pretty quick.

These insecticides are the ones most often used for battling turf pests:

- Imidacloprid. This newer systemic insecticide will control soil- and crown-loving insects and is extremely effective on very young grubs, so it's important that the insecticide be applied prior to egg hatch, in June or July. It also works well on aphids and most other sucking insects, and isn't harmful to earthworms and most beneficial insects.
- Cyfluthrin. This is a broad-spectrum synthetic pyrethroid that's effective against most insects on plant foliage but not in the ground. It works on caterpillars, aphids, adult Japanese beetles, most other beetles, and ants. But it is toxic to beneficial insects.
- Trichlorfon. This older insecticide is one of the few remaining products that control grubs throughout their life cycle—in spring or fall, not just spring.

- Carbaryl (brand name Sevin). Another older insecticide, introduced commercially in 1958, and one of the most widely used products, it's effective on a wide range of insects. It's also moderately to very toxic, depending on formulation.

Insecticides come in a wide variety of formulations, including concentrates, wettable powders, soluble powders, baits, dusts, pellets, and granules. Control varies from formulation to formulation; for example, control with sprays is highest within twenty-four to forty-eight hours after application. Granules must be moistened before they're effective. For soil-dwelling insects, products need to sink down to the roots to be effective, which means you'll have to water them in so they don't just stick to the turf, where they won't do any good. Surface feeders are best attacked with products applied to leaves, stems, and thatch. Baits are only effective on soil dwellers, are ruined if they get wet, and are best applied late in the day for nabbing night-feeding pests like mole crickets and cutworms.

If there's more than one formulation for the pest you're battling, check with the experts for the best choice.

Insecticides should be the last resort. For this reason, applying them isn't something you have to be proficient at to become a lawn geek. It's definitely something to stay away from if you have qualms about handling chemicals or simply would rather have someone else do it. On the other hand, a simple application of a product like Merit in granular form is as routine as applying fertilizer; people do it all the time and I think you do need to do it preventively if you know European chafer or Japanese beetle grubs are present in other people's lawns.

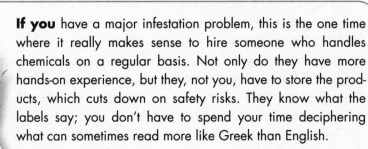

If you have a major infestation problem, this is the one time where it really makes sense to hire someone who handles chemicals on a regular basis. Not only do they have more hands-on experience, but they, not you, have to store the products, which cuts down on safety risks. They know what the labels say; you don't have to spend your time deciphering what can sometimes read more like Greek than English.

That said, here's what you need to know about working with these chemicals should you decide to do it yourself.

- Read labels carefully. They'll list the pests the products will control and the plants you can use them on.
- Read application instructions carefully. Make sure you understand them. This is imperative for you, your pets, and the environment. Follow them exactly. Free-styling is against the law.
- Mow your lawn and reduce thatch, if necessary, before application.
- Don protective gear—gloves and glasses or goggles—before mixing, and wear them while spraying. A face mask is a good thing to wear if you're working with powders.
- If you're spraying, load your sprayer carefully to avoid product spills. Spray on a calm day to minimize chemical drift to plants that don't need treatment. Hold off if rain is expected, as it can wash chemicals away before they get the chance to work well and increase the chance of their going places they shouldn't go, like storm drains.
- If spraying for leaf-feeding insects, put irrigation on hold for forty-eight hours after spraying so the product will stay on grass blades as long as possible. If treating root chewers, you will want to help the product move deeper into the soil by watering after it's applied. Follow label directions.
- Also follow label directions for product and container disposal. Store your equipment and any unused chemicals in clearly labeled containers far, far away from children and pets. Never use the same equipment for applying other products.

THE TOP TEN MOST PESTY AND UNDESIRABLE

The following insects are the ones that, when I go around and listen to my entomologist friends talk, are discussed the most often. They're by no means the only ones that can cause turf problems, but they're the most common criminals. They're grouped by where they inflict their damage—at the roots, on the leaves, and in the ground—not by peskiness.

Control recommendations for each insect follow the IPM least-harm model. Treatment windows are approximate because many factors—location, temperature, rainfall, and the product being used—vary so much. So check with local experts if you need help with determining the best time for control. Keep in mind that all products do their best work when applied at the insect's most vulnerable stage, which for many is when they're larvae or nymphs.

If, after going through this list, you think you're dealing with something else, check with local experts for advice. County extension offices are a good place to start.

Remember, the best approach with all insect invaders is to take better care of your lawn in general. Healthy lawns are the best control, as they will be most able to coexist with minor insect attacks.

Root Chewers

These insects munch on grass roots and damage grass plants by severing the root system so that the grass easily breaks away below the crown. They're the biggest insect invader category, and they include both native and introduced species. Introduced species, which have no natural predators, are the biggest threats to home lawns.

Grubs   "Grub" is a general catch term for the larvae of a bunch of different beetles, including Japanese, European chafer, May, and June beetles. The specific problem-causers depend on the area; they have similar looks and they cause similar problems. Adult beetles, while a problem in trees, shrubs, and other landscape plants, leave grasses alone.

Grubs are C-shaped, milky-white critters with brown heads. They range from a half inch to one and a half inches long and have three sets of tiny legs. They'll attack the roots of almost all grasses. Damage from their feeding appears as brown grass in large, irregularly shaped patches. Grass will be thin and wilted; your lawn will look like it's desperate for water when it's not. Infestations typically occur in late summer to fall, but can also occur in late spring. If the grass is producing enough roots to support both itself and the grubs, you may never see a problem (this is often the case in an irrigated lawn under good growing conditions, as the turf can outgrow what

Japanese beetles and European chafers go through an entire life cycle in one year. June beetle grubs can feed on grass roots for three years before they turn into adults.

the grubs can eat). Reverse the scenario and grub damage can be severe, if not devastating.

Positive identification of grubs starts with tugging on grass plants in suspect areas. They'll probably come right up, as their roots will be destroyed. If you see grubs at the surface, know that there are many, many others lurking beneath. You might also simply come across pieces of turf that look like they've been pulled out of the ground. This indicates animal activity, as grubs are good eats for moles, raccoons, and skunks. (If so, turn to chapter 15 for more advice on dealing with them.)

More than ten grubs per square foot call for control. The best time is when they're actively feeding on roots in spring or fall. Try to get them young; the larger they get, the harder they are to control.

- Soil moisture plays an important role when adults are laying their eggs. If Japanese beetles seem to be the invaders, try letting your lawn go a little dry in late July, which is prime egg-laying time. Do the opposite for European chafer beetles. They prefer dry soil, so watering can make them turn up their little noses and look for more hospitable places to drop their spawn.
- Predatory nematodes are an effective control for many grubs. If you're dealing with a Japanese beetle infestation, try milky spore, which is a biological control specific to that beetle's larvae. Milky spore will take several years to become truly effective, so pair it with an insecticide the first year for best control.
- Parasitic nematode products containing *Heterorhabditis bacteriophora* may control grubs if applied during August or early September.
- Halofenozide (brand name Mach 2) is an IGR that's effective on grubs and most caterpillars but doesn't harm other insects

or organisms. Apply prior to egg hatch, usually between June 1 (if you live further south) and August 1 (if you live in the North).

- Apply imidacloprid (Merit, Grub-X) prior to egg hatch, usually between June 1 and August 1.
- If you miss the application window and grubs hatch out, carbaryl and trichlorfon are also registered for grub control. Apply from August to mid-September if damage is severe and again the following spring before the grubs change into adults. Make sure to get it into the root zone by watering before and after application.

Adult control is not effective, although neem oil can discourage adults from visiting your turf.

Cutworms and Armyworms Although they differ in behavior—cutworms are solo feeders, armyworms munch across lawns en masse (hence their name)—these larvae of night-flying moths inflict similar damage and the controls are similar for them. Both are thick-bodied, robust little worms. Cutworms range from gray to black, depending on species, and have dark brown or gray heads. Poke at them, and they'll curl up and play dead. Armyworms vary from gray to yellowish green with a pink tint. They have stripes on their backs and sides, and their heads are light brown with a distinctive honeycomb pattern. There are also fall armyworms, which—you guessed it—time their attacks for cooler months. They range in color from pink to yellow-green to almost black. They also have stripes and sport an inverted Y on the front of their heads. All can grow up to two inches long.

These caterpillars feed at night and will attack the leaves and crowns on all grasses. Cutworms cut grass blades near the crowns, hence their name. Damage begins as small, irregular spots and spreads to larger patches, about two inches wide, as the worms mature. Armyworms also feed at night. When they're young, damage in the form of skeletonized grass blades often shows up before the larvae are visible. As they get older, they'll eat everything that's aboveground. The grass will look like it got a buzz cut, and like it was done in circles. Some cutworms can overwinter in colder climates; armyworms typically can't overwinter. Instead, their parents migrate northward in spring.

Irritating these worms is the best approach for diagnosis and threshold measurement. You might see larvae feeding at plant crowns if you scrape soil away from them. Control if you find more than three larvae per square foot.

Controls:

- dethatching, as larvae will hide in the thatch layer during the day
- watch your watering; wet areas favor adult egg-laying
- parasitic nematodes
- Bt, but only effective on very young larvae
- neem oil
- insecticidal soap
- traditional insecticides containing carbaryl or cyfluthrin

Billbugs   Billbugs are small weevils, which is a type of beetle. There are several species and they can be found almost everywhere. Both adults and larvae can cause serious damage, especially in bluegrass lawns. Most perennial ryegrasses and fescues, especially if they contain endophytes, are billbug-resistant.

Adults are a half inch in size and have long, curved snouts that they use to eat holes in plant tissues. Their larvae, which look like tiny white grubs, feed on grass stems and then move to grass roots. Damaged areas start small and can resemble dollar spots. As damage intensifies, the patches can increase in size. A severe infestation will completely destroy your turf.

Billbug damage is greatest during midsummer, when grass is stressed out from battling heat and drought, but it will remain long after the insects have departed. Neighboring lawns will green up when temperatures drop and moisture increases. Yours won't.

To confirm these pests, grab and pull a suspect plant. If it breaks away at the crown and there are hollowed-out stems with a sawdust-like material at their cut ends, billbugs are to blame.

Check infestation levels by looking for migrating adults near sidewalks or dig into the ground to seek out larvae. More than two adults marching by per minute or more than four larvae per square foot calls for control. Another approach is to dig a hole and put a plastic cup flush with the surface and simply let the billbugs fall into the cup.

Billbugs are notoriously difficult to control. Insecticides have a hard time piercing their tough little bodies and they don't ingest much insecticide when they feed. By the time you start seeing damage, their eggs are safely nestled in grass blade sheaths where most insecticides can't penetrate. When the eggs hatch, the grubs move deep into soil to pupate and can't be killed. So, the best time to control these pests is at the adult stage before they can lay eggs.

Controls:

- Plant resistant bluegrass varieties.
- Apply parasitic nematodes, which work on larvae and adults.
- In areas prone to billbug infestations, apply halofenozide or imidacloprid as soon as adults become active in the spring and before the eggs have hatched in the stems. This will give you season-long control because eggs only hatch once a year.
- Applying a traditional insecticide before adults lay eggs in spring. Liquid sprays, which cling to foliage and crowns and increase the chances of the bugs contacting it, are preferred over granules. This approach requires some monitoring and may not prevent damage if turf is drought-stressed.

Blade Runners

These insect pests feed by chewing or sucking on leaf, stem, and root tissues. Some release toxic chemicals that can damage plants.

Sod Webworms   Like armyworms and cutworms, these are the larvae of a night-flying moth. They get their name from the silky, web-lined tunnels they hang out in during the day. They're a problem just about everywhere, but they're less so in the central United States. They'll attack pretty much any grass, but they particularly like to go to town on Kentucky bluegrass and tall fescue.

Webworms measure about three-quarters of an inch and resemble their buff-colored adults in color. They also sport rings of darker brown spots. As they feed on the grass blades, they leave behind small, irregular dead patches that gradually expand into larger dead patches. Some species will also go after crowns and roots. Damage is most noticeable in dry lawns and if thatch layers are thick.

In some parts of the country adult sod webworms are called lawn moths; they're miller moths elsewhere. Either way, these moths flutter over grass at night, darting about as they drop their eggs. If you see a lot of them in late spring, you can count on caterpillars in about ten days to two weeks after they're gone.

To confirm webworms, get out your flashlight and hunt for them at night when they're happily munching away. Or do a daytime search by sinking a trowel into the thatch layer and looking for the worms in their tunnels. An irritating flush works well for determining their numbers. Control if you find more than two worms per square foot.

Here's how to control these critters:

- Take good care of your lawn. Control thatch layers. New growth can outpace damage, especially if irrigation is consistent.
- Replace existing grass with webworm-resistant turfgrass varieties.
- Bt can be effective on very young larvae.
- Apply parasitic nematodes. *Steinernema* nematodes are the most effective.
- Use insecticides labeled for controlling sod webworms. Traditional chemical controls include carbaryl and cyfluthrin. Permethrin is also effective. Apply at night when webworms are feeding.

Chinch Bugs These tiny insects—adults are one-sixteenth of an inch—can attack almost anywhere and can be extremely destructive when they do. There are a number of different kinds, but they all inflict similar damage, which typically appears in mid- to late summer during hot, dry periods. The nymphs, which are red and wingless, cause the most damage. All of them suck plant juices, which results in small yellowish areas of turf that quickly turn into larger dead patches as damage progresses, typically first observed in late spring or early summer.

Chinch bug damage is often misdiagnosed as drought damage. Turf will appear dry but won't recover when irrigated.

Confirm chinch bugs by seeking them out in grass crowns next to damaged areas during the heat of the day, when they're most active. Adults are white and black and may or may not have fully developed wings. Count their numbers by floating them out of your turf or dunking a piece of turf in a bucket. Control if more than five adults come up for air.

Chinch bug controls include:

- Regular watering, which will help control the damage they inflict. (A light application of urea fertilizer, by the way, will boost your grass's recovery.)
- Pyrethrins.
- Carbaryl. Water your lawn twenty to twenty-five minutes before applying liquid or granular products for optimum results.

Greenbugs   Also called greenbug aphids, these tiny, almost transparent egg-shaped insects are a particular problem in the shade on northern lawns—and especially Kentucky bluegrass lawns—when summer temperatures are at their highest. They congregate on grass blades, where they have a fine old time sucking away on plant juices. Affected grass changes from healthy green into yellow, burnt orange, and finally brown. Populations can grow to epic proportions quickly as the female produce offspring without fertilization. Baby greenbugs can reach maturity in a week.

To confirm greenbugs, get down to turf level and inspect suspect grass blades. If greenbugs are present, you'll see them sucking away.

Beneficial insects like ladybugs and lacewings typically do a great job of keeping greenbug populations under control. Insecticidal soap is the recommended control if these natural predators can't keep up with greenbug populations and your grass is showing measurable damage.

Leafhoppers These are tiny, wedge-shaped insects that typically measure less than a quarter inch long. Adults fly or jump short distances when disturbed; young nymphs resemble adults but are smaller and wingless. Both adults and nymphs suck juices from grass shoots, causing discoloration and stunted growth. Replanting is sometimes necessary if they attack seedlings, as baby plants lack the defenses to weather invasions well.

Since they hop around quite a bit, leafhoppers can be tough to control. Try neem oil or insecticidal soap. Acephate will control them and other sucking insects.

Down-and-Dirty Diggers

Insects in this category tend to be more of a nuisance than anything else, as their activities make turf look bad. That said, one member of this group—the fire ant—is definitely not something you want in your yard, no matter what.

Ants, Fiery and Not There are more than twelve thousand ant species in the world. Most are important contributors to turfgrass ecosystems, where they do things like feed on other pests and decompose dead animal tissue. Most of the time you want to let them go about their work, as they really are harmless. Maybe annoying at times, especially when they disrupt picnics or attack Fido's food bowl, but harmless.

If lots of ants are coming inside your house from nests they've built close by, or for some reason they've decided to turn into the Donald Trumps of the insect world and they're kicking up huge mounds from their excavating efforts, decreasing their numbers can make sense. First, make sure you're dealing with an active mound by raking it down. Wait a couple of days to see if the ants rebuild it. If they do, rake the mound level again and sprinkle a small amount of ant bait containing avermectin or hydramethylnon or an IGR such as fenoxycarb. Spread the bait around the entrance to the mound and the ants will carry it into the nest. You should see a noticeable decrease in the ant population after the first application. If not, repeat as necessary.

Fire ants, on the other hand, are nothing to mess with. They look a lot like their meek and mild kin, but you can tell them apart by their significantly more aggressive behavior, especially around their nests, which are shaped like mounds and are a good distinguishing trait. If you suspect their presence, don't even think about doing anything other than calling in the experts. These babies are aggressive, and their bites and stings (they do both) hurt like the dickens. You do not want to get into a fight with them, period.

Another reason for not messing around with fire ants is that there are native and imported species. The natives are very similar to the imported varieties, but they can help control the imported species, so it's in our interest to spare them.

Mole Crickets   Like their mammalian namesakes, these insects live underground. As such, they can be difficult to monitor and control, which means they can absolutely devastate warm-season turf, and their activities can lead to a host of long-term problems that affect overall turf quality.

Mole crickets feed on grass roots, but the damage they cause moving through the soil is the bigger problem. Like moles, they have strong forelegs and they use them to tunnel near soil surfaces in search of food, loosening the soil and uprooting plants as they go. They wreak their havoc at night and can tunnel up to twenty feet in one nocturnal session. During the day, they hang out in their burrows and rest up for another nighttime attack.

These critters are primarily southerners and will eat almost any warm-season grass. They're particularly fond of bahiagrass and bermudagrass. Adult females lay eggs in subterranean chambers beginning in April or early May. They'll build anywhere from three to five chambers, which they'll fill up with 100 to 150 eggs. The eggs hatch from late May through July. Nymphs will feed from then through the fall and even into the winter, depending on the weather.

Check mole cricket levels with an irritating flush. Control if more than one per square foot comes out of hiding.

Mole cricket control is challenging, as it's hard to get insecticides deep enough to reach their tunnels. The best results come when treating right after the eggs hatch.

Controls include:

- Predatory nematodes. Three are specifically marketed for mole crickets. One of them has shown a residual effect—it reproduces in the crickets it kills and its offspring stick around in the ground, where they can nab more crickets.
- Insecticides can be effective on young nymphs, but not as much on adults, as they tunnel so deep. Most products must be watered in well to reach the crickets, but be sure to check application instructions, as some products, such as acephate, should not be watered in. Baits will encourage the crickets to come to the surface to feed on them, and also shouldn't be watered in.

Remember, taking good care of your lawn is the best way to deal with insect problems. Don't give these pests a reason for getting out of control in the first place, and you'll be able to live in peaceful harmony with them.

CHAPTER 15

Critter Control

Sooner or later, an unwanted animal is going to come along and do something to upset your lawn. Here's what to look for, how to figure out what you have based on visual evidence, and what to do about the offenders you're most likely to encounter.

Because lawns are part of the big ecosystem we call Mother Earth, and that ecosystem includes flora and fauna, sharing your patch of green with other beings, invited and not, is a given. These other beings, of course, include the four-footed members of the animal kingdom, both wild and domestic.

Your lawn would be a true aberration, and you'd be the rare home owner, if along the way one or more of these animals didn't do something to upset it. And you.

Your response? It depends on whether the animal is truly a nuisance or just an irritant to you. It depends on how bad the problem really is—that is, how much it disrupts your patch of green. And it depends on how controllable the problem is in general.

Say you live somewhere with a large tree squirrel population. Your lawn might look like it's been pelted with tiny bombs when these rodents are scurrying about and shoring up their food supplies in the fall. Unsightly? Yes. A nuisance? Sure. Something you can control? Probably not. There are too many to trap, you can't shoot them because it's against the law (you checked this), and poisoning them is also out of the question (you also checked this).

You might be able to cut down on their food sources, and their access to them, but in many cases this is difficult to impossible, especially if you have a softhearted neighbor who delights in feeding the danged things because they're "so cute." Given all this, your best bet is to ignore the holes or go out and stomp them down. And maybe try to talk some sense into your neighbor.

Animal intruders—wild ones, anyway—are a reminder that, for the most part, they were here first. At some point, they roamed freely over your lawn and everyone else's. Depending on where you live, that point could be in the not-too-distant past and your home might be near wild areas where animals still roam freely. If so, you might be dealing with a fairly significant animal population that will keep enjoying the benefits of your yard because they're animals and they lack the ability to realize that party time is over.

Either way, successfully dealing with animal problems has a lot more to do with changing your behavior than theirs. Whatever havoc animals wreak on your turf, they're not doing it to be intentionally malicious. They're doing it because, well, they're animals, and it's what they do. In other words, it's normal behavior for them. Moles burrow under turf because it's the only way they know how to get food. Dogs use grass as latrines because . . . well, no one knows for sure and we can't ask them, but of all the possible outdoor surfaces they can choose from, they tend to prefer grass.

All that said, it's also normal behavior for us humans to want to control our environment, which includes dealing with nuisance animals, both wild and domestic.

Let's look at wild animals first.

WHEN BAMBI AND THUMPER RUN AMOK

The furry little forest animals that are so cute and lovable in Disney cartoons and nature films turn into nuisances real fast when they cause problems in your yard. Even if they're royal pains in the butt, though, getting rid of them might not be easy, primarily because it's you against the wildlife kingdom, and you're decidedly outnumbered.

You might be able to minimize the problem in various ways—by putting up barriers, cutting down or eliminating their food supply, or employing repellents or scare tactics—which, by the way, are recommended Integrated Pest Management (IPM) approaches for dealing with wildlife intruders—but you'll never entirely get rid of nuisance animals if there are lots of them or they're highly prolific breeders.

IPM FOR PESKY WILDLIFE

IPM always emphasizes a least-harm approach. When it comes to dealing with wildlife, it begins with correct identification, as knowing the enemy goes a long way toward effectively controlling it.

Next up is altering the habitat—that is, your yard—to make it less friendly to animal invaders. This isn't always possible—you might not be able to control or change some of the things the animals find so inviting—but you might be able to do more than you think.

One of the reasons nuisance wildlife is becoming a greater instead of a lesser problem is because human beings tend to make things welcoming to wild animals without knowing it. Feed the birds, and your resident squirrel population is bound to increase. Leave scrap lumber or wood on your land, and you're inviting rodents to take up residence under it.

Let grubs take over your turf, and you can say hello to a bunch of different animals that like to feed on them, including moles, skunks, raccoons, and armadillos. Feed your dog outdoors, and you're inviting raccoons and skunks to join him at his kibble bowl.

The solutions here should be pretty obvious, but if they aren't . . . quit feeding the birds, clean up your yard, make it less attractive to insect intruders, and feed Fido indoors.

Making your yard less inviting also includes using repellents and scare tactics. I've found both to be hit-or-miss approaches. Some work well for a while, then decrease in effectiveness as the animals get used to them. You'll see and hear lots of anecdotes about how mothballs will get rid of skunks and putting human hair down gopher holes will make them scream and run. It's all pretty much bunk, and a waste of time, effort, and money.

PLAYING KEEP-AWAY—PERMANENTLY

Control is the next rung on the wild animal IPM ladder. Methods here include poisoning, fumigating (gassing), flooding, shooting, and trapping. The goal here, obviously, is permanent elimination. As such, none of these approaches are pretty, but they can be very effective. That said, depending on where you live, there might be stringent rules in place regarding the permanent measures you can employ, and what you can do with the animals once they're in custody.

"Protected species" is a term you'll probably get to know if you're dealing with nuisance wildlife. It means that at some point someone decided to enact a mini Bill of Rights to protect certain wild animals. Depending on where you live, the laws and regulations might be federal, state, or local, or a combination of the above. They can differ quite a bit, but most allow removing small nuisance animals—squirrels, raccoons, and so on—if they're damaging your property and if you go at it the right way, which means following whatever guidelines are in the laws and/or regs. Typically, these guidelines cover trapping, shooting, poisoning, or gassing.

This means that if you don't follow the legal approach, removing your critter, or critters, can put you at risk of running afoul of your local animal control laws and ordinances. What's more, if the laws and ordinances where you live are particularly Draconian, you could even end up experiencing some control of your own in the local lockup (though big fat fines are typically the punishment meted out).

What you're allowed to do with these animals, once captured or killed, can also vary quite a bit. Some areas might allow trap and release. Others will spell out exactly how and where animals can be released. Still others will allow trapping, but not releasing, on the grounds that doing so makes problems worse, not better. So, if you decide that trapping's the way to go, once you capture the animal, you then have to kill it and dispose of it. Or find someone else to do the dirty work for you. The same thing goes for controls like gassing and poisoning. Once animals are dead, they can't just be left to rot. You have to dispose of them in a way that won't harm other wild animals, kids, or pets.

Now that that's said, permanent control choices also depend on a

I'm a big believer in hiring experts to do things that I'm not good at, or, better put, don't do often enough to be much good at. Dealing with wild animals is one of those things. If it is for you, too, here's my best advice: If you really have a nuisance animal problem, and modifying your surrounds isn't doing the trick, get some help. Hire an expert if you have to. Choices here include animal-control officers, wildlife-control experts, pest-control companies, and so on. There are even companies and organizations that specialize in dealing with nuisance wildlife. It might take some time to track them down, but doing so can be worth the effort.

couple of other factors: how squeamish you are about such things, and having the right equipment on hand (or being willing to buy or acquire it some other way). And, I suppose, a third factor—if there are others around who might not look at you in quite the same way ever again should you expose your inner great white hunter.

Poison Pills

Poison baits are fairly easy to find, which makes them a popular choice for critter control. Keep in mind, however, that these products can also be effective against other things you don't want to control, like wildlife that's not causing problems, household pets, and children. If you choose to use them, you'll have to be extremely careful about where they're placed—ideally, below ground or in places far away from things you don't want to kill. Clean up any spills immediately, and dispose of all dead animals you might come across, whether you know for sure that they ingested the poison or not.

Smoke Out

Fumigating involves dropping a gas-filled canister into animal burrows or runs. It's not very effective against the majority of nuisance animals for various reasons—for example, gophers and moles can sense

I once came out to a home (at the request of a nervous neighbor) of a guy who was running a hose from his car's exhaust pipe into mole tunnels to smoke out the little critters. When I pointed out that the chances of the exhaust getting to the target were akin to the ability of a screen door to hold back water, he gave up. You can gas a contained area, but not an infinite one.

the presence of noxious fumes and will quickly wall off treated tunnels to prevent their spread. The ground also has to be saturated for gases to work properly. If it's not, the fumes will disperse through the soil and won't be concentrated enough to do any good.

These products are also highly toxic to wildlife, and most of them are restricted-use pesticides, meaning that only certified pesticide applicators can apply them.

The Great Flood

Sticking a hose into a run or burrow and flooding the critters out might seem the humane way to go, but it isn't very effective on most of them. Moles, for example, can just swim their way out, hang out somewhere else until things dry out, and enter right back in when they do. Plus, there's little guarantee that the run or burrow you choose to flood actually contains the animals you're trying to get rid of—nuisance-animal bunkers can be extremely extensive and complex.

Caught in the Act

By now it's probably apparent that trapping is the best permanent control for dealing with nuisance animals. If you're dealing with a casual intruder, or a couple of them, it can provide immediate control. If not, it's a temporary solution at best, as it will have little to no effect on the resident population.

Trapping is a touchy subject and one that people tend to have strong opinions about. If those opinions are negative, they can be pretty vocal

> **Closure** is trapping's biggest benefit. You have a confirmed kill, or a confirmed live nabbing, as opposed to simply wondering about it.

about expressing them, too. That said, what you do on your lawn is your business. You don't have to tell the world about it. Plus, the nature of trapping is such that your activities will probably go unnoticed anyway. So if this is something you personally don't find repellent and, after doing the research, you think it's the solution to your problem, and it's legal where you live, trap away.

Keep in mind, however, that while trapping is the recommended approach for controlling most nuisance animals, they can be very good at evading capture. You can do everything right when it comes to figuring out how and where to trap them, and you can still end up feeling like Elmer Fudd, who, no matter how wily he got when stalking Bugs Bunny, was always out-wiled by the wascally wabbit.

If, after all this, you still want to trap the animal yourself, buy, rent, or borrow the appropriate trap for the species you're dealing with. Various sizes and styles are available; you'll see them described as "raccoon size" or "squirrel size." You'll also see some described as "live traps." These capture the animal for release or disposal. Those that aren't labeled as such, don't. Most experts recommend buying a single-door trap, as they do a better job of containing the critter than double-door models do.

If you have to buy a trap, try sporting goods stores, lawn and garden centers, farm-supply stores—basically anywhere testosterone runs a little high. Some wildlife-control and animal-protection organizations rent live traps. Make sure you get one that's fairly easy to set up and bait; a trap that keeps snapping shut when you're trying to bait it is both a hazard and a deterrent to taking this approach in the first place.

I'll give you some setup and baiting tips, where appropriate, along the way. If they don't work for you, get some live help from the experts.

STEALTH ATTACK

Regardless of the approach you take, your efforts—or the efforts of whoever you hire to actually do the badda-bing work—will be substantially more effective if you can determine the species that's raising a ruckus with your turf. This, too, can be harder than you think.

Wild animals tend to visit when you're not looking. Or their preferred transportation mode is subterranean. For these reasons, trying to visually identify the animal is pretty much a waste of time, because you'll probably never catch it in the act of messing up your lawn. You're better off knowing what kind of damage they cause, and then tying the visual evidence to the most likely troublemaker.

The ones here are the worst offenders.

Long Ridges of Brown Grass

Moles are the most likely culprit. These small mammals spend most of their lives in underground tunnels, which means your chances of actually seeing one going about its normal affairs are slim to nil. You're not missing much; if you were to set eyes on one you'd be hard-pressed to find anything cute about these beady-eyed little animals. But there are a few things about their anatomy worth noting. They have huge, paddle-like forefeet studded with prominent toenails. They use these features to literally swim through soil, typically practicing their strokes pretty close to the surface. This is what damages your turf and makes the grass turn brown, as they disturb grass roots as they go. They also have soft, directionless fur that lets them travel forward or backward through their tunnels with ease.

Moles are very fond of moist, sandy loam soil. If this is what your lawn is all about, and you live near woods, pastures, or fields, there's a good chance a mole or two will stop by and tunnel about in search of their favorite food—earthworms and white grubs.

Tunnels plus soil mounds—"molehills"—indicate that moles aren't

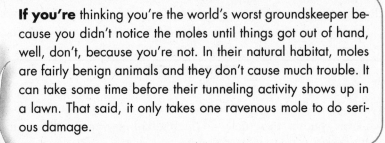

If you're thinking you're the world's worst groundskeeper because you didn't notice the moles until things got out of hand, well, don't, because you're not. In their natural habitat, moles are fairly benign animals and they don't cause much trouble. It can take some time before their tunneling activity shows up in a lawn. That said, it only takes one ravenous mole to do serious damage.

just traveling through. They've established underground nests and permanent tunnels to get to them, and the molehills are the by-product of their excavation work. If you see molehills, you're most likely dealing with a well-established mole colony. Their charter is in place and they're probably working on their flag and motto. At this point, they can be difficult to get rid of. Unless your yard is starting to look like it's crisscrossed with miniature truck tracks, leaving them alone and peacefully coexisting is an option. It's an option to give serious thought to if your home is near a mole-friendly habitat, because you'll end up dealing with the problem over and over again.

People have tried numerous humane approaches to moles with varying degrees of success, ranging from making their yards less habitable by getting rid of the insects they like to feed on to stomping down their tunnels and hills every time new ones appear. There's even a castor-oil-based mole repellent called Mole-Med that's supposedly effective on some moles, and in some circumstances. Most people find that these approaches are better at giving the animals time to get established and become real problems than at getting rid of them. Lowering the numbers of the insects they feed on can even make the damage worse by causing moles to increase their activities out of frustration before they leave, leaving you with a bigger mess to clean up and a big fat pesticide bill.

Poisoning isn't a good option for moles, as most poison baits are grain-based and moles aren't grain eaters. Zinc phosphide is the poison that the feds register for use against moles, and grain baits containing it can be found at nurseries or garden supply stores, but since the moles

> **Moles are** solitary travelers, most of the time. But mother moles and their babies can also take up residence in lawns during the spring.

don't like grain in the first place, don't make this the first line of defense in your battle.

If you do decide to take this approach, place the poison in active burrows—you can tell which are active by smashing them down with your foot or punching a couple of holes in them. Mark the spot and check it in about a day. If the smashed-down area is raised again, or the holes are covered up—moles hate light, so they'll scurry to cover up any holes they come across—you have a live burrow. Punch a couple more holes or remove a small section of the roof over the tunnel, drop the poison in, then cover the access spots with sod, a large stone, a board—basically anything that will keep the poison inside and away from children or other animals.

Three fumigants—aluminum phosphide, calcium cyanide, and gas cartridges—are approved for use on moles. Most are restricted-use pesticides, meaning they have to be applied by experts. Success with these is greatly enhanced if they're placed in deep burrows, not in surface runways.

Trapping is the best permanent control for moles. The main reason you can take this for gospel is that there are people who get rid of moles

> **Trapping** is a lot like fishing; casually dropping a line in the water and checking it every so often won't yield many fish. If you truly want to catch fish—or moles, or other animals—you'll have to be serious about it, and you'll have to stick with your plan once it's set.

for a living in certain parts of the United States (that's right, you pay them for every mole they get in your yard). Their method? Trapping. That said, moles are wily critters with a strong ability to sense danger and get out of its path. This makes them a challenge to nab. If you're going to try it, you'll need to understand some mole behavior or you'll end up with an empty trap and happy moles.

The most important mole behavior to know about, at least when it comes to getting rid of them, is this: They are creatures of habit and they look for food at the same time—early morning and/or evening— every day. So, if you can figure out where they're looking for that food, and get your traps set in that particular area, you might just catch your culprits. To do this, smack the tunnels down, then watch to see which ones pop back up. The ones that reappear signal ongoing mole activity and a good place to trap.

Because moles live underground, live trapping them isn't very effective. To make it work, you have to somehow drive the mole out of its burrow or tunnel and into the trap, which means you have to catch it in the act, which almost never happens. This isn't to say trapping isn't effective. It is, but you won't be using a live trap.

Spear, scissor-jaw, and choker loop traps stick down into mole tunnels and nab them where they live. They also effect a quick kill, meaning the mole's goose is cooked the second it's snared, which is actually about the most humane way of going about things if the area you live in doesn't permit trap and release.

These traps will only work on areas where the moles are still active (duh). You can figure out which ones they're using by smacking down the ground over every tunnel you can find. When the moles reestablish their routes, pick one active tunnel and jump on it hard enough to col-

Once you've figured out which runs the moles are using, you might even catch one or more as they're actually swimming along. Jam a pitchfork or shovel at just the right spot, and you might be able to simply flip the animal right out. The odds are against it, but it's cheaper than buying a trap.

lapse it. You want the mole to come along and think, "Gee, I gotta repair this." Put your trap right here, set it according to directions, and test it once or twice to make sure it's working right and not getting hung up on a rock or a tree root. Ideally, the mole will spring the trap when it repairs the tunnel. If it doesn't, you probably didn't jump hard enough to collapse the tunnel's innards. This time, jump a little harder. If you're not sure the tunnel's still in use, punch a small hole in it near the trap. Remember, moles abhor sunlight, and they'll plug the holes if they're still using the tunnel. If the trap isn't sprung and holes aren't plugged, move it to another location.

Spring and fall are the best mole-trapping seasons. Heat and cold drive them deeply subterranean and make them much more difficult to nab.

Large Mounds of Soil

Mounds of soil ranging from eight to twelve inches in diameter indicate pocket gophers, especially if you live in the West or Southeast.

Like moles, pocket gophers make extensive underground tunnels but they go deeper. As such, the soil they kick out around their entry holes are often the only indication of their presence. But they can also cause more extensive turf damage by burrowing holes and runways, which can leave larger soil mounds at tunnel entrances. Just one pocket gopher, in fact, can excavate as much as two and a quarter tons of soil in one year.

Like moles, pocket gophers are best controlled by trapping, and, since they also burrow like moles, the most effective traps on them aren't live. Get the appropriately sized trap, seek out active burrows and runs as above, and set the trap in spring before the females breed for best control.

Fumigating isn't effective against pocket gophers, as they'll sense the presence of the chemical and seal off treated areas. Poisoning can be effective if the bait is placed in a burrow or run, but you won't know for sure if you really got the animal.

Other possibilities with this type of damage are ground squirrels and voles, or meadow mice. Ground squirrels are considered varmints just about everywhere—tree squirrels are not, however, so be sure you know what you're dealing with here—so you can control them any way you see fit. Poisoning and fumigating works on them; the former is most effective in spring or late summer, when squirrels are actively feeding. Flooding them out by sticking a hose into their burrow can also work, but you'll need to deal with the animal when it comes out.

Trapping and poisoning are both effective against voles. Since they're so small, plain old mouse traps are fine here, but you'll need to set a lot of them. Put them along their established routes, at right angles to the runways and with the trigger end in the runway. The animals will set them off as they go by; you can bait if you want with apple slices or a peanut butter–oatmeal combo.

Ripped-Up Lawn

If your lawn looks like someone basically peeled back the top layer, suspect skunks or raccoons. They love to tear up turf for grubs, which is their primary food source. If you can cut down on their favorite food, they might eventually leave your yard on their own. Both animals are very good at setting up residency in and around houses, however, especially when the inhabitants of those houses make things hospitable for them. Woodpiles are great places for skunks and raccoons to hang out. They also like to crawl into empty spaces in foundations. Raccoons like to forage for food in garbage cans. If you keep yours outside, use containers that lock down tightly to keep them out.

If making your yard less hospitable to these animals doesn't get rid of them, they can be trapped. It's an especially good idea to do so if either animal is acting strangely. Both are disease carriers—skunks are particularly susceptible to rabies; raccoons fall prey to rabies and distemper.

 **Wondering if** a skunk or raccoon has taken up residence under your home? Sprinkle some powdery stuff—flour or corn starch works well—at likely entry points. Check those points in about a day or so. If you see marks or footprints in the powder, suspect an invader.

Trapping skunks can be problematic, for the obvious reason—you run a very real risk of getting sprayed, which is nothing you want to subject yourself to, believe me. If you think it smells bad when you catch a whiff of skunk stink while driving, there's nothing to describe the purely awful stench of a skunk bomb going off near you. When you set up a trap, put something over it—a heavy tarp or a big piece of burlap works well—to shield you and everything else in the area from the inevitable.

Live trapping is the preferred approach here. A raccoon-sized live trap will work for either animal. Canned fish packed in oil, fish-based cat food, or a fifty-fifty mix of peanut butter and honey or molasses works on raccoons. For skunks, go with the fish-based baits; the peanut butter blend isn't effective on them. Check regulations where you live regarding relocation and disposal.

Other controls are not recommended for either animal.

Lots of Medium to Large Holes, Yard Looks Like a Minefield

If you live in Texas, Florida, Georgia—well, just about anywhere in the South—suspect armadillos. These days they're even found, albeit a little rarely, as far north as Missouri, and their range is expanding.

Armadillos are practically blind. To compensate for their lack of sight, they have amazingly well-developed olfactory glands and can smell their favorite foods—beetles, grubs, ant larvae, and whatnot—as deep as six inches underground. They're also prolific eaters and will spend their waking hours seeking out their meals by rooting around in the ground, which is why they're so destructive. They dig with their noses, and when they hit pay dirt, they suck it up faster than fast. When they exhaust the supply in one spot, they move on to the next.

Like most nuisance wildlife, armadillos are nocturnal, and they burrow, big time. In fact, their burrows can go on for twenty-five feet or more and can also damage things like trees, shrubs, and foundations. They like wood and will often take up residence in wood piles or stumps; rock piles aren't off the possibility list either. If you have any of these on your land, get rid of them.

Live trapping is the best way to control armadillos. Since they're nearly blind, however, you just about have to take them by the paw and lead them into the trap. A raccoon-sized live trap will fit an armadillo. Set up the trap where the damage is taking place, then place a long narrow board or piece of plywood on either side of the opening, in an open wing formation, to guide the animal in. Bait the trap with over-ripe fruit such as bananas or apples, or earthworms placed in thin netting—panty hose work well. Check local regulations regarding release and/or disposal.

Now that we've conquered the wide world of wild animals, let's take a look at the most prevalent and potentially disruptive intruder of all. The Latin name is *Canis familiaris*, but it's better known as Fido or Fifi or Duke or Daisy or whatever name you happen to use when calling to man's best friend.

Dealing with Fido and Fluffy

If your turf is sporting brown patches ringed with bright green grass, chances are good that the intruder critters you're dealing with are domestic, either yours or your neighbors'. These are urine spots, caused by the chemicals in dog urine.

Dog urine contains nitrogen and other salts. When applied directly to grass—in other words, when your dog answers nature's call—these substances literally burn your grass, just like misapplied fertilizer can do. Remember, grass has no defense mechanisms and can't recognize trouble. So it's going to soak up those salts. It doesn't know any better.

The result—circular patches of yellow or brown grass, surrounded by one-to-two-inch rings of dark green grass. The light-colored grass indicates the exact spot where your dog relieved itself; the dark green ring is actually healthy grass enjoying the extra nitrogen boost from the urine that seeped into it. If your lawn is underfertilized for some reason (you should know better by now, but things can happen), the dark ring

Dogs are by far the bigger culprit than cats when it comes to pet spots. As a rule, cats have smaller bladders and different peeing preferences. Unlike dogs, which prefer grass over just about anything else, cats put up "scent posts" by marking bushes or trees. Or they'll bury their waste in gardens. This isn't any fun if you happen to be poking around in your garden sans gloves and you hit a cat deposit spot, especially if it's a fresh one, but at least it won't make your lawn look bad.

will be especially noticeable, as it will stand out in stark contrast to the pallid, light green of your starving grass.

Dog pee damage will be most prevalent in areas where your dog is confined, or if your dog likes a particular area of your yard and keeps going back there to do his or her thing. Of the two sexes, female dogs are the bigger problem, as they squat to urinate. Males typically don't, though male puppies will until they learn how to lift their legs. Plus, males, even neutered ones, tend to mark their territory by peeing as they walk. Even if their urine is fairly concentrated, they only leave a little bit behind as they move about. Females, instead of marking their territory, tend to squat and dump out their bladder in one spot instead of many. Some males will do this as well.

Fortunately, pee spots are unsightly more than anything else. Here's how to minimize or eliminate them:

- Don't let your dog urinate on your grass. Take it for walks so it can go in out-of-the-way places, preferably in uncultivated areas. If you don't appreciate spots on your grass, your neighbors probably won't appreciate them on their lawns either.
- Train your dog to go in a specific part of your yard, preferably one that's away from your home, from other people's homes, from high-traffic or use areas and that affords your dog and you some privacy. If your dog isn't real picky about its toilet environs, you can install an absorptive surface—pea gravel or mulch are two possible choices—to soak up the urine. If it is, and it

really, really likes squatting on grass, just kiss the grass in this area good-bye.

- Dilute the salts in the urine by watering things down as soon as Fido's done. Don't just sprinkle the spots with a watering can, flood them with a hose. This is a very effective solution, by the way, but you have to hit the puddle right away.
- Litter-box or paper train, if appropriate for your breed and your situation. This can work extremely well with toy breeds, many of which don't like doing their duty outside in the first place.
- Stick to male dogs, and make sure they learn how to lift their legs.
- Own small dogs. Smaller dogs produce less urine. Less urine equals less nitrogen waste.

If it's someone else's dog and you can't catch the culprit or its owner in the process of actually committing the crime, you have another set of problems that you might not be able to control very well. A solid fence will work. If neighbors are violating leash laws, you can try having a nice chat about it.

Repellants are available but most aren't all that effective. In fact, some of them actually encourage dogs to pee more so they can overcome the strange smell with their own smell.

A fairly new tactic, and a pretty effective one, is a motion-activated sprinkler. When doggie comes near, doggie gets sprayed. Presumably, so

Some people, especially those who appreciate the convenience of shoving their dogs out the front door to do their duty, or are simply too lazy to walk the poor mutts, have tried to deal with dog spots by modifying their pooches' diets. Most of these approaches merely change the pH of the urine, which has little or nothing to do with dog spots. What's more, they can put dogs at greater risk of developing bladder stones.

If you're thinking about trying any of them, check with a vet first to make sure what you're going to try won't be harmful to your dog. That would be another way to solve the problem, but probably not the preferred approach.

does the person at the end of the leash if doggie is leashed. Most likely, this nice Pavlovian experience for both dog and owner is one that won't have to be repeated. Very often, anyway.

Depending on what you're dealing with, you can get the upper hand with critters, but don't count on it. This is very much an area in which a "live and let live" attitude can serve you well, and save you from the unpleasant task of stomping out Bambi's friends.

CHAPTER 16

When Good Lawns Go Bad

Good lawns can go bad for lots of reasons, but many if not most lawns can be saved. Some can't. Here's how to know if yours is salvageable or not, and what to do either way.

Good grass can go bad for many reasons. Years of neglect, ongoing disease or insect attack, poor drainage, soil compaction, even growing the wrong grass . . . it can all result in lawns that are more frustrating than pleasurable.

If you're to the hair-pulling point with your lawn, perhaps even ready to pull the plug, cement it over, and put up a parking lot, this chapter will come to your rescue. And your lawn's.

BAD LAWN, BAD LAWN, BAD, BAD LAWN

Problem lawns can be overwhelming. Everywhere you look, it seems, there's something wrong. Bad lawn here, bad lawn there, bad lawn everywhere. It can be enough to make you want to surrender your lawn geek status for something more sensible and turn your lawn into something other than lawn. The southwestern look—gravel and a scattering of cacti—is becoming more appealing by the minute. So what if you live in North Dakota; you'll find prickly plants that can handle the cold. Or maybe huge perennial gardens with smatterings of turf as accents. The neighbor down the street went the natural approach. You're thinking you could live with a lawn that looks more like a meadow. Maybe.

The catch here is that problem lawns typically have more than one problem, and you don't know where to look first, not to mention where to start. Chances are that things aren't quite as bad as you think they are; you just have to get a grip. But how?

There's an old saying that goes something like this: How do you eat an elephant? One bite at a time.

Let's follow the "one bite at a time" approach with your turf. A micro view, instead of a macro view. Things are usually less daunting this way.

Start by taking a deep breath. Two if necessary. Maybe even three. Now let's take a walk. Not around the block, around your yard. Walk slowly. Stroll, even. Really take the time to look at what's going on and think about what your lawn is trying to tell you. You might spot one or more of the following:

- a shady area, maybe more than one, where grass is struggling or won't grow at all
- a soggy area that stays wet or where water pools when the rest of your lawn is dry
- patches of brown grass
- patches of weeds
- slopes or exposed areas where grass looks thin and listless
- a well-worn Fido path along your fence line
- weedy, thin turf everywhere

The good news? You can fix all of these things. Some fixes are easier than others, some remedies will work faster than others, but nothing here spells give up the ghost.

Ready to get to work? Here goes.

ON THE SHADY SIDE

You should know enough about how grass grows by now to also know that it typically doesn't do well in shade. Sure, some species and some cultivars are better at it than others, but let's say you have an extremely shady yard, or areas that are very dark and very shaded. Try as you might, grass simply won't grow or it comes in puny and thin.

Shade situations call for a reality check. The big piece of reality to get your mind around here is this: There's not a turfgrass on this green earth that grows well in deep shade. Look at naturally created shady spots. See any grass? So why do you think you should be able to get grass to grow in spots where even Mother Nature caved in?

You have two options when dealing with shady areas. Both center on changing the microclimate in them.

Changing Up

The first fix requires bidding adios to the grass. It's not doing anyone any good anyway, so why spend additional time and resources trying to make it grow? Remove the turf—what's left of it, anyway—and put something else in its place. Choices here include:

- Ground covers, such as wood chips, gravel, and so on. Crumb rubber, which you'll read more about later, is another possible choice.
- Living ground cover. There aren't many creeping perennials that do well in deep shade, but there are enough to afford some selection. Depending on where you live, choices include sweet woodruff, bishop's weed, periwinkle or vinca vine, some ivies, wild ginger, and redwood sorrel.
- Shade gardens. Like ground covers, perennials for deep shade are somewhat limited. Choices here include lily of the valley, hostas, ferns, bleeding heart, anemones, trilliums, and meadow rue.

Most ground covers spread by creeping. Some can be invasive, so make your selections carefully if you don't want them taking over your entire yard.

Always check moisture levels in shady areas and adjust your watering accordingly. Grass in shady areas needs less water in general, and shady areas are also spots where soggy soil can easily develop.

Another approach to shady areas is to learn to love them by creating reasons to use them. Maybe your kids would appreciate a shady play area on hot summer days. Or how about an outdoor seating area for alfresco dining?

You'll find tips on turf removal toward the end of this chapter.

Whack Things Back

The second microclimate fix requires removing some of the stuff that's causing the problem. If you've owned your house for a while and you can't remember the last time you had your trees professionally pruned, they're probably long overdue for it. Tree overgrowth is not only unsightly, it's dangerous. Shrubs run amok are also great hangouts for animal intruders.

Unless you're an experienced arborist and you have the requisite equipment to trim things up right, call in a tree specialist to do the pruning for you. Shrubs you can handle yourself with a good pruner or lopper. Be sure to get under the bushes and thin or remove whatever's growing there as well.

Both efforts—and especially cleaning up those shrubs—will vastly improve air movement and the amount of light reaching the ground in these areas. Their humidity levels will be more in line with other parts of the yard, too. Guess what? You might even get grass to grow. Be sure to plant shade-loving cultivars or mixes anyway.

OUT, OUT, DAMNED WATER

Your kids might love to watch the little birdies play in the puddles that remain on your lawn after a good rainstorm. You might get a kick out of them, too. If you do, buy a birdbath for your feathered friends, because you're going to kiss those puddles good-bye.

Soggy sod or standing water on turfgrass indicates drainage problems. They put your lawn at risk for diseases. What's more, that sod, when it dries, tends to turn into something resembling concrete. In other words, soil compaction. No turf area worth its weight in salt has ever been able to succeed long term with drainage issues.

Drainage problems can happen at the surface, down below, or both.

Skimming the Surface

Lawns should slope evenly and continually. Any interruptions, even fairly slight ones, and water will find them as sure as I'm writing and you're reading. This is why good subgrade preparation is so important. But even the best-prepared lots can and usually do develop low spots for a variety of reasons—soil settling, erosion, even normal wear and tear can disrupt site continuity. Instead of water exiting gracefully from your yard, it sticks around and causes problems.

If low spots aren't apparent—they can be very subtle—you can identify them by watching how the water runs during the next rainstorm. Or create your own storm and flood suspect areas with a hose. Irregularities should show up pretty quickly.

Adding soil to low-lying areas is the fastest and easiest fix for surface drainage problems. Installing a drain in problem areas is the more permanent solution, but it's also costlier and beyond what you might be able to do on your own. Another option, should you be so inclined and it works for your yard, is establishing a water feature. This one I won't go into, as it's really more about decorating your lawn than caring for it.

Adding Soil   If there's still grass growing in your low spots, you can't just dump a load of soil in them and call it a day. It will smother the grass, which I'm pretty sure is not your goal. Slow and steady wins the race here. Shovel it on in thin layers, no more than a half inch at a time. Use soil that's compatible with what's already in your lawn to avoid soil layering. Remember, soil layers grab water instead of letting it filter through. If you don't know what lies beneath, this is a good

Drainage problems can be complex. If yours is, call in the experts. Look under drain specialist in the phone book. You can spend lots of time and money on your own fixes, only to have them not work or, worse, make the problem worse.

time for a casual or official soil test. Using soil that's a little heavier in sand than what's already there would be erring on the safe side. Wait a week or so, check how the grass is doing, then add the next layer if necessary.

If there's little to no grass growing in the area, which is a real possibility if the area has been under water for a while, then go ahead and dump in enough soil to bring the low spots up to par. Again, match the current soil texture or make it a little sandier. Seed or sod over the area.

Drained, Simply Drained Diverting standing water by installing a French drain is the faster fix and the one for more serious drainage problems, like water that's ending up in your basement. They're not that difficult to construct, but they do call for some digging and knowing where to place them for the best results.

Here's what a basic DIY installation looks like. After reading it through, you decide if it's something you want to do or if it's best left to the experts.

1. Have the area marked for utility lines.
2. Find the lowest point in the problem area (this is pretty simple, it's where the water collects first).
3. Dig a trench there. Make it about two feet deep, about six inches wide, and long enough so it can carry water safely away from the problem area. If it has to go a long way, rent a trencher.
4. Compact the bottom of the trench, either by walking on it or using a small tamper.

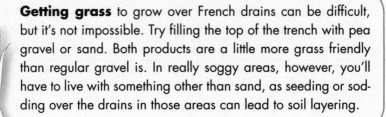

Getting grass to grow over French drains can be difficult, but it's not impossible. Try filling the top of the trench with pea gravel or sand. Both products are a little more grass friendly than regular gravel is. In really soggy areas, however, you'll have to live with something other than sand, as seeding or sodding over the drains in those areas can lead to soil layering.

5. Add a plastic trench pipe. This is the conduit for the water. They have holes in them. Be sure the holes face down, not up.
6. Cover the pipe with clean gravel about one inch or larger. Filling the trench to the top is best for controlling surface water, but then you have to contend with a line of gravel running through your yard. If it works for your yard, you can disguise it somewhat by building a footpath along it. If you want to sod or seed over the area, stop the fill at six inches or so below the soil surface. Fill in with soil and seed the area or sod it.

A dry well is another option. These devices channel water from soil surface to subsoil. Dry wells can involve some fairly extensive digging to install underground holding tanks and whatnot, depending on the severity of the problem, and are usually best left to the experts. If you think one's in your future, it's probably time to make a call or two.

Wet Down Below

If your lawn's slope looks okay but water's still standing around, you have an internal drainage problem. The topsoil and subsoil might have been a little questionable to begin with, and got worse over time. There might be soil layering going on. Excessive tree root growth can even cause internal drainage problems.

Aerating the topsoil might help some, but the problem usually lies below it. A French drain can help in these areas, but again, it's probably time to call in the experts.

Every spring, as regularly as clockwork, I'm asked if going over lawns with a weighted roller will smooth out their bumps and wrinkles. The answer is pretty much no. Rollers don't do much good, as the ones light enough to maneuver easily are too light to have much effect on the turf below them, and soil compaction is a risk with heavier ones. Aerating is the best approach for smoothing out slight hills and valleys, short of starting over from scratch and paying more attention to your lot's final grade. Do a good core aeration and drag the cores over your turf. They'll gravitate to the low areas and fill them in. It will take some time, however. Plan to do it for at least a couple of years.

PATCHING THINGS UP

Try as you might, some dead spots will come into your life sure as bluebirds are blue. Before you fix them, try to determine what's causing them. If you don't, they'll keep coming back.

Next, patch 'em up. For cool-season lawns, seed or sod; be sure to go with products that match what's already in your yard so your patches don't stick out like sore thumbs. For warm-season grasses, patching with turf dug from your own yard is usually the best approach. (Take from areas close to the house.) Not only are many of them great at filling in bare spots, but they might not be available as seed.

Bare spots tend to come back like a bad penny. So don't get discouraged if yours do. You can keep trying to figure out why they do,

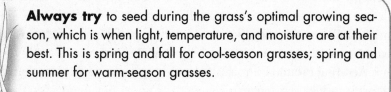

Always try to seed during the grass's optimal growing season, which is when light, temperature, and moisture are at their best. This is spring and fall for cool-season grasses; spring and summer for warm-season grasses.

but patching them is usually the course of least resistance. Watch for straight lines or patterns; remember, turf doesn't die naturally in either.

BUNCHES OF WEEDS

Remember, weeds are opportunists, and they'll grow wherever they can find space. If there are weeds in your yard, you've somehow given them the chance to establish residency. Take a close look at the turf in the area. If it's thin, maybe there's a circulation problem going on. The soil could be compacted, or maybe there's excessive thatch growth.

If weeds outnumber grass plants in some areas, smothering them out and starting over from scratch in those spots is probably your best bet. Turn to the description of field bindweed in chapter 11 for how to do it.

HITTING THE SLOPES

Grass doesn't mix well with hills and slopes, as water runs off these areas before it can do the plants much good. Add sunlight to the problem and you've got a double whammy. What's more, they can be dangerous to mow. If you're tired of climbing that particular mountain, think about making a change.

Sun-loving ground covers are one option for these areas, and a low-maintenance one as well. Choices here include snow-in-summer, snow-on-the-mountain, sage, pussytoes, moss pinks or creeping phlox, hen and chicks, prostrate speedwell, creeping potentilla, and pineleaf penstemon. Beds of ornamental grasses are also a possibility here; their deep roots are also good for controlling erosion.

Modifying irrigation systems on hills and slopes is another way to whack mountains down to molehills. Drip systems, which apply moisture slowly at ground level, are better at keeping water in place than traditional sprinkler systems.

AT THE DOG TRACK

Dogs that spend a significant amount of time outdoors, and that have fences to run along, will typically do so unless there's something preventing them from it—say they're also tethered to a chain that doesn't let them reach the fence line. Over time, the grass along your fence thins out or dies completely because it's trying to grow into something that's more like concrete than dirt.

You can aerate the tracks, of course, but this is a short-term fix if you don't do something about the cause. The better approach, especially if you plan on keeping your dog and allowing it free access to your yard, is to give your dog something else to run on. You can replace the grass with something that can take the constant trampling, like wood chips or pea gravel. Or you can leave it in place but cushion the blow with something called crumb rubber.

Crumb rubber is recycled from beat-up, worn-out automobile tires. The refining process sterilizes it and makes it safe for grass, dogs, kids, and anything else that comes into contact with it.

Crumb rubber can be put down in place of grass or in addition to it. Adding it to turf, especially in high-traffic areas, helps reduce soil compaction and improves drainage. It can also reduce pesticide use and lower water and fertilizer needs. What's more, it lasts a long, long time. Use it in your lawn, and you won't have to replace it for at least twenty-five years. In short, it's pretty amazing stuff, and a great reuse of a product that used to end up in landfills or ditches more often than not.

If your dog track is still sending up grass shoots, a half to three-quarter-inch layer of crumb rubber will protect the plant crowns and

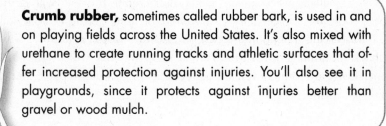

Crumb rubber, sometimes called rubber bark, is used in and on playing fields across the United States. It's also mixed with urethane to create running tracks and athletic surfaces that offer increased protection against injuries. You'll also see it in playgrounds, since it protects against injuries better than gravel or wood mulch.

give the plants a chance to recover. It will also protect new seedlings if you decide to reseed the damaged areas before you put the product down. Here's how to apply it:

1. Determine how much product you'll need by measuring the fence perimeter and the width of the dog track. As an example, let's say your fence measures forty by sixty feet and the dog track is two to three feet, give or take a few inches in spots. You'll need to cover five hundred square feet (forty plus forty plus sixty plus sixty equals two hundred feet, times 2.5, the average of the width of the dog track). Purchase the same number of pounds as you have square feet of dog track area. This will be enough for a half-inch layer. Multiply the total by 1.5 if you want to add another quarter inch.
2. Aerate and water the affected areas. Seed if desired.
3. Spread the crumb rubber with a rake.
4. Keep your dog off the area for a few days.

That's all there is to it.

Crumb rubber, since it's black, does a great job of soaking up heat. This is something to keep in mind if you're putting it down during the summer and you want to reseed the area, as it can heat up the soil beyond favorable germination temperatures. Applying it and seeding in the fall is the better approach for cool-season grasses. Warm-season grasses love the heat, so you can put the crumb rubber down anytime.

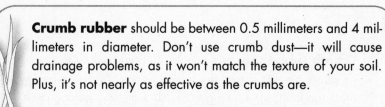

Crumb rubber should be between 0.5 millimeters and 4 millimeters in diameter. Don't use crumb dust—it will cause drainage problems, as it won't match the texture of your soil. Plus, it's not nearly as effective as the crumbs are.

THE CHANCES ARE THIN

Weedy, thin, butt-ugly turf might look like it's fodder for the compost bin, but chances are that it's not. It can be saved, and doing so might be easier than you think. Even if your turf looks like a lost cause, simply try treating it right. You have nothing to lose and everything to gain.

Fertilize and water regularly, mow at the proper height, and you might be amazed at what you, with some help from Mother Nature, of course, hath wrought. All those problems that once plagued you? Gone. Weed control? Maybe a little spot treatment for some of the peskier ones, but nothing drastic. Resident bug population? Under control. Diseases? Nary a one in sight.

Amazing what a little TLC can do, isn't it?

STARTING OVER

Sometimes, no matter what you do or what you try, your lawn problems retain the upper hand. Your best efforts don't bring the desired results. Your lawn still looks a mess. You're still frustrated, probably even more so than you were before.

Putting your lawn out of its misery and starting over again might seem drastic, but it might be the better approach in the long run.

Renovate or Reestablish?

Like starting over in inside spaces, there are various levels of starting over outside. If the problem is in the grass, not in the site itself—in other words, the soil's in good shape and things are sloping the way they should—renovating might be all that's necessary.

Consider renovation if you're battling things like:

- Excessive, hard-to-kill perennial weeds. If you can't see the grass for the weeds, this is a battle you're not going to win. Easily, anyway.
- Diseases and/or insect damage that erupts every year. You'll save time and money in the long run by replacing the old grass with a more resistant species or variety.

- Your yard is getting more wear than what it was originally designed for. The previous owners might have had a show lawn. You, on the other hand, have a passel of kids and they have a passel of friends. Your pretty show grass can't take the wear. Replace it with something that can.
- Dead grass due to drought or flood.

Renovating calls for killing off everything that's green, or should be green, while leaving the bare bones of your yard untouched, and seeding or sodding a new lawn right over all the dead stuff. Here's how to do it:

1. Kill, kill, kill. Spray a nonselective herbicide (glyphosate) over the renovation area. If there are particularly persistent weeds about, you'll have to live with dead grass and weeds for a while, as you'll want to make a second application to make sure you killed off everything.

2. Mow low, very low. Yup, this is a time when it's okay to scalp your grass. The plants are already dead; there's nothing you can do to further harm them. The lower you mow, the better the seed-to-ground contact. Set the mower blade as low as it will go.

3. Cut things up. Rent a power rake or a sod cutter and slice through the dead stuff. Really dig into what's there. Doing so will further improve future seed-to-ground contact. Rake in both directions.

4. Hook up the oxygen. Core aerate the area. Rake out the plugs. You want the site smooth, and there won't be enough time to let the plugs decompose naturally.

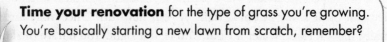

Time your renovation for the type of grass you're growing. You're basically starting a new lawn from scratch, remember?

You can save a little time and a lot of effort by renting a slit-seeder, which cultivates and seeds at the same time.

5. Seed it. Use the same amount you would for establishing a new lawn. Get the seeds down to where they need to go by running that power rake again.
6. Feed 'em. Starter fertilizer, which is higher in growth-supporting phosphorous, is the choice here.
7. Water 'em. Keep the area uniformly moist until you start seeing green.

Reestablishment is called for if there are problems at ground level or below. This is the route to take if you're battling things like:

- Serious drainage problems.
- Soil fertility issues. If your lawn simply doesn't respond well to your cultural efforts, there's a good chance that the soil is lacking nutrients. Be sure to test it.
- Thin topsoil. Ideally, topsoil should be four to six inches deep. Thinner than this and there's not much for roots to dig into.

Chapter 5 is the place to turn for site preparation advice; chapter 6 for help with starting your new lawn from scratch.

Your lawn isn't the only thing that's getting a second chance. You are, too. Start things off on the right foot by being a good lawn geek. You've created life where there wasn't life before. Be proud of that, and let your pride show by doing right by your new turf. Once more and finally, mow it right, water it right, and feed it right. You'll have the lawn of your dreams.

GLOSSARY

acid soil—soil with a pH below 7

aerating—punching holes in the soil to improve oxygen, water, and nutrient flow

alkaline soil—soil with a pH above 7

amendment—a substance added to soil to change its physical composition

annual, summer—grass that goes through a complete life cycle in one growing season, from spring to fall

annual, winter—grass that starts growing in fall, overwinters, and dies after producing seed the following spring

bedknife—the fixed blade on a reel mower

blade—the upper portion of a grass leaf

blend—a mix of two or more varieties or cultivars of a single turfgrass species

bunchgrasses—grasses that grow by adding shoots or tillers at their crowns

carbohydrate—an organic compound consisting of carbon, hydrogen, and oxygen, used as a food and energy source by humans, animals, and plants

clippings—the leaves and stems cut off when mowing

collar—the part of the leaf where the blade and sheath join to-gether

cool-season turfgrass—a grass that grows well in cool weather

core aeration—increasing oxygen, water, and nutrient flow in soil by removing small plugs, or cores, of soil

creeping grass—grasses that spread laterally via stolons and/or rhizomes

crown—the center of the plant's activity, where the leaves, roots, and stems originate

cultivar—a specifically developed grass variety of a certain species

cultivation—working the soil

cultural practices—the things that are done to take care of a lawn—mowing, cultivating, feeding (fertilizing), watering, and so on

cutting height—on mowers, the distance between the blade of the mower and the point at which it cuts grass

dethatching—removing excessive thatch accumulation

disease—a disorder with recognizable signs, often with a known cause

ecosystem—a group of interdependent organisms together with the environment they inhabit and depend on

endophyte—microscopic fungi that grow inside blades and leaf stalks of grasses

evapotranspiration—the return of moisture to the air through soil evaporation and plant transpiration

fertigating—applying fertilizer through an irrigation system

fertilizer burn—dehydrated plant tissue caused by excessive fertilizer

fertilizer rate—the amount of fertilizer applied to a defined area

fertilizer ratio—the ratio of essential nutrients in fertilizer

fungicide—a pesticide applied to battle fungal diseases

grade, grading—the elevation and contours of a site; also, establishing these elements prior to planting

grass canopy—the uppermost layer, or ceiling, of vegetation in turf

grub—the wormlike larvae of beetles

herbicide—a pesticide applied to remove undesirable plants, such as weeds

hybrid—a grass developed by breeding dissimilar grasses of two species

hydromulching—applying a mixture of water and mulch over seeds already in or on the soil

hydroseeding—applying seed in a slurry mixture of water, fertilizer, and mulch

infiltration rate—the amount of water soil can absorb in a given period

insecticide—a pesticide applied to combat insects

interseeding—seeding into turf to improve its density or to change its composition

lateral shoot—a stolon or rhizome

liquid fertilizer—fertilizer in liquid form

mat—the layer of living and dead plant matter that accumulates between plants at the surface of the soil

metabolism—the ongoing, interrelated series of chemical interactions in living organisms that provide the energy and nutrients to sustain life

microclimate—a mini-climate

microorganism—tiny living organisms, such as fungi and bacteria

mixture—a combination of two or more grass species

mowing height—the height at which grass is cut

mulch—a protective covering of organic material laid over the soil around plants to prevent erosion, retain moisture, and sometimes enrich the soil

nitrification—to introduce nitrogen or nitrogen compounds into the soil to increase fertility

nodes—enlarged portions on grass stems where new leaves develop

nonselective herbicide—herbicides that kill anything they come into contact with

overseeding—seeding a cool-season grass into warm-season turf to provide winter color

overwinter—to last through the winter

perennial—a plant that survives from season to season

pesticide—a chemical substance used to kill pests

pH, soil—the measure of a soil's hydrogen ion activity level, used to determine whether it's alkaline or acidic

photosynthesis—the process by which green plants produce simple carbohydrates from carbon dioxide, hydrogen, and sunlight

plugs—pieces of sod used to establish turf

postemergence herbicide—an herbicide applied to kill weeds after they germinate

potash—a form of potassium used in fertilizer

preemergence herbicide—an herbicide applied to kill weeds as they germinate, before they establish

preventive application—applying pesticides prior to problems cropping up

recuperative capacity—a grass plant's ability to recover from damage

reel mower—a mower that cuts grass with a rotating reel that passes across a blade attached to the mower frame

resiliency—a grass plant's ability to stand up to adversity

rhizomes—jointed, underground stems

roots—the underground network that anchors plants and provides water and nutrients to support their growth

rotary mower—a mower that cuts with a rotating blade

scalp, scalping—cutting a lawn so low that the crowns are damaged

seed—the plant part resulting from reproduction

seed head—the flowering or seeding part of the plant

selective herbicide—an herbicide designed to target certain plants while leaving others alone

sheath—the tubular portion at the base of the leaf that wraps around and encloses the stem

shoot density—the number of shoots in a defined area

slow-release fertilizer—fertilizer that dissolves slowly either by water breaking it down or by microbial activity

sod—strips of turfgrass with soil attached used for vegetative establishment

sod cutter—a device used to cut sod when harvesting

sodding—establishing turf with sod

soil layering—stratification from soils with different physical characteristics placed on top of one another in layers

soil mix—prepared soil used for growing grass

soil probe—a tool used for testing soil or obtaining soil samples

spreading grass—a grass that grows by sending out stolons and/or rhizomes

sprig—a small piece of sod, typically just a tiller, stolon, or rhizome, used to establish turf

sprigging—establishing a new lawn or filling in an existing lawn with sprigs

stand—an area of grass

stem—the vertical center of the grass plant that supports the seed head of the plant

stolons—lateral, joined stems that originate from the crown, travel above the ground, and develop new shoots and roots along the way

subgrade—the bed of ground on which the foundation of a building or lawn is based

syringe, syringing—watering grass plants lightly during periods of high heat to bring down temperatures in the grass canopy

texture, leaf—the relative size of a grass blade

texture, soil—the size of particles in soil

thatch—the matted layer of dead plant material that builds up next to the soil at the base of lawn grasses

tillers—shoots that develop in the crown but don't creep along or under the ground like stolons or rhizomes

tip burn—leaf tips that turn white, usually from dehydration

topdressing—a thin layer of soil spread over established turf or seeds; also the act of doing this

transpiration—giving off water vapor through a plant's surface

turf—a dense, thick, even cover of grass and roots in the top layer of soil

turfgrass—a species or cultivar of grass specifically used to establish turf

turfgrass community—the turfgrass family

urea—a nitrogen-based compound

variety—a specific type of grass species, also called cultivar

vertical mower—a machine with vertically rotating blades used for dethatching

wear—the effects of continually damaging turf by scuffing or tearing leaf blades

wind burn—death and browning of grass leaves caused by dehydration

winterkill—damage to turfgrass during the winter

APPENDIX A

RESOURCES

Books

Virginia Scott Jenkins, *The Lawn: A History of an American Obsession* (Washington and London: The Smithsonian Institution Press, 1994).

   Jenkins isn't a lawn geek, merely a historian curious about the American obsession with front lawns. Her curiosity turned into a doctoral dissertation, and her dissertation turned into this book. As such, it sometimes reads like a dissertation, but if you want to learn why and how the American lawn became what it is today, there's no better guide out there.

George Teyssot, ed., *The American Lawn* (New York: Princeton Architectural Press, 1999).

   Another fairly scholarly book, but an interesting read, as it's a collection of essays that tackle lawns from varying viewpoints—historical, political, artistic, literary, and so on. If nothing else, it's worth picking up for its illustrations of green spaces dating back many centuries.

Internet Sites

http://grounds-mag.com. The online version of *Grounds Maintenance* magazine. Geared more toward professional groundskeepers, but lots of good geeky information here, too, especially since it's coming from the front line.

www.ntep.org. Home of the National Turfgrass Evaluation Program (NTEP). Lots of good information on grass, high on the geekiness level.

www.jaitire.com. If you're having problems finding crumb rubber, this site can point you in the right direction. In the interest of full disclosure, I developed Crown III, the topdressing product featured here, with one of my associates.

www.lesco.com. LESCO is where the pros shop, and where you'll find equipment, pesticides, and fertilizer that big-box and garden stores don't stock. Their Internet site has some good general information on lawn care, plus a LESCO service center locator.

www.weedalert.com. Billed as "The Turf Professional's Online Source for Weed Control Options," this site contains alphabetical and regional weed locators and thumbnail images of unwanted plants.

www.briggsandstratton.com. The online home of Briggs & Stratton. If you're looking for a new lawn mower, you can go here and compare the features on lots of B & S machines.

www.yarddoctor.com. My own little patch of green on the Internet.

www.ipminstitute.org. If you're interested in learning more about Integrated Pest Management, the Web site for the IPM Institute of North America is a place to start.

www.turf.msu.edu. This Web site, maintained by the Department of Crop and Soil Sciences at Michigan State University, contains detailed information on a wide variety of turfgrass subjects, gleaned from the front lines—MSU's Turf Team. You'll also find information on various turfgrass programs offered at MSU should you be interested in exchanging amateur lawn geek status for professional.

www.msuturfweeds.net. Need help identifying those pesky weeds in your yard? This site, also maintained by MSU's Department of Crop and Soil Sciences, offers extensive weed ID help. You can search for weeds by family, common name, or Latin name. Also here are 320 weed images for double-checking your weed sleuthing.

www.irrigation.org. There's some good information on irrigation at this site, including advice on hiring an irrigation contractor.

www.seedsuperstore.com. Online source for Supina bluegrass.

APPENDIX B

LAWN-CARE CALENDARS

GEOGRAPHIC REGION

A) Northwest
B) Mountain West
C) Southwest

Cultural Practice	Jan	Feb	Mar	Apr	May	Jun	Jul	Aug	Sep	Oct	Nov	Dec
Fertilization				C	ABC	ABC	BC	C	ABC		AB	
Cultivation				ABC	ABC	BC	C	BC	ABC	ABC		
Overseeding				AB	AB	B		AB	AB	A		
Seeding and sprigging			C	C	C	C	C	C				
Overseeding cool-season grasses									C	C	C	
Cool-Season grass fertilization		C							C	C		

Weed Control	Jan	Feb	Mar	Apr	May	Jun	Jul	Aug	Sep	Oct	Nov	Dec
Preemergence crabgrass control		C	C	AC	AB	B						
Postemergence broadleaf control			C		A	B				AB		C
Dormant grass winter weed control	C	C										C

Pest Control	Jan	Feb	Mar	Apr	May	Jun	Jul	Aug	Sep	Oct	Nov	Dec
Sod webworm						A	AB	B				
European crane fly			A	A	A							
White grubs							AC	ABC	ABC			
Bluegrass billbugs				AC	AC	ABC	ABC					
Bermudagrass mite			C	C	C	C	C	C	C			
Bermudagrass scale			C	C	C	C	C	C	C			
Armyworm			C	C	C	C	C	C	C	C		

GEOGRAPHIC REGION
A) Central Southeast
B) Gulf Coast & Florida

Fertilization	Jan	Feb	Mar	Apr	May	Jun	Jul	Aug	Sep	Oct	Nov	Dec
Bermuda and zoysiagrass				B	B	B	B	B	B			
Bahia- and centipedegrass					A				A			
St. Augustine- and bermudagrass			A	A	A	A	A	A	A			
Cool-season grasses	A	A								A	A	A

Cultural Practice	Jan	Feb	Mar	Apr	May	Jun	Jul	Aug	Sep	Oct	Nov	Dec
Cultivation				AB	AB	AB	AB	AB	AB	AB		
Seeding and sprigging			A	AB	AB	AB	AB	AB				
Overseeding cool-season grass										A	A	A

Weed Control	Jan	Feb	Mar	Apr	May	Jun	Jul	Aug	Sep	Oct	Nov	Dec
Preemergence crabgrass control		AB	AB	AB		A						
Postemergence broadleaf control				AB							A	AB
Dormant grass winter weed control	AB	AB										AB

Pest Control	Jan	Feb	Mar	Apr	May	Jun	Jul	Aug	Sep	Oct	Nov	Dec
Mole cricket					A	AB	AB	A				
White grubs							AB	AB	AB			
Bermudagrass mite			AB	AB	AB	AB	AB	AB				
Bermudagrass scale			B	AB	AB	AB	AB	AB	AB			
Armyworm				AB	AB	AB	AB	AB	AB	AB		
Southern chinch bug			A	A	A	A	A	A	A	A	A	
Sod webworm					A	A	A	A	A	A	A	

TRANSITION ZONE
A) Cool-season Grasses
B) Warm-season Grasses

Cultural Practices	Jan	Feb	Mar	Apr	May	Jun	Jul	Aug	Sep	Oct	Nov	Dec
Fertilization	B	B	B	AB	AB	AB	B	B	AB	A		A
Cultivation			A	AB	AB	B	B	B	AB	AB	A	
Seeding and sprigging				B	B	B	B	B				
Overseeding			A	A	A				A	A	A	
Overseeding cool-season grasses									B	B		
Cool-season grass fertilization		B								B	B	

Weed Control	Jan	Feb	Mar	Apr	May	Jun	Jul	Aug	Sep	Oct	Nov	Dec
Preemergence crabgrass control		B	AB	AB								
Postemergence broadleaf control				AB								AB
Dormant grass winter weed control	B	B										B

Pest Control	Jan	Feb	Mar	Apr	May	Jun	Jul	Aug	Sep	Oct	Nov	Dec
Sod webworm						A	A					
White grubs							AB	AB	AB			
Hairy chinch bugs						A	A	A				
Mole cricket						B	B					
Bermudagrass mite				B	B	B	B	B				
Bermudagrass scale			B	B	B	B	B	B	B			
Armyworm			B	B	B	B	B	B	B	B		

MIDWEST AND NORTHEAST
A) Northern Half
B) Southern Half

Cultural Practices	Jan	Feb	Mar	Apr	May	Jun	Jul	Aug	Sep	Oct	Nov	Dec
Fertilization				B	AB	AB			AB	B	A	B
Cultivation			B	AB	AB				AB	AB	B	
Overseeding			B	AB	AB			A	AB	AB	B	

Weed Control	Jan	Feb	Mar	Apr	May	Jun	Jul	Aug	Sep	Oct	Nov	Dec
Preemergence crabgrass control			B	AB	A							
Postemergence broadleaf control				B	A					A	B	

Pest Control	Jan	Feb	Mar	Apr	May	Jun	Jul	Aug	Sep	Oct	Nov	Dec
Sod webworm						AB	AB					
White grubs							AB	AB	AB			
Hairy chinch bugs							AB	AB	B			
Bluegrass billbug				A	A	A	A					

APPENDIX C

ESSENTIAL GEAR, AND ESSENTIALS ABOUT GEAR

Being well equipped is part and parcel of being a lawn geek. You can be extensively equipped or take the minimalist approach. Either way, the list below contains the ten "must-haves." Without them, you're nothing.

Before we start, some quick advice from the front line. You don't have to buy the most expensive equipment, but you definitely don't want to base your decisions on money alone. Wise geeks will do some comparison shopping to find the equipment that offers the best value for the money, but they'll stop short of analysis to paralysis.

Years of being a lawn geek have taught me this: You definitely get what you pay for when it comes to tools of the trade. Nothing's more frustrating than having tools or machinery break down in the middle of a project, and cheap equipment is almost guaranteed to do exactly this. So, be prepared to spend a little dough here. You won't regret it.

Mower
Since mowing is the cultural practice that affects a lawn more than any other, your mower is the one piece of equipment that will make or break your lawn-care program. There's no one perfect mower, but there's a right mower (or two or three) for you and your lawn.

For help on choosing a mower, turn to chapter 7.

String Trimmer
These devices make fast work of tidying up the edges of your green space. Get one to match the size of your yard. I like gasoline-powered trimmers, as I hate

dealing with power cords. You'll find more information on the different types in chapter 7.

Gasoline Cans
You'll need one or two, depending on the size of your mower and if you have to mix gas and oil for your trimmer or other implements. If this is the case, be sure to clearly label each can—you don't want to put a gas-and-oil mix into an engine calibrated for pure gas.

Rotary Spreader
Definitely don't cheap out on this piece of equipment. Inexpensive spreaders simply don't last and they're frustrating to use. Buy the better spreader and you'll take it with you every time you move. LESCO and Scotts make the best ones.

Sprayer
A two- to three-gallon sprayer comes in handy for large-scale herbicide application. Match sprayer size to your lawn. The Hudson Company makes good ones.

Shovels
Okay, I lied about there being only ten tools. You'll need two shovels—a square shovel for edging, digging straight lines, and cleaning up flat surfaces; a round shovel for digging holes. (Buy yourself a good pair of leather gardening gloves, too. Your hands will thank you.)

Rakes
Oops again. You'll need two—a wooden or plastic fan rake for attacking leaves and cleaning up your yard in the fall, and one with metal tines for smoothing out soil before planting. You can also use the latter for dethatching small areas.

Hose
Yet another oops. Hoses, not a hose, might be in order, depending on the size of your lawn. Either way, buy rubber or flexible plastic to keep crimping and tangling to a minimum. Brass fittings will last as long as the hose does. Longer, actually.

A patch kit is another good thing to have around. Good hoses aren't cheap, and even the best can spring a leak. Patching them is pretty easy.

Pruning Shears or Loppers
Your landscaping will determine which and how big, and what the heck, we're well beyond just ten items now, so you might even want to spring for both. Long-handled loppers are good for pruning trees and bushes. Pruning shears work well for thinning and trimming back shrubs.

Safety Glasses
You only get one pair of eyes in this life, and taking care of your lawn presents lots of opportunities to mess them up. Don't take a chance with your eyesight. Wear safety glasses or goggles when mowing, trimming, mixing chemicals, whenever your eyes could be at risk.

TAKING CARE OF YOUR GEAR
Lawn-care equipment falls into two basic categories: with moving parts and without. The ones without moving parts are fairly easy to take care of. The ones that move, a little more complex. But definitely doable by you.

Mower Maintenance
You'll have a happy relationship with your mower if you take the time to read the manual that came along with it, and if you follow the manufacturer's instructions for taking care of it. The basic care tips here are always best practices for these machines:

- Check the oil and oil filter regularly; add or change oil and change filter when necessary. Do this at least annually or when you sharpen your blade.
- Occasionally check and tighten nuts and bolts.
- Visually inspect mower blades regularly.
- Hose down the mower deck after you're done mowing. Get all the debris out; leaving it in will make your mower run less efficiently. Be sure to clean under the deck too.

Keeping Things Sharp
A sharp blade is essential for grass health. Remember, you want to cut the grass, not shred it.

Here's how to sharpen a rotary blade. These are general guidelines; be sure to check your manual for specific instructions. You'll need a wrench, a vise, and a file.

1. Be sure the mower is off.
2. Disconnect the spark plug.
3. Remove the blade with a wrench.
4. Secure it in the vise.
5. Sharpen the beveled edge with your file. File in smooth, long strokes. Be sure to follow and maintain the existing angle on the blade.
6. Unclamp the blade and check the balance by centering it on the top of your finger. If it tips to one side, file a little more off the heavier end.

7.   Put the blade back on the mower. Make sure it's right side up, and
      that the locking nut is tightly secured.

Or make life easy on yourself by having a spare blade or two on hand
when the one you're using gets dull or twists and warps. They don't cost that
much.

You can sharpen a reel mower yourself, too, but it's typically easier and
better to have a professional do it.

Powering Up in the Spring

You aren't going to yank your mower out of its winter home, plop it down
on your grass, and fire it up when spring comes. You just aren't going to do this.
Mowers aren't the most delicate pieces of machinery, but like all machines,
they'll run better if you take a few minutes to check their welfare.

Here's what to do in the spring:

- Remove the engine casing.
- Clear away any debris that might have collected around the fans dur-
  ing storage.
- Change the oil.
- Check the air filter. Clean or replace as necessary.
- Change the spark plug.
- Clean the top and bottom of the deck.
- Lubricate the moving parts.

Going to Sleep in the Fall

You're not just going to dump your mower in your garden shed in the fall,
either. Here's how to put it to bed right:

- Fill the fuel tank and add fuel stabilizer or additive. Less than a full
  tank opens the door for condensation (read water in the fuel, which
  you definitely don't want). You can now add stabilizer continually
  through the winter via a smart-fuel filter from Briggs & Stratton. If it
  gets really cold where you live, you might have to drain the tank.
  Check the manual.
- Remove the spark plug and drop a teaspoon of oil into the cylinder.
  Run the engine briefly to distribute the oil, then replace the plug.
- Remove all dirt and debris.

Store your mower in a dry, well-ventilated area. Keep it away from
heaters, stoves, pilot lights, basically any heat source. If it's a battery-powered
electric, check your manual for information on charging the battery during
winter storage.

Staying Trim

String trimmers are pretty simple devices. You can keep the motor on yours running right by clearing debris from the motor casing after you use it. Check the filter above the motor fan regularly, and clean or replace it when necessary. On gas trimmers, replace the air filter and spark plug annually. Lubricate the shaft between the engine and the cutting unit annually as well.

Be sure to replace worn trimmer line with the right type for your trimmer, and be sure to install it correctly. If you don't, a jammed line is the result.

Tooling Up

Implements like shovels and rakes can last you a lifetime if you treat them right. Here's how:

- Never use a tool for something it wasn't meant to do.
- Wash and dry the blades, tines, and so on after you're done using the tool. Rust buildup makes it tougher to move blades through the soil. If they get rusty, remove the rust with a wire brush, sandpaper, steel wool, a grinder, whatever it takes. Prevent rust from building up again with a light coating of machine or vegetable oil. Grab the Pam; spray-on cooking oil works great for this.
- Keep them sharp. You'll need something called a flat bastard or mill file for this. Follow the steps for sharpening a rotary blade above. Be sure to match the blade's original angle.
- Keep wood handles in good shape by rubbing them down with boiled linseed oil in the spring. Remove roughness by smoothing with a medium-grit emery cloth.
- If heads come loose, fix them right away. Don't reach for the duct tape; no matter how well you tape the head back on, it will loosen up again when you use it. You'll need heavy-duty epoxy glue for this. Coat the tool head, then reinsert the handle.

Spreading Love . . . er, Fertilizer . . . All Around

Spreaders are pretty durable pieces of equipment, as they're relatively simple in design and they don't have cutting edges to sharpen. But they need proper care and maintenance, too.

Always wash and dry your spreader after you use it to keep it from corroding. Do so even if you're using a cheap plastic crank spreader—they have metal parts inside and they can also rust.

Spreaders have settings that govern how much fertilizer is put down. Making sure these settings are calibrated correctly will ensure you're putting down the right amount, no more and no less.

Calibration gets a little long and involved, but stick with me here. This is good information to know.

Broadcast News

If you're using a broadcast spreader, you'll want to check the spreader's coverage area first. Here's how to do it:

Measure off a sixteen- to twenty-foot line. The length can vary, but it should be at least 1.5 to three times as long as the spreader's recommended swath width. You want to have at least two containers on each side that are placed beyond this width. (This might seem confusing, but you'll see why in a moment.)

Place same-sized containers about a foot apart along the line. Use containers that are large and deep enough so the product doesn't bounce out of them. When you have them in place, remove the container in the center. You're going to walk your spreader through the gap you just created.

Make sure the spreader hopper is closed, and then load it with a little fertilizer. Line up a few feet away from the gap in the center of the line, then open the hopper and walk through the gap a couple of times.

Check the containers. Coverage is going to be highest in the center of the pattern and will gradually taper off. This translates into the containers closest to where you walked being fullest. When product depth is about 50 percent that of the fullest containers, you've reached the edge of the effective coverage area. You now know how far your spreader is distributing the product. Sweep up what's on the ground and dump it and what's in the containers into your fertilizer bag. You can reuse it.

Another, simpler way is just to watch the pattern while someone else operates the spreader. And, of course, if there is an issue, it will show up in time in a distinctive pattern in your lawn.

Calibration is next. Using a catch pan under the spreader, which collects the product as it exits the spreader, is the easiest approach. PennPro is the brand name to look for here, or you can make your own by attaching a fairly sturdy box to the bottom of your spreader with a rubber or bungee cord. Choose a box that covers the entire spreader opening and that's deep enough to catch all the product.

Here's what you'll do:

- Measure a fifty-foot path on your driveway or other flat surface. This is your calibration test area.
- Set the spreader calibration level to about halfway.
- Make sure the hopper is closed, then fill it about halfway.
- Place the catch pan under the spreader.
- Move the spreader to the beginning of the test area. Open the hopper and start walking at the pace you'd use if you were actually applying the product.
- Shut the hopper when you reach the end of the test strip.
- Remove the catch pan.
- Weigh what's in it. Put the loaded tray on the scale first, weigh it, then

dump the contents back into the fertilizer bag and weigh the empty tray.

Now you have the information you need to factor the application rate, which is calculated by dividing the pounds of product collected by the area of coverage. As an example, let's say you dropped 1.5 pounds during the test and your coverage area was twelve feet wide. First multiply 1.5 by 1,000 (remember, application rates are calculated per thousand square feet). Then divide 1,500 by 600 (the measured coverage area, times the length of your test strip). The answer is 2.5, or 2.5 pounds of fertilizer per 1,000 square feet.

Are you golden? Let's see. The fertilizer bag weighs 15 pounds and it says it will cover 5,000 square feet, so that's 3 pounds per every 1,000 square feet. Your spreader applied 2.5 pounds per 1,000 square feet. That's pretty good, as you want your measured rate to be within 10 percent of the desired rate, but you're still a little short. You'll need to adjust the setting and test again.

Dropping Down

Testing a drop spreader is pretty simple, as the application area is fixed and more easily measured. You can also dispense with the catcher, if you want to, and sweep up the product when you're done. Simply follow the same calibration test as above.

Spraying Away

Liquid tank or canister sprayers are pretty easy to maintain. The only real area of concern is the O-ring at the end of the plunger. If it's leather, it needs to be soft and pliable or the sprayer won't seal properly and won't stay pressurized when you use it. The easiest way to keep the O-ring in good shape is to remove it when you finish spraying and drop it into a small container of oil. You can use cooking oil or light machine oil.

If the O-ring is nylon or rubber, check it periodically for wear. Replace as necessary. Also be sure to check the seal on the bottom of the pump housing every so often. Clean the sprayer every time you use it; pesticides and herbicides are corrosive. Lubricate metal parts with light oil; spray-on products are good for this. If the sprayer head clogs, carefully clean it out with a pin or paper clip. If it leaks, replace the O-ring.

Sprayer calibration should also be checked. Here's how to do it:

- Set the nozzle opening to the desired spray pattern.
- Put a measured amount of plain water in the canister. Fill it about halfway.
- Pressurize the sprayer, then start walking and spray the water on a hard, flat surface. Walk at the same speed as you would if actually spraying. Apply the water evenly; be sure to cover everything with minimal overlapping, just like you'd do if you were actually spraying.

Measure the sprayed area when the canister is empty. Multiply the area covered by the amount you sprayed for application rate, which, for sprayers, is expressed as gallons per 1,000 square feet. As an example, let's say you sprayed 1 quart of water over a 20-by-50-foot area (1,000 square feet). One gallon of spray (4 quarts), therefore, will cover 4,000 square feet. Compare the results to the recommended application rate on the product, and adjust as necessary.

INDEX